Arrival of Eagles

Dedication

For my grandson Alfie Blaney

Arrival of Eagles

Luftwaffe Landings in Britain
1939 –1945

Andy Saunders

Grub Street • London

Published by
Grub Street Publishing
4 Rainham Close
London
SW11 6SS

A CIP record for this title is available from the British Library

ISBN-13: 9781909808126

Design by Roy Platten, Eclipse, Hemel Hempstead
roy.eclipse@btopenworld.com

Printed and bound by Berforts Group, UK

Grub Street Publishing uses only FSC
(Forest Stewardship Council) paper for its books

Previous page: Captured enemy aircraft were always great intelligence 'prizes' and here RAF
personnel examine a Messerschmitt 109 G abandoned at a former Luftwaffe airfield in France
during September 1944.

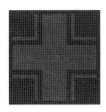

Contents

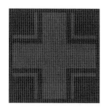

Acknowledgements

I MUST RECORD MY INDEBTEDNESS to a number of individuals and organisations for assistance in the production of this book. Not in any order of merit I must thank the following: Chris Goss, Winston Ramsey, Gail Ramsey, Christopher R. Elliott, Steve Brew, Martin Mace and *Britain at War* magazine, Peter Cornwell, Steve Hall, Nigel Parker, Simon Parry, Tony Holmes, Robert Forsyth, Dean Sumner, Norman Franks and Sue Eagles.

I should also record my gratitude to the late Peter Foote and Ken West from whom much information was gleaned over many years of co-operative research and the sharing of information and photographs.

A very special thank you, though, must go to Captain Eric 'Winkle' Brown for writing what is a much-valued foreword to this book. It was, Sir, a very great honour indeed that you should have agreed to write for a book that covers a number of aircraft with which you have had a very intimate connection. I cannot thank you enough. Many thanks also to the Fly Navy Heritage Trust for providing a wonderful photo of him.

I must also thank my friend of many years, Dr Alfred Price. Alfred has very much become the doyen of aviation history researchers and authors and also a prolific and greatly-respected writer. His early works of the late-1960 period very much sparked my enthusiasm for the subject and I have avidly read all of his published works since. During the 1970s and early 80s I was privileged to help him in some small ways with his various Battle of Britain and other projects, and I felt honoured recently to be gifted substantial parts of Alfred's archive upon his retirement in 2012. Alfred has generously allowed me to draw on his documentary and photographic material and to use it howsoever I please. Thank you, Alfred.

Again, I must thank the superb team at Grub Street Publishing for their enthusiasm for this book and their dedication in ensuring a quality production as ever, especially Natalie Parker and Sophie Campbell, and the ever patient John Davies. You are always a pleasure to work with.

Lastly, but by no means least, I must thank Zoe for her continued support and understanding as I put this book together and as I spent long hours shut away in my office. Without her encouragement and input, and frequent tea, sandwiches and cake it would have all been impossible. Thank you.

If I have forgotten anyone, please accept my apologies. Any oversight was entirely unintentional.

# Introduction

URING WORLD WAR TWO AROUND 1,200 Luftwaffe aircraft arrived on the ground in the UK or in its surrounding coastal waters, although not all through 'conventional' combat circumstances. Some had got lost, others were brought by defectors, and some fell foul of electronic countermeasures implemented by the RAF. Occasionally they were brought down in unusual combat circumstances or were aircraft of specific interest to RAF intelligence and in a number of instances, these aircraft were repaired and test flown by the British.

This book, though far from exhaustive of aircraft losses of the genre, looks at a selection of interesting cases and related events from among the plethora of arriving German aircraft during the period 1939-1945 and draws upon the author's own research, interviews with participants and survivors, official reports and other eye-witness accounts. In addition, each account is richly illustrated with high-quality photos to bring alive this selection of truly unconventional arrivals of some of the Luftwaffe's eagles.

Never before has such a colourful and varied mix of stories relating to Luftwaffe losses over Britain been brought together in one book. The scope of stories and the author's treatment of them will provide the reader with a variety of accounts that each, in their own way, can be described as nothing less than utterly astonishing. These range from a diminutive Luftwaffe mail courier aircraft lost in English Channel fog, to the extraordinary arrival in Britain of Rudolf Hess in a Messerschmitt 110, a dramatic dog-fight and chase leading to the 'ramming' of a German fighter right through to the supposed and yet utterly fantastical, if not completely surreal, plot to kidnap Hitler and bring him to Britain in his personal Focke Wulf 200 Condor.

This book is a journey through some of these amazing episodes and turns up many stories that are little known or else certainly deserve closer examination and wider exposure. Others, like the arrival of Rudolf Hess in Britain, are rather better known. Often, though, this eclectic bag tells of events that are truly stranger than fiction.

Andy Saunders
East Sussex
April 2014

Foreword

By Captain Eric Brown CBE, DSC, AFC, Hon FRAeS, RN
Former CO Enemy Aircraft Flight, RAE Farnborough

I N ANY FORM OF WARFARE, one of the most vital elements to success is true knowledge of the enemy's weaponry. This may be obtained by intelligence methods, or best of all by procurement of actual hardware, by fair means or foul. This book concentrates on the aviation hardware that came our way in the course of World War Two, and was to prove invaluable in assessing where we stood in relation to our enemy's air forces.

In a police state such as Nazi Germany the chances of defecting by air to Great Britain were rare indeed in the early years of the war, and the penalty for failure was dire. In such a situation we had mainly to depend on hardware from downed combat aircraft which were inevitably damaged, but in some cases could be repaired to flyable status.

Although virtually all these captured enemy aircraft passed through RAE Farnborough for testing and evaluation of both the machine and its equipment, they were then sent on to a specialist service unit of maintenance test pilots. Formed at Duxford on 21 November 1941, 1426 (Enemy) Aircraft Flight expressly exhibited them to RAF and USAAF operational units based in the UK.

1426 was finally disbanded on 17 January 1945, and all responsibility for captured enemy aircraft passed to the RAE whose experimental test pilots would now deal with the more advanced types likely to be found in defeated Germany. This was an astute move as the degree of sophistication found in the captured German jet and rocket aircraft was quite remarkable as the British public learned at the Captured Enemy Aircraft Exhibition held at Farnborough during October and November 1945.

Although this book deals with the pre-capitulation arrival of eagles, it is this very fact that gives it such an expectant aura of mystery and anticipatory excitement, because the stakes were high for both sides, and the scenario was electric.

As I was German speaking I was given a leading role in the post-World War Two flight-testing programme and flew fifty-five different types of Luftwaffe aircraft, and was generally suitably impressed and occasionally suitably tensed.

Eric Brown

CHAPTER 1 First Eagle Down

WHEN PRIME MINISTER NEVILLE CHAMBERLAIN broadcast to the nation with his solemn announcement of the declaration of war at quarter past eleven on the morning of Sunday 3 September 1939, there had existed a very clear expectation on the part of the British public that the country would almost immediately be attacked by waves of German bombers. It was a fear that had been considerably heightened by the sounding of air raid warning sirens in London just a few moments later, at exactly twenty-seven minutes past eleven. That was only a test, but the realisation now dawned on everyone in the country that the threat of air attack was very real. For the next five years it would be ever-present and although it was a few weeks before any real Luftwaffe activity would be seen (initially in the north of England and Scotland) there were a few more scares beyond the sirens that had wailed that day. And it wasn't just the civilians who were twitchy.

On 6 September, just three days into the war, came what at first seemed to be a very real and present threat to London itself as searchlight batteries on the Essex coast reported aircraft at high altitude flying over West Mersea at 06.15 hours. The sequence of events that unfolded was complex and convoluted, but suffice to say that RAF Fighter Command scrambled Hurricanes of 56 and 151 Squadrons from RAF North Weald to meet the supposed threat, along with Spitfires from 54, 65 and 74 Squadrons from RAF Hornchurch.

Exactly what unfolded over the ensuing minutes is still shrouded in a degree of mystery, but the fact of the matter is that the aircraft reported at altitude over the Essex coast turned out, in fact, not to be hostile. Nevertheless, the scrambled fighters had no way of yet knowing this. So far as they were concerned, this was an interception. What followed, though, was a somewhat inglorious baptism of fire for RAF Fighter Command. Confusion reigned, and mistaking the Hurricanes of 56 Squadron for enemy aircraft, the Spitfires of 74 Squadron swept in to attack. In moments it was all over, but before the terrible mistake was recognised, and the engagement broken off, two of the Hurricanes had been brought down with Plt Off M. L. Hulton-Harrop killed and Plt Off F. Rose being forced to crash-land, albeit unharmed.

The repercussions were immediate and serious, with flying personnel and ground staff alike being relieved of their respective posts and court-martialled. Fighter Command, though, had suffered its first fatality of the war, and by its own hand. It was an event that later became known as 'The Battle of Barking Creek'. The bigger picture of this story has, of course, been very well documented elsewhere but it is important to view the mistakes of that day in the context of setting the scene for what would be five years of enemy air assaults against the British Isles.

Nervousness, very often on the part of civilians and military alike, frequently played an important part in events that were to unfold in the varied and individual dramas surrounding the downing of Luftwaffe aircraft and their aircrews. Such events, collectively, might truly be described as an arrival of eagles. And that first eagle finally came just weeks later.

56 Squadron; Plt Off F. C. 'Tommy' Rose (rear row, right) Plt Off Montague Hulton-Harrop (front, left). This photograph was taken on 3 September 1939.

At 09.15 hours on the morning of Saturday 28 October the three Spitfires of Red Section, 603 Squadron, got airborne from RAF Turnhouse for a routine patrol at 14,000ft over the River Forth whilst, at around the same time, the three Spitfires of Red Section, 602 Squadron, were patrolling over RAF Turnhouse. Already, and in a little over one month of war, Luftwaffe raiders had operated against targets in and around Scotland and the very north of England with 602 and 603 Squadrons claiming victories over the North Sea against Junkers 88s and a Heinkel 111 on 16 and 22 October respectively.

Operating at long range over the North Sea from their base at Westerland on the island of Sylt, the raids were clearly risky. Conducted during daylight hours, and with no possibility of any fighter cover, the raiders were flying into a sensitive and well-defended area. Here was the strategically-important Scapa Flow and the shipyards and docks of Greenock off to the west, with the region patrolled almost constantly by sections of the various squadrons of RAF Fighter Command's 13 Group.

It was into this 'hot' area, then, that Lt Rolf Niehoff brought his Stab./KG26 crew that morning, as captain of Heinkel 111, Werke Nummer 5449, 1H + JA. His mission that day was an armed reconnaissance, first to Glasgow and then back eastwards to look for British naval ships in the Firth of Forth. As the first Luftwaffe aircraft to cross the coastline of the British Isles that morning,

Niehoff was under orders to transmit a weather report once he had reached the coast at around 18,000ft. Later, he would conclude that this wireless transmission had been his undoing and had been heard by the British, thus alerting them to their presence. However, that was not the case.

Returning from the west coast, but now down to around 15,000ft, Niehoff discovered that the earlier cloud cover had thinned over the Forth area and gave him a much better opportunity to photograph any shipping. Unfortunately, this was very much a two-edged sword; it also gave anti-aircraft gunners a better view of the roaming Heinkel 111 that could be heard and seen overhead and immediately the gunners are reported to have put up an effective barrage. However, since the 3rd (Scottish) Anti-Aircraft Division reported that none of their guns opened fire that day, the barrage must presumably have originated from naval shipping laying at anchor at Queensferry, including HMS *Belfast*, HMS *Edinburgh* and HMS *Mohawk*.

Rolf Niehoff takes up the story:

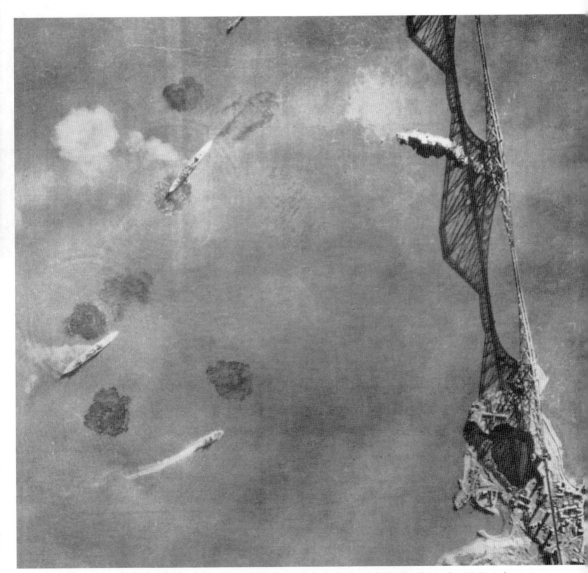

This aerial view of Queensferry shows the attack on shipping in the Firth of Forth, 16 October 1939. Here, by the famous Forth Bridge, bombs burst around HMS *Edinburgh*.

"When we returned from the area of Glasgow, flying at a height of about 12,000 to 15,000ft, we were greeted by anti-aircraft fire. One shot must have been a hit because I heard the explosion and felt the impact, but I do not think much damage was done."

Whilst Niehoff judged the damage from the anti-aircraft fire to have been non-critical, it might still have sealed his fate. Already in the area, Red Sections of 602 and 603 Squadrons were alerted to the Heinkel's presence by the bursting AA shells and were quickly in hot pursuit. Again, we turn to Niehoff's account:

"A short time after the anti-aircraft fire four Spitfires appeared and began attacking, one after the other. My two rear gunners were, of course, at their weapons and alert. They were Gefr Bruno Reimann and Uffz Gottlieb Kowalke. Twice before we had had contact with enemy fighters but this time my gunners started shooting back far too early, so the first Spitfire killed them both as they were changing their spent ammunition drums. Before I could go to look after my gunners, my young but very able pilot, Uffz Kurt Lehmkuhl, was hit in the back by two bullets and I had to stay with him in the cockpit in case he fainted.
    "Now, of course, the Spitfires received no more machine-gun fire from our aircraft and they flew very close to our rear. Therefore, most of their bullets hit our wings and engines which soon stopped. Only a few more bullets hit the cockpit, which is why I and my pilot survived. The four Spitfires were shooting at us, one after the other, right up until we hit the ground."

Rolf Niehoff's crippled Heinkel 111, 28 October 1939.

Meanwhile, and on the ground at RAF Drem, Yellow Section of 602 Squadron were ordered off to find and engage the enemy after an over-flying Heinkel 111 had been spotted but, in unfortunate and uncomfortable echoes of the recent 'Battle of Barking Creek' episode, the three Spitfires instead found what turned out to be an RAF Anson off May Island. Flt Lt Hodge, mistaking the Anson for an enemy aircraft, led his section in for a line-astern attack and raked the RAF aircraft with gunfire before the error was realised and the interception called off. This was not before the unlucky Anson pilot had been hit and wounded in the jaw, however. Unfortunately, two such episodes just weeks apart would hardly be unusual in terms of the frequency of so-called friendly-fire incidents which were a far greater problem during air fighting than is generally appreciated.

The attacking pilots of 603 Squadron's Red Section had been Flt Lt P. Gifford, Plt Off C. Robertson and Plt Off G. K. Gilroy in Spitfires L1050, L1070 and L1049 respectively and although Red Section of 602 Squadron were reported to have engaged the Heinkel first it would seem that only their leader, Flt Lt A. A. McKellar, actually did so with any success. This would sit both with Niehoff's account of being attacked by 'four Spitfires' and with McKellar's combat report which mentions 'three other Spitfires' attacking the Heinkel. However, far from Niehoff's air gunners necessarily opening fire too early it is noted that, in his combat report, McKellar refers to one Spitfire being rendered unserviceable during this engagement due to a bullet through the starboard main wing spar and an ammunition pan. Obviously, and with 602 Squadron's Spitfires first into attack, they had been fired upon before the Heinkel's defensive fire could be silenced.

Although wounded in the back, weak from loss of blood and still under relentless attack by four Spitfires that were queuing up, one after the other, to pump more lead into his aircraft, Uffz Kurt Lehmkuhl did a more than creditable

Flt Lt Pat Gifford, 16 October, stands alongside Spitfire L1050, LO-A, the aircraft he flew during the action of 28 October 1939.

job of maintaining control of the Heinkel and getting the aircraft down to a very reasonable crash-landing in less than ideal terrain. With insufficient height to bale out, and with two smoking and dead engines, he had little choice, though. In a rapidly descending glide over the Lammermuir Hills, Lehmkuhl selected the only place available to him, a piece of sloping and heather-covered ground that he could see directly ahead. Lehmkuhl eventually set the bomber down between

High Latch and Kidlaw, just to the east of Humbie village. It thus became the first enemy aircraft brought down intact on mainland British soil during World War Two.[1]

Crashing and careering over the rough terrain and demolishing a dry-stone wall, where it left behind its starboard tailplane, the bullet-riddled bomber eventually came to rest on an uphill incline with its nose smashed in and its back broken. And it wasn't only the Heinkel that had a broken back. The bumping and jolting landing had, indeed, been literally bone-jarring and Rolf Niehoff, unhurt in the sustained fighter assault, was later found to have also suffered a broken back as the Heinkel juddered to a halt. However, his injuries were not so incapacitating as to prevent him helping his wounded pilot out of the aircraft as they waited for the arrival of the authorities. Clearly, Reimann and Gottlieb were beyond any human aid and Niehoff tended instead to his pilot before the first people started to arrive at the crash site.

In this view of the Heinkel 111 the liberal distribution of bullet holes across the airframe can clearly be seen as locals come to gape at the spectacle.

Of course, the arrival on the ground of German aircraft within the British Isles was always the cause of great interest and excitement for civilians nearby and this was certainly the case with the Humbie Heinkel. Such was the novelty, then, of Luftwaffe aircraft landing under such circumstances that the BBC later broadcast an interview with Mr John K. Irvine of nearby Long Newton Farm:

1 A Junkers 88 had previously crashed and exploded on the Island of Hoy, Orkneys, on 17 October 1939 but had been smashed to pieces, along with three of its crew. A fourth man had been taken prisoner, wounded.

"I was filling up sacks of barley about a quarter past ten when I heard a noise like the hurling of a barrow. That's what I thought it was at first, but it went on and on and came nearer, and then I knew it was the noise of guns. Then we saw a big black machine with two engines coming over the trees from the north-west. There were four British machines with it. They were circling round and round and rattling bullets into the German as hard as they could do it.

"I thought we ought to take cover, there were women workers there, but curiosity brought us out again. We saw the German go over the houses, so low that it almost touched the chimneys. Then they all went out of sight up over the hill, and a few minutes later I saw our fighters going back, all four of them. They seemed to have finished with the job, so I ran up to see what had happened.

"Two of the crew were dead. I expect they were the gunners and they must have been shot before they came into my view, because I never saw them firing at our 'planes. The machine had scraped its tail over a dyke and then came down on the moor on an even keel. One of the crew was not hurt at all. He was pulling out his mate. By the time we got up there he had him lying on the ground.

"We tried to talk to the unwounded man but he did not know what we were saying, although he spoke a little English. The wounded man said he wanted a drink, but the doctor said he ought not to have one. He had two bullet wounds in the back.

"The police took the unwounded man away and before he went he shook hands with his mate. We used a gate off one of the fences to carry the wounded man down to the road and waited there for the ambulance."

Albeit that John Irvine thought one man (Niehoff) was unwounded, we now know that not to have been the case and a contemporary photograph shows Rolf Niehoff with the arresting police officers as he holds his hand to his hurt back. Niehoff himself takes up the story of events following the crash-landing:

Lt Rolf Niehoff holding his injured back after being taken into custody.

"A few minutes after the crash some men arrived on the scene and among them was a doctor who took care of my wounded pilot. He was later taken to an Edinburgh hospital.

"I was taken prisoner by some friendly policemen and escorted to a police station. As far as I remember this was in a town called Dalkeith. Here I waited some time until an army captain arrived and took me in his private car to the HQ of an army unit located in a country estate. Here, a colonel received me and asked me for my name and home address, but then added 'I don't suppose you will answer any other questions?' Of course, I wouldn't! Then he introduced me to the officers' mess where I had some conversations with the men there. Then, at about noon, the captain invited me to lunch in his room and afterwards I was taken to Edinburgh Castle where I spent the afternoon in the guard room.

"During that afternoon I was interrogated, or I had better say interviewed, by two RAF officers. They asked me which of the four Spitfires had shot me down. Of course, I didn't know which one. Furthermore, they seemed very interested in our self-sealing fuel tanks and the fuel injection system.

"That night I was taken to London by train, guarded by four armed soldiers. On arrival I was taken straight to the Tower of London where the treatment was very correct but strictly military. It was not always so with the interrogation that followed.

"The interrogator was a man in RAF uniform, but I got the impression that he was a civilian. He spoke German fluently, but with a strong Viennese accent. His questioning was rather primitive and several times he contradicted himself and wasn't always telling the truth. His methods were not always very decent and I was interrogated by him six times and, later, another three times when I was in hospital. He wanted information from me that he knew I had, but refused to give.

"In the Tower I shared my room with Oblt Heinrich Storp who had been shot down over the Firth of Forth on 16 October 1939 in a Junkers 88 that crashed into the sea. Strangely, I had been on the same raid. During that sortie I had taken photos of the British ships *Edinburgh* and *Southampton* and to my huge surprise I saw these same photographs later in the British magazine *Picture Post*. I then heard that my photographs had been distributed around the world.

"After some days in the Tower I was taken for x-rays on my troublesome back at Westminster hospital, and then on to the Luftwaffe POW ward at the Royal Herbert military hospital in Woolwich. Here, I had treatment for a broken back. I was prisoner number thirty-two, but would have had a much earlier POW number if it were not for my long stay at hospital before being sent off to the POW camp at Grizedale Hall."

In many respects, Niehoff's experiences were typical of the those of many Luftwaffe airmen taken prisoner over Britain; friendly treatment on capture, the taking of drinks and lunch whilst being 'entertained' by British officers, armed escort by train to London, sometimes aggressive interrogations and, if needed, treatment at the Royal Herbert. Only in his incarceration at the Tower of London did Niehoff's early imprisonment differ significantly from most of those captured later.

In the early part of the war the British had not yet established the procedures for housing and processing prisoners during the first days of their captivity and what became known as the London Cage. Thus, the Tower of London was used initially for this purpose and it was something that Niehoff later rather regarded as a badge of honour. "After all," he said, "the Tower of London was traditionally used to imprison enemies of the British monarch. And here was I, most definitely an enemy of the King!"

If Niehoff's interrogators, and those initially investigating the wreck of his Heinkel, had been keen to learn what they could about the self-sealing tanks, fuel injection and, perhaps, the operational details of KG26 they were, in fact, missing a bigger 'secret' that lay hidden in the aircraft. It was only much later, however, that this 'secret' and its huge importance to the conduct of electronic countermeasures would become apparent; and only then as very much an almost accidental afterthought. For now, though, an initial examination of the airframe and engines took priority.

As the first intact enemy aircraft to fall into British hands it was, of course, of considerable technical interest and it was decided that a thorough examination of the DB 601 engines would be undertaken at the Rolls-Royce aero engine works in Derby, and both motors were duly despatched there. Here, comprehensive reports on the DB 601 were produced, setting out metallurgical and performance properties and examining every single technical detail including the quality of engineering and production.

As for the fuselage and remnants of the airframe, these were despatched to the Royal Aircraft Establishment at Farnborough. Again, a careful look was taken at the instrumentation, radio fit, armour, armaments and general matters such as cockpit layout and overall construction methods. Scrutiny of the instruments, for example, also looked at issues such as how they were constructed and the names and locations of the factories which had made them. One thing, though, caught the investigating technician's eye; the blind-landing receiver was extremely sensitive. He thought it just an odd anomaly having no other particular significance and promptly forgot about it. Now, however, we need to fast-forward eight months to the early days of rather more sustained Luftwaffe attacks on Britain.

On 12 June 1940 the scientific intelligence expert, Professor R. V. Jones, was summoned to meet Gp Capt L. F. Blandy, head of the RAF's 'Y' radio listening service that monitored all German wireless traffic. Blandy handed a slip of paper to Jones. On it was written: *'Knickebein, Kleve, ist auf punkt 53 grad 24 minuten nord und ein grad west eingerichtet.'*

It was a recently picked-up Luftwaffe transmission and Blandy admitted that it had stumped all in the 'Y' service as to what it might mean. Did Jones have any idea? Translated, it meant:

'Cleves Knickebein is established at position 53 degrees 24 minutes north and 1 degree west' and immediately it made sense to Jones. It was confirmation that the Luftwaffe was operating a blind-bombing system by using intersecting radio beams as he had earlier suspected. The name Knickebein meant crooked leg, and to Jones this reflected the shape that might be made by the crossing of two radio beams. The story of the so-called 'Battle of the Beams' is, of course, well known. However, it was Niehoff's Heinkel that would subsequently unlock some if its early secrets.

The question was what equipment on board Luftwaffe bombers was being utilised for receiving the Knickebein beam signals. At this point in the war nothing had been found on the now-plentiful German aircraft examined on the ground by RAF intelligence officers. But if the system was in use then there must be *something* reasoned Jones. Exasperated, he went to Sqn Ldr S. D. Felkin, head of A.I.1(k), the department responsible for the interrogation of Luftwaffe prisoners. Was there anything, asked Jones, which had been gleaned from prisoners that might offer a clue? No. There was nothing.

Professor R. V. Jones, British scientific intelligence officer.

However, from then on Felkin started to ask very specific questions about beam-bombing and once the prisoners who had been so interrogated were put together their 'private' conversations were covertly recorded. Finally came a clue, although, in truth, it was more of a confirmation. In a recorded conversation one of the prisoners had said to his colleague: "No matter how hard they look for the equipment they will never find it." Once this was relayed to Jones he realised that there must be something obvious, in plain sight, that had simply been missed. Jones takes up the story:

"This could not have been a better challenge because it implied that the equipment was in fact under our noses, but that we would not recognise it. I therefore obtained a copy of the full technical examination of the Heinkel that had been shot down during the Firth of Forth raid, and looked especially at the various items of radio equipment. The only thing that could possibly fit the bill was the receiver that was carried in the aircraft for the purpose of blind landing. It was labelled E.Bl 1 (which stood for Empfänger Blind 1 – blind-

Sqn Ldr Denys Felkin who headed the RAF's Air Intelligence A.I.1(k) department.

landing receiver type 1) and was ostensibly for the normal purpose of blind landing on the Lorenz beam system which was now standard at many aerodromes.

"I ascertained that the equipment had been examined by Cox-Walker at Farnborough and so I telephoned him. 'Tell me, is there anything unusual about the blind-landing receiver?' I asked. 'No,' he replied – and then 'but now you mention it, it is much more sensitive than they would ever need for blind landing.' So that was it. I now knew what the receiver was, and the frequencies to which it could be tuned, and therefore on which frequencies the Knickebein beam must operate."

After all, and despite the RAF's initial interest in the Heinkel's self-sealing fuel tanks, engine fuel injection systems and the composition of Niehoff's KG26 unit, there had been a much more important intelligence prize waiting to be found. In all probability, the subsequent three visits of the RAF interrogation officer to Niehoff (most likely Sqn Ldr Felkin) whilst he was hospitalised came after R. V. Jones had realised the significance of the blind-landing receiver in the Heinkel. This would certainly make sense of Rolf Niehoff's comment that his interrogator: '... wanted information from me that he knew I had, but refused to give.'

In the case of the Humbie Heinkel the discovery really was more than highly significant in the establishment of countermeasures, and in the understanding of how the Luftwaffe was conducting its bombing campaign against the British Isles. Arriving eagles sometimes carried the most surprising and unexpected secrets.

To a large extent, the downing of the very first eagle at Humbie was typical of Luftwaffe arrivals in Britain throughout the war, but its inclusion is merited not only because it was the first of many but, additionally, because its engines became the focus of detailed examination by Rolls-Royce Aero Engines and, significantly, its instrumentation had helped British intelligence fathom out some key elements of the German blind-bombing system. Not only that but it rather sets the scene, or even establishes a benchmark, for what were other far less ordinary arrivals. And into that category surely falls the Heinkel 111 that came to grief in Berkshire during the very early hours of 29 July 1940.

For the most part, Luftwaffe aircrews coming down in Britain were almost immediately apprehended or quickly sought to give themselves up. After all, escape from the island was considered nigh-on impossible. And, in any event, the crews who were downed during the early part of the war took the view that their captivity would surely only be very temporary with an expected German invasion reckoned to be just around the corner. Not all Luftwaffe airmen, though, would decide to give up quite so easily.

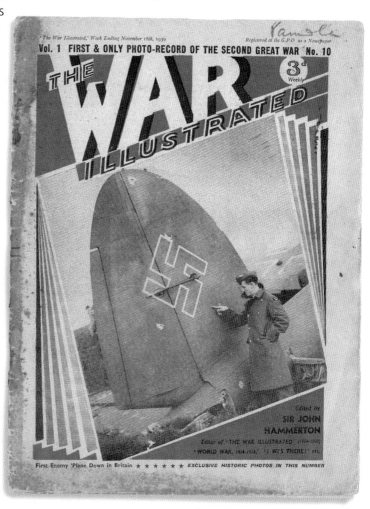

Extensive coverage was given to the downing of the Heinkel 111 at Humbie on 28 October in the British press and this was the cover of the *War Illustrated* journal from 18 November 1939.

CHAPTER 2 On The Run

WHEN THE STAFFELKAPITÄN OF 8./KG55 briefed his nominated crew for a single-aircraft sortie on the night of 28/29 July 1940, radio operator Uffz Kurt Böker couldn't help but notice the chalked symbol against his crew that the orderly clerk had marked onto the 'state' board; a cross signifying a casualty. Although Böker's blood ran cold when he saw the chalk mark he tried not to dwell on it. But, under the circumstances of a risky night raid over British territory, it was difficult not to – or to see that cross as anything other than an omen. Collectively, the crew nervously laughed it off as they busied themselves with pre-flight preparations and checks of their aircraft and equipment. "We aren't dead, yet!" one of them quipped. Eventually, G1 + CS finally taxied out for its heavily-laden take-off from Villacoublay, France, with its four x 250kg bombs at around midnight and set course for the south coast of England. In the pilot's pre-flight checks, Böker caught a glimpse of the unit emblem as it flashed briefly into view on the waggling rudder; three little fish painted onto a shield. The emblem reflected a German saying that implied the message: 'it will be easy.' Momentarily Böker was reassured. It would, after all, be easy. And to start with it was.

Uffz Kurt Böker of 8./KG55.

Crossing in over the Dorset coast, pilot Fw Theodor Metzner held his course on a north-westerly heading, on track to his target at Bristol.[2] However, the crew were not long over English soil when their aircraft was caught in a cone of

---

2 Whilst some sources indicate that the Bristol Aeroplane Works was to have been the target, other sources reckon the actual intended target to have been the Avonmouth Docks area.

searchlights whilst flying at just over 15,000ft. Eventually, though, Metzner shook off the searchlights and continued on. When the crew were nearing Bristol the aircraft came under intense anti-aircraft fire and eventually took a serious hit in the port wing. Almost at once, Metzner ordered the bombs to be jettisoned and they were dropped hastily when the aircraft was over the centre of Bristol. Böker, who in the terror of the moment had the image of the chalked cross on the briefing room blackboard flash before him, takes up the story:

Fw Theodore Metzner, pilot of the Heinkel.

"The hit tilted the aircraft sideways through thirty degrees before we settled back onto a normal attitude, but after that nothing would function properly. The port engine and flying controls were damaged and the Heinkel kept veering further to the left and, in this manner, we lost a lot of height. When we had dropped to about 9,000ft the pilot decided to give the order to bale out. I sent a radio message and made ready to jump.

"First, the flight engineer and youngest crew member, nineteen-year-old Gefr Ernst Ostheimer, jumped. Then, the air gunner, twenty-two-year-old Gefr Heinz Morgenthal jumped – then, it was my turn. There was nothing to see through the escape hatch except a black gaping hole. I knew I had to jump; there was no longer any time to hesitate or think about it. Right hand on D-Ring. Legs closed. And jump! In seconds the aircraft has passed above me but to start with I couldn't get the rip-cord to come free from its covering with my right hand.

"Then, my left hand came to the rescue and there was a crash as a jolt went through my entire body. The parachute cracked open. Quietly swinging with its load, it gently sank to the English soil below. It was completely quiet; in the distance there was the sound of an aircraft, otherwise nothing. No one could have seen the spot where I fell in the darkness with only the pale moon shining down as my sole witness.

"Once I was on the ground I got rid of my flying suit and equipment and took a good look around. I had landed next to a fence in a field, and although I had sprained my left leg

Gefr Ernst Ostheimer, seen here during an excursion to the recently-occupied Channel Islands.

on landing I set off at dawn to give myself up to the police. After all, it was impossible to leave the island. After a short while I heard a car coming behind me. I stood still and saw a police car approaching and pull up next to me. I was taken straight away to a police station where the bobby's wife gave me a good cup of tea and biscuits, for which I was very thankful. My imprisonment, though, had begun."

Whilst Böker had taken a pragmatic view about the possibility of escape from the British Isles, and the futility of doing anything other than giving himself up, three of his comrades had taken a rather different view. For the time being at least, their own particular wars were not quite over.

Just like Böker, the pilot of Heinkel 111 G1 + CS, Fw Theodor Metzner, had little time on the ground before being captured although for the other three, Fw Josef Markl, Gefr Ernst Ostheimer and Gefr Heinz Morgenthal their adventures were only just beginning. As for their aircraft, however, the stricken and now un-manned bomber flew on for a short distance before finally impacting into gardens adjacent to labourers' cottages in Fullers Lane at Woolton Hill, East Woodhay, in Berkshire. Here, a Mr and Mrs Frank Bray and their daughter Alice and Mr and Mrs Roland Drage lived side-by-side in the two cottages. Mr Drage was a member of the LDV and was quoted on the episode in the *Newbury Weekly News* of 1 August 1940:

"We were awakened by the back-firing of an aeroplane engine. The 'plane seemed low and then the engine was cut off every few minutes. The pilot seemed to be in difficulty. We heard a terrific screaming noise followed by two explosions and then a blinding flash."

The impact had caused the bomber to break into several large sections, with one wing ending up some forty yards from the main wreckage which had come to rest on top of an air raid shelter that, by great good fortune, neither the Brays not the Drages were occupying. The surrounding produce, planted by the two families, had however been destroyed in the crash. What hadn't been ruined was subsequently trampled by eager sightseers over the following days.

This was the scene at Fullers Lane, East Woodhay, on the morning of 30 July 1940.

Certainly, the two families had had a lucky escape although Mrs Bray suffered a heart attack (from which she subsequently recovered) and Mr Drage's terrier bolted in panic, with the dog eventually being found the following morning. Whilst Patch the terrier was at large, however, so were three German airmen and they, of course, were of considerably more concern to the police and military authorities.

Initially, it was assumed that one crew member was dead in the wreckage of the aircraft (this being reported in one of the preliminary RAF intelligence reports of 30 July 1940) and although this was quickly discounted it did, of course, mean that at least some of the crew had apparently survived and were most likely on the run. However, we know that Böker and Metzner were quite quickly apprehended. We know that Böker was picked up by a local policeman, whereas Metzner was captured by LDV man, Albert Admans.

Admans, a local taxi-driver, was a veteran of World War One and had been awarded the Military Medal in the conflict and came on duty that night about half an hour after the crash. It was some three hours later, however, that a special constable had approached Admans' post to report what he described as "…a queer sort of fellow standing in a ditch smoking a cigarette about a mile down the road". The LDV man decided to investigate, and, taking his rifle, he set off in his taxi to see what he could find. To begin with he discovered nothing at the place the special constable had indicated, but then he spotted a man ahead of him walking along the edge of the road. Taking his rifle from the car he approached the man and called "Halt!" At once, the stranger stopped and raised his hands and Admans cautiously approached him, his rifle levelled. Later, he told the local newspapers:

> "He was in overalls and looked more like a navvy than anything else. He was a young man of about twenty to twenty-three years, about five feet ten inches in height and stockily built. When I halted him he turned and started to talk in German. He handed me his oxygen apparatus which he had hung in front of him and took off his belt and revolver. After this I ran my hands over him to see if he had any more arms."

Admans took his reluctant but somewhat resigned captive in the taxi and drove back to his post where he collected one of the other LDV men on duty. The trio then set off for Newbury police station and, passing the spot where Metzner had just been captured, noticed his parachute hanging in nearby telephone wires. Handing their captive over, the German indicated by hand signals that he was a pilot and although one other man, Böker, had already been taken prisoner it was quickly apparent that the type of aircraft heaped in an untidy pile at Fullers Lane usually carried more than two men. In confirmation, the captives had asked about their comrades and thus word was quickly sent out to police and military units that they should be on the lookout for German airmen.

At first, the search was perhaps not so desperately urgent. Surely, the men would be found, and quickly. Of course, there was always the possibility that they were no longer still alive and although not many German airmen had been captured in Britain those who had had been taken quickly and with little fuss. There was certainly no reason to suspect that it would be any different.

The relatively remote rural location into which the crew had baled out, and the fact that their parachute descent had been at night, had surely aided their ability to slip away unnoticed and were it not for the fact that Metzner and Böker hadn't actively tried to avoid detection they too might have been able to go into hiding like their colleagues. However, it wasn't difficult to estimate the area into which the airmen had most probably descended and with news of the escapees spreading fast there were many eyes and ears on the lookout as well as the teams of soldiers, LDV men and policemen who were actively scouring the countryside for any sign of the fugitives.

The net was certainly closing in, and it was felt that they could not have got far. Ill-equipped for escape, and wearing clothes that would immediately attract attention, the men stood little chance if they ventured too close to towns or villages or onto roads or footpaths and there was no hope that they could get onto public transport. In any event, what was the point? And where could they go?

The point, perhaps, was that they were giving their enemy the slip and tying up effort and resources in the manhunt rather than having made any realistic or conscious effort to consider a serious escape attempt from Britain. However, two of the men, Gefr Heinz Morgenthal and Gefr Ernst Ostheimer, had happened to meet up with each other not long after they had landed and the pair managed to lay low and tried to hatch an escape plan.

By the time the second night had passed since their enforced descent into enemy territory the pair had perhaps become emboldened in their plans. Between them, they realised they had a few English coins and a few bits of confectionary, cigarettes and matches that had been picked up on a very recent trip to the German-occupied Channel Islands. Quite how the objects could help them in their attempts to remain at liberty was something of a challenge that the pair hadn't quite yet addressed by the time they were finally detected and taken POW some forty-eight hours after landing.

In the end it was sheer bad luck which resulted in their capture after a determined effort to find them in woods at White Oak by Canadian soldiers had initially failed following a day-long search. As the soldiers returned to their trucks, unsuccessful in their hunt, one of the Canadians wandered off to relieve himself in the undergrowth when an urgent shout suddenly went up. "Over here!" The startled soldier had found himself urinating on an equally-astonished Heinz Morgenthal and Ernst Ostheimer before the two were hauled out of their hiding spot under a Rhododendron bush and hurriedly 'interrogated' by a local man who could speak German.

Almost at once, the two Germans were marched at gunpoint back into the woods as eleven-year-old Anthony Gale looked on, boyishly excited by the unfolding drama. To him, both men looked drab and dirty in their blue-grey uniforms. Both were muddy, unwashed and unshaven although their yellow collar tabs gave a vivid flash of colour to two men who, to young Anthony, were "entirely grey young men". Evidently, the return into the woods with the two captives was to search for one of the airmen's pistols which the group returned with some while later.

Whilst the war was now over for Morgenthal and Ostheimer, there was still one man at large and although we know little of these two men's adventures over that forty-eight-hour period, and there is no clue in surviving RAF Air Intelligence reports, the story of the fifth man is recorded in some considerable detail. His experiences in the game of escape and evasion are surely unique in wartime Britain; a nation that was on a paranoid lookout for fifth-columnists, spies and German paratroopers where many thought that such parachutists would almost certainly be in disguise and probably dressed as nuns!

When Fw Josef Markl, the observer on board G1 + CS, had jumped into the inky blackness that night he probably did so in the complete and certain expectation that he would almost immediately fall into captivity. That alone was a worrying thought, especially as he, too, remembered the omen of that chalked cross on the briefing room blackboard. He had heard rumours that he could expect to be treated badly at the hands of the British public. After all, hadn't he just dumped the bomb load of four 250kg bombs and seen them all explode violently on the city below? From the very moment he had tried to exit the Heinkel that wretched chalk cross had repeatedly flashed in front of his eyes.

As he jumped, disaster! His foot had become caught in the exit hatch and Markl was momentarily suspended; buffeted by the slipstream and battered mercilessly against the lower fuselage of the bomber. In the howling maelstrom that tore at his body his parachute pack had blown outwards from him and he only became free

Fw Josef Markl, the observer of the Heinkel 111.

when the man behind him, Theo Metzner, released his foot thus allowing a relieved but somewhat bruised Markl to tumble earthwards. For a few seconds he had all but given up, but now he had to wrestle his parachute pack back to his body in order to try to pull the D-Ring. Finally, and much to Markl's intense relief, the parachute canopy billowed open above him although he now had to endure a strenuous descent in a high wind, being buffeted and tossed from side to side like a wildly oscillating pendulum.

„DER SPIEß AUF ABWEGEN."

Markl's erstwhile comrades back at 8./KG55's French airfield placed this cartoon in the unit's Christmas 1940 souvenir booklet. The caption roughly translates: 'The Spieß [nickname for Feldwebel rank] on his journey.'

As he drifted earthwards, Markl spotted what he thought might be water in the pale moonlight and made determined efforts to try to steer away from it, but as he got lower he realised that what he was seeing was in fact a town. Almost certainly Newbury. Finally, he crashed through the branches of a pine tree – but wasn't yet on terra-firma. Hopelessly entangled in the tree's branches with the lead from his flying helmet, and now draped in shroud lines that were pulling taut while the canopy flapped in the wind, the likelihood of strangulation might have seemed a distinct possibility as Markl struggled to stop himself from slipping from his tree-top perch.

Finally, and with some considerable effort, he managed to free himself from his flying helmet with the troublesome radio lead and choking neck strap with its tightly fitting throat microphone and was finally to be able to operate the release box of his parachute harness. Now, he sat on his high branch and methodically destroyed everything on his person that he thought might be of any military value; his papers, his life jacket and anything he could find in his pockets. Having taken stock of his situation, and his surroundings, he gingerly climbed down and hid his parachute, flying helmet and combination suit and struck out across the countryside to find the nearest road. His intention was clear. He would walk into the nearest town and give himself up. There really wasn't much option, he considered.

Trudging off towards Newbury, dressed in his Luftwaffe uniform and clumping along in what were bulky flying boots, he reckoned that it wouldn't be long before he was spotted and taken. But when he was actually in the town, he hesitated. Thus far, nobody had even seen him. And what if the locals were hostile?

Suddenly, his mind was made up; he would rather be taken than surrender and he quickly headed back out of Newbury to a spot about 500 yards past the first houses on the edge of town. Here, he found some scrub and settled down amongst the nettles and bracken and waited. Hungry, he tucked into a bar of chocolate that he had kept in his uniform pocket but cursed the loss of a larger box of ration chocolate, the Luftwaffe-issue Scho-Ka-Kola that had tumbled out of his flying overalls during his rumbustious parachute descent. Thirst, too, started to take its toll and his craving had probably not been helped by his chocolate consumption. There was little hope of getting water without the risk of showing himself so, in an ingenious improvisation, he soaked up moisture from the heavily dew-laden grass onto his handkerchief and wrung out a few precious drops. It was a laborious process, but it gave him at least a little water in his parched mouth.

Undiscovered, he decided to stay put at this location for a few days and was sustained further when he managed to find a little trickle of water to drink as he foraged edible roots from nearby fields. Bored and restless in his bracken and nettle hide, he eventually elected to venture up to a high ridge that he could see in the neighbourhood and from where he thought he might be able to study the landscape. He might also find a better food and water supply, or so he reasoned.

Under the cover of darkness he headed out at around midnight for the ridge, travelling along roads but taking cover if he heard people or vehicles. After about an hour and a half he reached his objective and stayed put in the woods there for five or six days during which time he saw or heard no-one albeit that a massive manhunt was going on in the countryside all around to try to find him. In fact, Josef Markl had found his way to Pilot Hill above East Woodhay and it was here, wandering around the Lower and Upper Eastwick Copses, that he would spend most of his time on the run. It wasn't long, though, before it seemed that the game might be up.

Exhausted, Markl was resting under a beech tree with a red handkerchief draped over his face against the sun when he suddenly heard voices nearby; voices that were far too close for comfort or for him to consider moving lest he might draw attention to himself. Instead, he froze and waited as two men, farmers he thought, passed within a mere thirty yards of the spot where he lay as they went off to examine a nearby hay field. Once they had passed, he quietly slipped away to hide when he realised that by some miracle he had not been seen by them. However he was becoming weaker and weaker from lack of nourishment and growing more and more indifferent to the prospect of capture, although he still managed to evade other civilians despite this. Thoughts, too, of his wife in far-away Bonn who was expecting their child concerned him greatly.

The longer it was before he was officially in British hands, the longer it would be before any word could reach her that he was at least safe. But still, for the time being, he clung onto his freedom such as it was. By now, and although he didn't know it, the RAF no longer believed that at least one man had died in the wreckage of the Heinkel 111 when 'the charred human hand' found in the burnt remnants of the cockpit turned out to be nothing more than a leather glove left behind by one of the crew. Somewhere, Josef Markl was likely still out there. And he needed to be found.

On day eight the sound of shooting alarmed him. Were they now coming to get him and shooting into the woods? Cautiously, Josef spied out where the shots were coming from and watched a man out shooting pigeons with his Spaniel dog. Here was a double danger. A man with a gun who also had a dog; one that could doubtless sniff him out. As quickly as his weakened body would allow, Markl climbed a tree and sat on a branch as the unwitting hunter and his dog both passed beneath the branch where the Luftwaffe airman sat nervously fingering the holster of his Luger pistol in the event that he might need it. As he did so, the futility of his situation dawned ever more clearly on him. The prospect of using his pistol, even in self-defence, was ludicrous. Killing or even wounding a civilian could only be a virtual death sentence. If he was subsequently captured, he might expect the severest of punishments.

In all probability, he thought, those who might now be out looking for him would be rather more intent on shooting him than capturing him alive. He needed to have a complete re-think about what to do, especially as hunger and thirst were both increasingly taking their toll on his physical and mental state. First, he wanted to get some rest before deciding on his course of action but the woods on this Sunday also seemed popular with courting couples and he spent some time avoiding them, although they perhaps were less of a danger to him. At least they were preoccupied with other things, he thought. Once the coast was clear, and exploring as far as he could manage, Markl found an unlocked hut on a clay pigeon shooting butt where he took shelter and spent the night, deciding that tomorrow he would eventually give himself up.

On day nine, Tuesday 6 August, Josef Markl decided that the time had finally come to face the world and he wearily made his way to the nearest road. This time, there was no need to be cautious. Quite the opposite, in fact. However, giving himself up didn't prove to be as easy as he had hoped. This dishevelled and unshaven man in a strange uniform, and a pistol holster at his hip, did not exactly lend himself to unexpected close encounters in a quiet country lane. Here the first person he chanced across was a young lady, a Miss Jessie Ballard. As soon as she saw him a somewhat alarmed Jessie ran off at full pelt and did not stop until she had reached Highclere post office where she knew there to be a telephone. It is presumed that the young Jessie called the police to report how she had encountered the missing German airman but, as it happened, events rather overtook both Jessie and Josef.

Next, after Jessie, a man and a girl on bicycles hove into view and approached Markl but simply looked very startled and pedalled away, somewhat faster. Later, a lone man in a car looked rather more than surprised and refused to stop to offer him a lift. He, too, drove away quickly. Was he that frightening, wondered Markl? Giving himself up was almost becoming harder than evading capture, or so it seemed. Surely somebody would accept his surrender? In the event, he didn't have much longer to wait.

Riding out with her chauffeur from her home at nearby Woolton House, Lady Buckland drove almost serenely into view as Markl stood his ground in the roadway and indicated for the car to stop. Lady Buckland didn't hesitate. Ordering chauffeur Nicholls to pull over, she wound down her window and spoke to the exhausted Luftwaffe airman. In relatively good English, Markl explained who he was and that he wanted to be taken to the nearest military commander. Undeterred by this dirty and somewhat smelly flier, the feisty Lady Buckland ordered Nicholls to let the German, still armed, sit in the front of the car with him and for the chauffeur to drive straight away to Newbury police station. Clearly, her ladyship didn't want this scruffy German sharing the back seat with her but she was, nevertheless, quite happy to engage in conversation with him.

En route to the police station, Lady Buckland explained that she was not in the least bit surprised or perturbed to come across a German airman under such unusual circumstances. After all, the bomber had crashed onto her land and a manhunt for him had been underway for several days, now.

Markl, it seems, told her ladyship that he had been made to believe that German airmen who gave themselves up in England would almost certainly be treated very badly. Perhaps concerned about his potential ill-treatment, and for how long he might have to endure it, Markl asked if she thought that the English would give up. "No!" she responded somewhat imperiously: "Why on earth should we?" If Josef Markl was dismayed by her sharp response, he nevertheless bowed to her ladyship when he got out of the car as they arrived at the police station and gratefully thanked her for her courtesy as Lady Buckland demanded of the arresting police superintendent that he immediately give the German airman a good meal. In a clearly deferential response, the arresting officer assured her that he would certainly do so.

Shortly afterwards, and having been duly relieved of his Luger pistol and its sixteen rounds of ammunition, a ravenous Josef Markl was generously fed and the fugitive airman hungrily tucked into his first meal since supper at Villacoublay on 28 July, now some ten days prior.

In his intelligence assessment following Markl's capture and interrogation, Sqn Ldr S. D. Felkin, head of the RAF's Air Intelligence A.I.1(k) noted:

'The prisoner of war handed in his Ausweis (pass book) which he had retained. This fact is especially interesting in view of the pains which he had taken to destroy all papers which he considered of military value. He had put all personal considerations aside but it would indeed have been to his own advantage to give himself up and have the news of his safety sent to his wife who was about to have a baby. The prisoner's morale is still very high and he suffered remarkably little from his experience.'

It would certainly be a long captivity for Josef and one wonders if his morale was still quite as high as it was when observed by Felkin by the time of the war's end. In fact, and by the time he had finally got back to Germany at the end of 1946, his child, unborn as he wandered about the Berkshire countryside, was now nearly seven years old.

Fw Josef Markl would hold the record for remaining at large and on the run in Britain for the longest single period of any Luftwaffe airman during World War Two; nine days in total. For most German airmen, though, captivity would come almost immediately when they arrived on British soil and in one notable instance that would even be before the engine of the airman's forced-landed aircraft had been switched off!

CHAPTER 3

The Lost Post

FLIGHT LIEUTENANT LAURENCE IRVING WAS an RAF intelligence officer attached to the army's XII Corps HQ in Tunbridge Wells during 1940 and it was his duty to liaise with the army on all matters pertaining to aerial activity. Clearly, there was a good deal of such action in the region during the summer of that year and, as mentioned in the previous chapter, some considerable nervousness existed over the possible intrusion of agents, enemy troops or fifth-columnists. There was certainly no shortage of reports to the police of people acting suspiciously, or of odd movements of vehicles or even aircraft. Much of the latter, of course, might well have been borne out of perfectly legitimate military activity that was observed by civilians who had no proper understanding of what they might be seeing.

To Flt Lt Irving, however, the reports regarding a repeated and unexplained dawn arrival of a Lysander over the South Downs near Lancing was cause for concern and he spent many days during July 1940 trying to unravel what was going on. In the event, it was all to no avail although he remained certain that there was some covert activity involving an

Flt Lt Laurence Irving, 1940.

aircraft that may have been captured in France and that was now engaged in the delivering of packages to a remote Sussex field.

What convinced Irving was the unshakeable testimony from soldiers of the 17th Lancers who told him they had seen a Lysander swoop low over farm buildings at Steep Down, circle, and then drop a package on 21 July. Minutes later, a black limousine with a white roof appeared and three people got out, retrieved the package and then drove off. Locally, the Observer Corps were able to confirm the presence of the aircraft but Irving's enquiries with RAF Lysander squadrons drew a blank. None of them had had aircraft operating in the area at that time.

Additionally, and further raising suspicions, the car number plate that had been noted by the soldiers was checked out by the local constabulary and found to be fake. Irving was sure he was onto something and, to be fair, these were certainly some very odd and unexplained circumstances that warranted further investigation. Not only that, but a few days later on the 24th at around 06.20 hours a similar event was observed with the Lysander circling low over Hill Barn when a person appeared from the farm buildings there, walked towards New Barn and then returned back to Hill Barn whereupon the Lysander flew off. Again, Irving checked with RAF squadrons and found that only 26 and 225 Squadrons operated Lysanders in the general area. Both units confirmed it was not one of their aeroplanes. For Irving, the mystery deepened and his suspicions grew.

Keeping watch over subsequent dawns Irving was accompanied by Wg Cdr Kaye of GHQ Home Forces, but although the Lysander failed to appear the pair certainly became convinced that something was afoot. As investigations gathered pace, Irving was involved in discussions with the local police, Scotland Yard and MI5 as to what had gone on. In his book *Great Interruption* Irving says of the event:

'….Kaye and I were convinced this was a line of communication between the Nazis and an underground subversive group in England – a kind of fifth column that I had seen so successfully employed in France.'

Going to his dawn vigil on the Downs one last time, Irving was astonished to see a car that fitted exactly the description given by the troopers and hoped the vehicle would continue on its route that led to a nearby military checkpoint and where the driver could be apprehended. Although armed, Irving had been reminded that he had no powers to stop the vehicle and followed his instructions to the letter. Unfortunately, and although Irving was sure that the vehicle's route would take it to the checkpoint, it turned off on a road that he didn't know about and was lost to view. He had, though, scrawled down the vehicle registration on the back of his map. Again, it was checked out. And again it was a fake. This time, it was registered as a two-seater sports car belonging to a female doctor in London.

Despite all of the unexplained circumstances, Irving was frustrated that no further actions were taken and the matter was dropped. Although the events remain a mystery they were most likely either innocent (at least, in the context of any covert activity related to security issues) or entirely explicable in some other way. It was definitely the case that rather excitable responses to 'odd' events were not exclusively the province of the civilian population. The military, too, were sometimes prone to seeing the proverbial fifth-columnist in every shadow.

Nevertheless, Irving was ordered to stand down his investigations and duly notified the various army and RAF officers who had been assisting him, including an officer of air intelligence A.I.(k), Plt Off Sankey, based at RAF Biggin Hill. For now, the matter was forgotten and Irving's war had moved on with matters relating to the defence of southern Britain in the event of invasion. Meanwhile, the Battle of Britain gathered momentum overhead.

A little over a month after the strange Lysander episode and during the sunny late afternoon of 28 August 1940, schoolmaster George Bennett and James Palmer of the East Sussex county surveyor's department were walking on Race Hill, at Lewes in East Sussex (not many miles from Lancing) when they heard the approaching sound of aircraft. It was not altogether an unusual occurrence for that period of the Battle of Britain but the pair were more than surprised to see a small bi-plane in German markings circle around twice and then land on the old Lewes racecourse. Overhead two RAF Hurricanes circled, but they flew away as Bennett, Palmer and a number of other locals approached the bi-plane which sat with its engine still running on the gallops, just to the west of the track leading from behind Lewes prison up towards Offham Hill.

The Gotha 145 bi-plane photographed shortly after landing on the South Downs near Lewes, 28 August 1940, attracts a crowd of intrigued locals.

Almost immediately, the pilot climbed from the aircraft and was approached by the two civilians and as Bennett was fluent in German he asked the pilot if he was alone. The reply was affirmative, but the young pilot was clearly in a state of some shock and confusion. Palmer then asked Bennett to enquire how the engine might be switched off, and after the pilot had vaguely indicated the switches to him Palmer leaned into the cockpit and turned off the still idling motor.

By now, other civilians and the Home Guard were arriving on the scene in some numbers and Bennett only had time to ask the German pilot one more thing; "Where are you from?" The reply "Stuttgart" was all the German was able to mutter before members of the Home Guard arrested the clearly agitated and severely shaken pilot. He was not in the charge of the local Home Guard for very long, though, before a party of police officers came puffing up the hill to the scene of the incident.

Taking charge of the pilot, Superintendent Holloway detailed Sgt Simmonds and other officers to guard the aeroplane from the ever-gathering crowd of curious civilians as he marched his prisoner back down the hill with Inspector Britton to a waiting car for conveyance back to the nearby Lewes police station.

Britton, interviewed in 1973, recalled how the German airman was very young and very frightened as well as being somewhat shocked by his untimely arrival in England and expressed considerable alarm as to what his commanding officer would say about it all. Britton and Holloway tried to allay his fears by telling him that he almost certainly wouldn't be seeing his CO for some while yet, to which the German replied: "Well, that's all very well so long as he doesn't get shot down and taken prisoner too!"

The aeroplane that had made this unusual arrival on British soil was, in fact, a Gotha Go 145B training and communications aircraft, Werke Nummer 1115, which was on the strength of Stab./JG27 based on the Cherbourg peninsula. This Messerschmitt 109 E fighter unit, just like most other fighter units on the Channel coast, was using the Go 145 as its communications 'hack' aircraft. On the day in question Uffz Leonhard Buckle was detailed to carry out routine mail delivery flights between the Channel Islands and JG27's bases around Cherbourg.

Unfortunately for Buckle, though, a sea fog had developed during his transit flight and he quickly became lost and disorientated, eventually finding himself a long way out to sea and with no land in sight. Quite what happened as the frightened young pilot contemplated his impending fate in the English Channel is unclear, although somewhere off the south coast of England a pair of patrolling Hurricanes evidently chanced across the bi-plane and escorted it to land, eventually forcing it down at Lewes.

Regrettably, and despite an extensive search, it has proved impossible to identify in any RAF operations record books or combat reports of the Hurricane squadron or pilots involved although it seems most unlikely that such an unusual encounter would have gone un-recorded. In

Uffz Leonhard Buckle, shortly after his ill-fated mission.

fact, and had Buckle not found himself being 'encouraged' to land by a pair of Hurricanes, his fate might well have been worse than captivity. Almost certainly, and by the time he had found himself approaching the Sussex coast, he would not have been able to make it back to the French coast given his fuel state and the maximum endurance of the Gotha 145.

For British intelligence there must surely have been a substantial coup in the sacks of mail found in the second cockpit of the Gotha, although just as it has proved impossible to identify the Hurricane aircraft involved in this episode, the author has been unable to source any specific intelligence summary or assessment of the documents retrieved at the National Archives, or elsewhere. Equally, or perhaps more surprisingly, there is no interrogation summary of Buckle in the files of A.I.1 (k) – the RAF's Air Intelligence 'k' branch who were tasked with the interrogation of Luftwaffe prisoners. Reports exist for many other prisoners taken at this time – but not for Buckle.

However, the value of the undelivered mail to RAF intelligence officers must have been quite enormous, especially when interrogating subsequent POWs from JG27, for example. It is not hard to imagine how disconcerting it would have been for prisoners to discover that personal and perhaps intimate information about unit personnel was known to the British.

As regards subsequent searches for detailed information on this coup, however, it is possible that some extensive and separate report was made on Leonhard Buckle and his unusual arrival with the haul of documents. Perhaps such a file, if it indeed exists, might conceivably be subject to future discovery in some other dusty and overlooked archive. However, what is certain is that both Buckle and his aeroplane came under considerable scrutiny almost as soon as they had arrived on the South Downs.

Buckle, having been initially searched at Lewes police station, was locked up in the cells there and at 18.36 Sgt Simmonds telephoned to RAF Biggin Hill requesting that an interrogation officer be sent. Returning to the aircraft (now being guarded by men of 325 Company of the Royal Engineers) Superintendent Holloway found a Pilot Officer Gibbs and three other RAF officers present at the site and was told by Gibbs that he had been sent to interrogate the prisoner. At around 8pm Gibbs interrogated Buckle at the police station, but was then notified by his superior officers that he should cease his task and that a Pilot Officer Sankey was on his way to carry out the interrogation instead. This, of course, was the very same man who had had some involvement with the mysterious Lysander episode.

At 22.15 Sankey arrived and started his interrogation of the prisoner, only to be interrupted in his task some three quarters of an hour later by the arrival of a Pilot Officer Birch. He too had been detailed to interrogate Buckle! Clearly, a great deal of interest was being placed on the prisoner and his astonishing cargo and Birch immediately demanded that he be given the letters and documents found in the Gotha. Sussex police reports tell us that Sankey declined to hand them over and it was not until two in the morning that an exhausted Buckle was allowed to get some rest and a bemused Supt Holloway bade farewell to Birch and Sankey – the pair of them still arguing about who should be in charge of the recovered documents.

It can only be speculation, but this unusual arrival of a light communications aircraft on the South Downs, just a few miles from the location of the reported 'Lysander episode' at Steyning, might well have rung some alarm bells for Sankey when it was reported to him. All the more so, perhaps, when he heard that the aircraft contained sacks full of mail. Sankey was almost at once heading out from RAF Biggin Hill to Lewes, and given the unsolved puzzle of the 'Lysander' and its 'packages' it is perhaps not surprising to discover his reluctance to hand over the mail bags to anyone else once they were in his hands.

Of course, there was absolutely no connection and any link that may have initially been formed in the minds of RAF intelligence officers was very quickly dispelled. If there was any supposed connection then it proved to be purely coincidental.

Intriguingly, Irving's personal diary notes that the very next day, 29 August 1940, Plt Off Sankey called on him at his HQ in Broadwater Down, Tunbridge Wells, when: '....we discussed various points'. It is inconceivable that the circumstances of Leonhard Buckle's arrival were not discussed, although it very clearly threw no light whatsoever on the Lancing incidents. Perhaps it showed, however, that this war could throw up some unexpected and often very hard-to-explain events.

As for the aeroplane, it was left under army guard until 31 August when it was flown from Lewes to the Royal Aircraft Establishment, Farnborough, by Sqn Ldr H. J. Wilson although not before RAF roundels had been hastily painted onto the wings and fuselage. Brief test flights were made at Farnborough, on 6 and 10 September, with the aircraft now allocated the RAF serial number BV207 and standard trainer aircraft colours applied – yellow undersides and fuselage sides with dark earth and dark green upper surface camouflage.

The Gotha did not fly again until 12 December 1940 when it was air tested before delivery, by air, to 20 MU at RAF Aston Down on 1 January 1941. By September of that year it had been allocated to RAF Maintenance Command and was given the maintenance serial 2682M. It was then issued to No 2 School of Technical Training, RAF Cosford, although its value to the RAF in terms of technical training might, perhaps, have been questionable. Nevertheless, a number of otherwise useless airframes were often used for air training by the Air Defence Cadet Corps (the forerunner of the Air Training Corps) or for ground trade training in such areas as airframe repair or the ground handling of aircraft. However, the Gotha did not last long and by 1 April 1942 it had been struck off charge.

Whilst Buckle languished in a POW camp in Canada, reflecting on his disastrous postal delivery flight, his aeroplane was eventually broken up for scrap. Somehow, however, at least one part had survived the scrap man's axe and the foundry smelter.

Under new ownership. The Gotha 145 in the national markings of the RAF.

In recent years an object originally described as 'a rudder pedal from a Junkers 87' turned up at a collector's market in the UK, although it didn't take long to identify the pedal as something else instead. Not only did it not look quite right for it to have originated from a Junkers 87 Stuka, but part number clues gave the game away. Fortuitously, German aircraft of the period had a clear type identifier number, always prefixed R8, which was marked onto cast alloy parts. The pedal was indeed a cast magnesium alloy, and this perhaps explains its survival as it would doubtless have not been of any use or value for scrap metal. However, as a cast piece it carried the all-important identifier – in this case R8 145.

Without a doubt this was the rudder pedal from a Gotha 145. Not only that, but it *had* to have come from Leonhard Buckle's aircraft and the reasoning for this was very simple. Not only had this item originally turned up in a scrap yard not far from RAF Cosford where the Gotha had ended its days, but amongst the very large number and variety of German aircraft types brought to this country, either through landing here or being transported to Britain post-war, there was only ever *one* Gotha 145 amongst them.

The landing of Leonhard Buckle must have been one of the most unusual Luftwaffe arrivals in the country during the Battle of Britain. On the face of it, here was an insignificant aircraft with a very lowly-ranked and relatively inexperienced Luftwaffe pilot. Neither the aircraft nor its pilot could have been of much intelligence value or particular interest to the RAF. The contents of the mail sacks on board, though, may well have been a veritable gold mine of information; a fact that might well be reinforced by the efforts of no less than three RAF intelligence officers, all vying with each other to interview the prisoner once he was in custody and to get their hands on the captured contents.

CHAPTER 4 Rooftop Pursuit

BY LATE SEPTEMBER, 1940 THE inhabitants of south-east England had generally become accustomed to a daily routine of aerial combat during the Battle of Britain; the staccato clatter of machine guns, interwoven vapour trails, wildly howling aero engines and the punctuation of blossoming parachutes. The people of the East Sussex market town of Hailsham were no exception to this familiarity with the on-going sight and sound of battle, but the noises reaching them on the morning of Friday 27 September were different; louder, and somehow more intrusive with an urgency that had been emphasised by the wailing of the town's air raid sirens. And yet, for all the distant noise that grew ever closer, there was no sign of the combatants.

From all around – at least, to the north and north west – the tonal rise and fall of aero engines in violent manoeuvre and the furious chatter of machine guns and harsher bark of cannon fire assailed the air. Then, suddenly, an explosion of noise and commotion erupted as two aeroplanes finally flashed into view and lifted themselves over the rooftops on the town's outskirts with just feet, if not inches, to spare. A Messerschmitt 110 with a Hurricane almost fixed to its tail. In an instant it was all over.

The Hurricane lifted momentarily away, banked slightly and dived towards the enemy aircraft – slicing with a fearful crunch into the twin tail. Like some insect dismembered in mid-flight, the severed tail flicked and tumbled away as the fuselage pitched violently forward and impacted into the ground with awful finality. Arcing fiercely around, and above the disintegrating Messerschmitt, the roaring Hurricane slammed into a mature oak tree with a splintering and ear-splitting crunch and dismembered itself across the fields.

It had been a transition from the deafening roar of combat to near silence in just a split-second. Only the very distant rumble of battle could now be heard above the crackle of fire as widely-scattered wreckage blazed. In that moment, a boyishly young fighter pilot had forever established his place as a hero in the hearts and minds of the residents of Hailsham. That he was never recognised for this singular act of gallantry has been a persistently niggling puzzle for many of the town's population.

In the combats that faced the German crews and the defending British forces on 27 September 1940 the outcome for the Luftwaffe would be serious. Indeed, it would be catastrophic for one particular unit, the V/LG1. That said, it was no picnic for RAF Fighter Command, either. It is no exaggeration to suggest that by the end of the morning some of the finest young men of both the Luftwaffe and RAF would lie scattered like fallen leaves across the autumnal landscape of Sussex, but in the examination of this particular case we need, first, to put the episode into context.

At 08.30 on that Friday morning, at airfields across northern France, the sound of Daimler-Benz and Junkers Jumo aero engines broke the countryside tranquillity as they roared into life amidst a

This was the severed tail of the Messerschmitt 110 brought down over Hailsham. The fin is marked with four roundels signifying victories over four RAF aircraft.

haze of blue exhaust smoke and formations of bomber aircraft with their fighter escorts taxied out before taking off for another attack on England. The bomber force comprised fifteen Junkers 88s of I./KG77, with eleven Messerschmitt 110s of V./LG1 and thirteen of II and III./ZG76 flying as close escort. Indirect escort was flown by forty Me 109s of I and II Gruppen of JG27. Target; London.

The objective was to draw British fighters into the air and thus weaken defences to the maximum extent possible in preparation for two much bigger raids that were planned for later that day – at noon, and in the afternoon. In the event, British fighters were certainly drawn into the air *en masse* to meet the threat and just as the Luftwaffe had intended.

Between 08.45 and 09.05 no less than 160 Hurricanes and Spitfires had been scrambled to intercept the threat – outnumbering, by a very considerable margin, the attacking force and, in this instance at least, shattering the enduring myth that defending British forces were always pitched against the fearful numerical odds that were stacked against them.

Certainly, in terms of total combat aircraft available to RAF Fighter Command the odds were, overall, in the Germans' favour. In terms of the individual actions fought within the context of the Battle of Britain those odds were not always translated into the actual numbers of aircraft participating within specific engagements. Such was the case during the morning of 27 September 1940. Crossing the coast between Hastings and Dover, the formation of Junkers 88s flew at approximately 15,000ft whilst the Me 110 formations lurked protectively some 1,500ft above them. Higher still, and just below the cloud ceiling at 21,000, flew the top cover of Me 109s.

Alerted to the enemy presence, to their location and course the RAF defenders were vectored, squadron by squadron, into positions for attack and interception. It was the Hurricanes of 213 Squadron, airborne from RAF Tangmere, who first crossed into the path of the north-bound invaders near Mayfield. Immediately, the Messerschmitt 110s had formed into two defensive circles (ZG76 and V./LG1) – a typical Me 110 manoeuvre that could be difficult and dangerous to break into for the execution of any effective attack.

Still circling, and still moving northwards with their charges, the Me 110 formations probably became rather more pre-occupied with self-preservation than with directly protecting the still advancing Junkers 88s. Whatever, the effect was still the same because the attacking fighters could not safely deal with lower bombers before first tackling their escort. That situation was about to change, though, as yet more RAF fighters sped in for the kill from across south-east England.

While the Hurricanes of 213 Squadron continued to nibble irritatingly at the heels of the Me 110s, the higher Me 109s had yet to come down to join battle. Perhaps they were biding their time to see what developed and were satisfied that the Me 110s below were adequately dealing with the existing threat. In any event, their pilots were certainly mindful of RAF fighters that might yet appear from above and engage them in a surprise 'bounce'. For now, altitude was their best ally. Not only that, but fuel capacity severely limited the range of the Messerschmitt 109 and petrol consumption was a serious consideration when engaging in combat so far inland. Meanwhile, the formation, with its harrying attackers, moved inexorably northwards although it wasn't long before other RAF fighter squadrons began to close and make contact.

Next were the Hurricanes of 1 RCAF Squadron, followed by 303 (Polish) Squadron and 253 and 501 Squadrons. As more and more defending fighters joined the battle, so the German formations became stretched out and – at last – were broken. Now, with the escorting Me 110s too busy to intervene, the Junkers 88s came under attack and lost several of their number in quick succession. By 09.40 the German formation had reached the critical moment when the main body reversed course, and just as more defenders roared in from the east and west. This time, it was Spitfires of 66 and 602 Squadrons with yet more Hurricanes of 17, 46, 73, 249 and

The Hurricane pilots of 249 Squadron. In this well-known and posed photograph, Fg Off Percy Burton is far left with the CO, Sqn Ldr John Grandy, third from right.

605 Squadrons joining the fray. As the chase spread out across southern England towards the coast, the Spitfires of 72 and 92 Squadrons got airborne from RAF Biggin Hill and joined the pursuit just as the homeward-bound Me 109s came into the melee. The interception was turning into a rout, and the RAF was in full chase.

Individual combat reports of participating RAF pilots that day tell a confused story and one where it is quite difficult to build an accurate picture of who attacked who and who downed what. What is certain, however, is that it was the Messerschmitt 110s of V/LG1 who were faring the worst. Once the defensive circle they were flying was finally broken, the unit's aircraft stretched out across southern England while they attempted to run for home. Attempting to escape the onslaught, and with all further protection of the bombers now utterly futile, the Messerschmitt 110 pilots pushed the noses of their aircraft downwards and, hugging the contours, headed hell-for-leather towards the distant glint of the English Channel. It was every man for himself.

At Mayfield, where the raiders had first been intercepted on the way in, schoolboy George Tuke, a Home Guard messenger, stood riveted to the spot in the roadway outside his home 'Newlands' on the Five Ashes Road. A Messerschmitt 110 now screamed southwards and passed the tall trees by the house with a Hurricane in hot pursuit. In George's own words "…..it was almost attached to the German's tail".

Whilst the Messerschmitt rear gunner fired continuously at his pursuer the Hurricane also blazed away, returning the fire. Empty bullet cases pinged and clattered off the tarmac around a stunned George as fired machine-gun rounds seared through the leafy branches which swayed in the slipstream as the aeroplanes flashed past. Then, as suddenly as they had burst upon the scene, they were gone.

Now almost out of sight and heading south towards Hailsham both were curving around buildings and tall obstacles. As a display of precision flying, George, who was later a flight test observer with the De Havilland aircraft company, had never seen anything like it. What he had witnessed was one of several pursuits that had developed as the Messerschmitt 110s fled southwards for home. In fact, he had watched brief seconds of what would be a duel to the death between the Austrian commanding officer of V/LG1, Hauptmann Horst Liensberger, his crewman Albert Kopge and a young South African, Flying Officer Percy Burton of 249 Squadron.

Moments after they had passed out of the sight of George Tuke, the pair of aircraft were passing over Horam, still at rooftop height and still firing. Again, those on the ground were startled by how quickly the battle was upon

Hptm Horst Liensberger.

Uffz Albert Kopge.

Flying Officer Percy Burton.

them and how fast it then passed. Phyllis Pitcher shouted to her husband Robert who stood atop a pile of hay in their yard at West Street Farm as he gaped at the amazing spectacle of two battling aircraft flashing by. She called for him to come down to avoid the hail of bullets that lashed the fields around them. Rooted to the spot, the danger had already passed before he could move from his exposed perch to join his wife behind the safety of farm buildings. Phyllis was agape, having clearly seen the faces of the flying-helmeted German airmen glancing sideways at her, practically at eye-level. Almost matter-of-factly, Robert later recorded in his diary: 'An exciting time with 'planes today. One down at Horam and two more at Hailsham.'

Seconds passed between the aeroplanes vanishing from view at Horam and being over the rooftops on the outskirts of Hailsham. Here, the guns of both 'planes finally fell silent and watchers on the ground just heard the roar of engines and had momentary glimpses of the wildly-manoeuvring aircraft. One of the best views was probably had by farmer's son Doug Weller as he stood near his father's farm. Approaching him, head on, he could see both machines plainly as they cleared the town centre, passed the railway station and then the town's gasholder before curving round towards George Catt's Hamlin's Mill. What happened next was so sudden and so unexpected that Doug could scarcely believe what he saw. He left this testimony of what he witnessed that day:

"That morning was bright and clear with only a few clouds in the sky and I was working in a field on New Barn Farm in Station Road. The siren sounded so I stopped the tractor and settled down near a deep ditch (in case bombs started dropping) to have my mid-morning break because the air raid warning provided a convenient chance to stop.

"The sound of aircraft north of Hailsham alerted me to the fact that they were coming my way. Then I saw a Messerschmitt 110 approaching at great speed over the rooftops of Hailsham with the German insignia clearly visible in the morning sunlight. At the same time I could see a Hurricane flying out and away in a wide sweep, turning to come into the flight path of the Messerschmitt. I was expecting there to be a burst of machine-gun fire but nothing happened and he just kept on coming and closing the gap all the time.

"As he passed slightly below and beneath the Messerschmitt he banked the plane so that the tip of the wing made contact with the tailpiece of the Messerschmitt. The timing of this manoeuvre was perfect and the tail broke off the German 'plane, but so too did part of the Hurricane wing. The Messerschmitt dived straight to the ground and then a huge column of black smoke rose up from the next field from me, where the Hurricane was now a blazing inferno with the pilot lying some 20-30ft away from the burning wreck. His parachute was extended but not fully opened and this was used to cover his body until the time came

Uffz Albert Kopge prepares for another sortie over England as he stands by his CO's Me 110 aircraft.

to take him away. Later, we found one of his flying boots in the field and this hung in the barn for many years as a sad and rather poignant reminder of his bravery."

The Messerschmitt struck the ground at Simmons Field in Mill Road and disintegrated. Its final careering path demolished a sewage pipe mounted on brick piers while one of the engines catapulted forward and on through a hawthorn hedge into Catt's Field behind Hamlin's Mill.

Meanwhile, the out-of-control Hurricane roared on, veering towards the young Douglas, slamming into a massive and unyielding oak tree not many yards from where he stood. The long chase was over. Horst Liensberger, Albert Kopge and Percy Burton all lay dead, their broken bodies just a stones-throw apart; Liensberger strapped into his seat as if still at the controls with his crewman Kopge laying on his back nearby, lifelessly staring into the blue sky that had so recently been their battleground. Across the fields from the Messerschmitt a fire still burned near the wrecked Hurricane.

Initially, no trace could be found of its pilot although clearly there could be no hope for his survival. The trail of wreckage, interspersed with huge tree limbs and smouldering foliage, was searched fruitlessly until farm labourer David Cottington found the lifeless body of young Percy face down in an adjacent ditch with his parachute pulled open behind him. Like his German adversaries, Percy was a long way from his native land and could not be sent home for burial. Instead, he was interred at St Andrew's Church near RAF Tangmere, West Sussex. The two German airmen, meanwhile, were buried in Hailsham's town cemetery with military honours on 2 October.

The main wreckage of the Messerschmitt ended up a short distance from the tail section and struck a culvert at the local sewage treatment works. A severed pipe is seen in the foreground of this photograph.

On the very same day, and on the other side of the English Channel, the remnants of V.(Z)/LG1 were being disbanded as a unit, such had been their losses over England during the Battle of Britain and, specifically, on 27 September 1940.

In the aftermath of the incident there was certainly a general consensus that Percy Burton's actions had been a deliberate act of ramming. Indeed, such a view was held both officially and by the public at large, the clear belief being that Percy, out of ammunition, had calculatingly severed the Messerschmitt's tail to prevent its escape. In so doing he had been too low to recover from the collision or escape by parachute. In truth, the loss of a wingtip and an aileron would have made the aircraft uncontrollable and the young pilot was doomed from the very moment he lost control.

Understandably, and quite appropriately, Percy Burton was accorded hero status locally for his brave and selfless deed. Under the circumstances it might be reasonable to question why no gallantry award for the action was ever promulgated. What is surprising, though, is to discover that consideration was clearly given to such an award. Sadly, no recommendation was ever carried forward and the name of Percy Burton slipped quietly from public awareness just as the name of another RAF fighter pilot, Flt Lt James Nicolson, very much entered the limelight with the award of what was to be RAF Fighter Command's only Victoria Cross of the entire war.

By coincidence, Nicolson was one of Percy Burton's pals. He was another member of 249 Sqn who had performed deeds of perceived heroic bravery, and survived them, just over one month before Percy met his death. What was perhaps not a coincidence, though, was the decision not to recognise Percy's bravery. Publicly, the first recognition of Percy's action came in what, for the time, was a surprisingly-detailed report in the *Sussex Express & County Herald* newspaper of 4 October 1940. Under the headline 'British Pilot Rams a Messerschmitt' it stated:

'On Friday, residents in a market town in the south east saw an enemy aeroplane and an attacking British fighter crash on the outskirts of the town. The RAF pilot appeared to ram his opponent deliberately. Spectators of the incident heard fierce machine-gun fire overhead before the two aircraft – the Nazi one a Me 110 – dived steeply from the clouds almost down to the housetops. The Nazi pilot attempted to make off when his opponent, after circling part of the town, appeared to ram the Messerschmitt deliberately. The Me 110 crashed into an overhead sewer carried on tall brick pillars and parts of the machine were scattered over a wide area in fields near a sewage works. In the collision the British aircraft lost a wing and it went on to hit a tree before catching fire.'

The graves of Liensberger and Kopge, together with the graves of other Luftwaffe airmen, were originally at Hailsham Cemetery. Liensberger was repatriated to his home at Mutters, near Innsbruck, during the early 1960s whilst the other Luftwaffe airmen were re-interred at the German Military Cemetery, Cannock Chase.

Journalistic licence and censorship aside, the detail outlined by the local newspaper pretty much fits the facts as they are known. However, rather more telling are the archives relating to the local ARP service. In correspondence to his superior officer we have Mr A. Carr, ARP sub-controller at Hailsham, writing on 1 October 1940 to RAF Fighter Command:

'I beg to report that Pilot Officer [sic. Burton had been promoted to Fg Off on 26 September 1940 often leading to him being referred to as Plt Off at the time of his death] P. R. F. Burton was killed in action when his 'plane crashed in Wellers Field, Station Road, Hailsham, on 27 September 1940. He had been taking part in an air battle over Hailsham and was first seen engaging an enemy bomber [sic] which he was forcing down. I enclose an original letter of the 29th ultimo from the head warden with the original signed statements to which it refers.

'I confirm the statements of the head warden that it is the general opinion of all who witnessed the occurrence that the act of gallantry performed by Pilot Officer Burton should be suitably rewarded. In saying that, I should state that the evidence of all the eye witnesses is quite spontaneous and has not been canvassed.

'I also enclose an original letter of today's date from Sgt Owen Golds, East Sussex Constabulary, regarding the state of the body and I should add my reports show that whilst the enemy bomber had ample ammunition Pilot Officer Burton's had none. I trust that the act of Pilot Officer Burton in ramming the enemy bomber [sic] will be reported to the appropriate authority with a recommendation for an award.'

Significant in this letter is the comment that Fg Off Burton's aircraft had no ammunition. Here we have contemporaneous evidence that Burton was out of bullets, a factor that cannot be ignored when considering the circumstances of Burton's reported ramming of the German aircraft.

Frustratingly, we do not have the letters and statements referred to in Carr's letter. Thankfully, though, it is abundantly clear from the letter what the nature and content of those documents actually was. What we do have, though, is a most revealing reply sent on behalf of Air Vice-Marshal Keith Park, the AOC of 11 Group RAF Fighter Command, to whom Carr's correspondence and reports had eventually been sent. In this letter, dated 23 October 1940, Sqn Ldr A. C . H. MacLean wrote: 'I thought you would like to know that I have recommended this pilot for a posthumous decoration and I very much hope that this will be awarded in due course.'

Significant in this letter is one single statement '...I have recommended this pilot for a posthumous decoration' – the significance here being that the only decoration which is available for posthumous award is the supreme award for valour, the Victoria Cross. No other gallantry decoration may be awarded posthumously. As

Sgt Owen Golds of Hailsham police.

we know, the VC was not awarded in this case. The question must be asked: why?

While the records of 249 Squadron, *per se*, do not reveal anything of a clue as to where this recommendation ended up (the operations record book for the squadron merely noting his death and not the circumstances thereof) it was probably what had been going on within the squadron at the time that militated against the promulgation of any Victoria Cross for Percy.

Indeed, Flt Lt James Nicolson's well-known action of 16 August 1940 over Southampton had already led to a recommendation for a VC for that engagement and this recommendation was certainly in train at the time of Percy's death.

Additionally, and by the time HRH the Duke of Kent paid an official visit to 249 Squadron at Boscombe Down during August, Nicolson's action had already taken place. Doubtless an account of it was relayed to the duke and it has been suggested that he added some weight or influence to the decision to promulgate the VC award. Nicolson's story is too well known to recount here, although it is perhaps significant that he survived the episode for which he was eventually decorated.[3] Cynical though it may sound to suggest it but perhaps a live VC winner was of greater 'value' to the nation at this period than was a dead one?

3 The announcement and accompanying citation for the decoration was published in the *London Gazette* on 15 November 1940: 'During an engagement with the enemy near Southampton on 16th August 1940, Flight Lieutenant Nicolson's aircraft was hit by four cannon shells, two of which wounded him whilst another set fire to the gravity tank. When about to abandon his aircraft owing to flames in the cockpit he sighted an enemy fighter. This he attacked and shot down, although as a result of staying in his burning aircraft he sustained serious burns to his hands, face, neck and legs. Flight Lieutenant Nicolson has always displayed great enthusiasm for air fighting and this incident shows that he possesses courage and determination of a high order. By continuing to engage the enemy after he had been wounded and his aircraft set on fire, he displayed exceptional gallantry and disregard for the safety of his own life.'

More important though is one consideration that the authorities *must* surely have taken into account – would two VCs on one squadron and in two consecutive months have been acceptable? How would this have been viewed within other RAF squadrons, groups and commands, or, perhaps, by the general public at large? Clearly, a choice had to be made. The risk of any perception that VCs were being 'given out with the rations' on one squadron had to be guarded against along with the scarcity value of the award itself, and thereby the decoration's real worth. Maybe it was either Nicolson or Burton?

As to the specific case of Percy Burton, some have previously suggested that the non-award might also be attributed to the fact that his action was not witnessed by other service personnel. However, that is clearly an entirely fatuous suggestion. The accounts from those on the ground including the ARP and police might, one would hope, have had more than a little influence on any decisions regarding the

Flt Lt James Brindley Nicolson VC of 249 Squadron.

formal recognition of Percy's gallantry. Indeed, the letter signed by Squadron Leader MacLean clearly implies this to be so. More importantly though, and so far not addressed in this account, is the testimony of Sgt Pilot George Palliser of 249 Squadron who was flying not too far distant from Percy at the fateful moment. In September 1990 he told *The Sunday Times*: "Percy was about 400 yards from me in what was quite a melee. It was as though someone had given him a punch on the nose and he went for him. It was a very deliberate ramming."

If we take Palliser's account at face value, and also take into consideration all aspects of the contemporary and retrospective evidence, the case for a deliberate act of ramming certainly seems a strong one. That is not to say, however, that any possibility of an accidental collision in the heat of a frantic chase can be excluded. Patently it cannot. The truth is that we shall never know for certain what happened in those fateful last seconds. Whatever the cause of the collision, the possibility that Sgt Palliser did not relay his version of events to the squadron intelligence officer obviously beggars belief.

Equally, we are faced with an ironic conundrum in the Nicolson/Burton VC scenario; Nicolson survived to tell his tale, Burton did not. More importantly, a very large question mark has to hang over the validity of Nicolson's claim to have actually destroyed the Me 110 supposedly downed by him in his VC action. Bluntly, there is no evidence whatsoever to support that claim.

In the case of Burton the claim for the destruction of 'his' Me 110 is unquestionable. None of this, of course, is to suggest that James Brindley Nicolson was not a brave and skilful pilot, nor that he was somehow undeserving of his hero and VC status. However, perhaps through unfortunate twists of fate Percy Burton was denied the Victoria Cross for which he was seemingly recommended. This might be considered an especially cruel outcome when other VCs have been awarded in instances that, perhaps, do not have such weight of contemporary evidence – or indeed apparent merit – as this case might have.

That said, it is not entirely the case that Percy's gallantry went completely unrecognised. On 17 March 1941 he was Mentioned in Despatches in the *London Gazette*, although in the absence of any details of the recommendation for that award it is impossible to say with absolute certainty that it was related to the action on 27 September although it is fair to assume that it was. Aside from the Victoria Cross, a MID is the only posthumous recognition available for an act of bravery in which the recipient lost their life although it might be difficult to categorise this as the 'decoration' to which Sqn Ldr MacLean had previously referred. In any event, some might consider a Mention in Dispatches to be a rather inadequate second.

Some may well think, and not unreasonably so, that proof to validate a Victoria Cross for Percy Burton was more than sufficiently satisfied. Whatever the truth of this dramatic and ultimately tragic rooftop pursuit, Flying Officer Percival Ross-Frames Burton was one of Churchill's 'Few'. That alone marks him out as a hero.

Whilst the arrival of these two Luftwaffe eagles ended in the deaths of Horst Liensberger and Albert Kopge it was an episode that was sufficiently dramatic and with circumstances behind the whole event so unusual as to make its inclusion in this book more than relevant. The operation which had cost their lives had, as we have seen, been a precursor to set the stage for later Luftwaffe raids planned for that day. It was during that afternoon raid of 27 September 1940 that another unusual episode occurred, and one which has become almost a legend in the narrative of the Battle of Britain. It might, of course, be just that; a legend.

Hptm Horst Liensberger, photographed in the cockpit of his Messerschmitt 110 as he prepares to take off on another flight over southern England in 1940.

CHAPTER 5

The Battle of Graveney Marshes

I N ITS ASSESSMENT OF LUFTWAFFE activity over England on 27 September 1940, and particular in relation to such actions against London and the south east, the Air Ministry subsequently observed of the late afternoon raid that:

'The enemy's major operations for the day were completed by this attack on London. They can have given them little satisfaction, if they knew the truth. Not one of the four attacks has been successful. Moreover, their losses had been suffered in the type of medium-altitude bombing raid that had been so successful earlier in September when mounted on a large scale.'

The same narrative observed that:

'...it is probable that the raiders were drawn from two of the Gruppen of KG77 as Junkers 88s from both were found on land after the attack. As they retired, they had relied on their own speed and evasive tactics to escape attack.'

Indeed, the Air Ministry assessment had been accurate in terms of the unit composition of the attack although, as it had observed, not all of the raiders had got home. By definition, therefore, not all had escaped attack by RAF fighters and one of the unlucky Junkers 88s of 3./KG77 had been engaged and harried by Spitfires flown by Sgt C. A. Parsons of 66 Squadron and Sgt H. Bowen-Morris of 92 Squadron, forcing it down to a crash-landing on Graveney Marshes at Seasalter on the north Kent coast. Of itself it was, undeniably, singularly unremarkable even for the period and Spitfires shooting down Junkers 88s were, by now, quite literally daily events. However, it is what occurred later that is, perhaps, remarkable. Leastways, the legend and myth that has grown up around the event might be regarded as such.

As the air battle raged above north Kent and the Thames estuary that afternoon, A Company of 1st Bn London Irish Rifles went about its daily military routine, with one platoon of A Company preparing for a full weapons inspection at its base in the Sportsman Inn at Graveney. Such was the daily round of air battles in these parts that very little heed was paid to the aerial fighting above as all of the platoon's rifles, revolvers and ammunition were laid out for inspection in one room at the pub. The inspecting officer that afternoon was to be Captain John Cantopher, commander of A Company with HQ at Mount Ephraim, Faversham.

With his men drawn up for pay parade and the arms inspection, Cantopher arrived at the pub and returned Sgt Allworth's salute, remarking as he did so that he had just noticed a German aircraft coming down. "Yes Sir!" replied Allworth. "I have sent some men." Glancing at the laid-out weaponry, Cantopher brusquely asked: "They took arms, I hope?" Allworth, snapping to attention, barked: "No Sir. The arms inspection, Sir!" No sooner were the words out of the platoon sergeant's mouth than the sound of short bursts of machine-gun fire rang out across the fields. "It looks as if they should have done, Sgt" commented the captain: "Forget the inspection! I am going over there. Tell Mr Yeardsley, (Lt Yeardsley) and bring some of your men with rifles....and ammunition!" With that, Cantopher checked his revolver, jumped into his truck and drove off at high speed towards the scene.

The Junkers 88 after its forced-landing with combat damage at Graveney Marshes, Kent, on 27 September 1940.

First to get anywhere near the Junkers 88, Cantopher had advanced along the nearby drainage ditches that criss-crossed the marsh, revolver in hand, and slowly approached the bomber. In the fields around him, presumably, were the other unarmed soldiers of A Company who had taken cover against the firing that had been heard coming from the Junkers 88.

Now, panting along behind Cantopher came Lt 'Paddy' Yeardsley, Sgt Allworth and ten men armed with rifles. Joining Cantopher, Yeardsley observed the downed bomber through his binoculars. The afternoon sun was glinting off the cockpit canopy as four figures moved quickly around the front of the aircraft. Yeardsley quickly drew up his plan. Leading five men from ditch to ditch as Sgt Allworth's party laid down covering fire, Yeardsley gradually closed on the Junkers 88 from where bursts of machine-gun fire rang out once more.

Eventually, Yeardsley's men were within fifty yards of the bomber and opened fire but, just at this point, the German crew immediately surrendered. Meanwhile, and as the German crew and the London Irish soldiers gathered around the Junkers 88, they were joined by Captain Cantopher just as one of the German airmen, in halting English, explained that the aircraft might explode at any moment.

According to London Irish Regiment sources it was initially suspected that the alarm might have been 'a typical Teutonic practical joke' but, all the same, Cantopher moved everyone away from the bomber as a precaution. If it wasn't a joke, he thought, then it might at least be a means of self-protection on the part of the German crew. Better to be safe than sorry.

As the main group moved away from the Junkers 88, Cantopher clambered into the cockpit looking for any obvious self-destruction charge. Unable to find anything, he was about to leave the aircraft when Sgt Allworth, observing from a distance with binoculars, called out: "What's that under the wing, Sir?" Going to investigate, Cantopher found a black box, and with no obvious means of making it safe he picked up the 'device' and deposited it in the nearby drainage ditch, whereupon he joined the rest of the party as the Luftwaffe crew were conveyed back to the London Irish HQ at Mount Ephraim. It was, as they say, all over bar the shouting. And that was just about to begin.

For his bravery in neutralising the destruction device Captain John Kelly Cantopher was awarded the George Medal, with the award being listed in the *London Gazette* of 22 January 1941. According to London Irish Regimental reports, Cantopher was 'very surprised' to learn that his deed had been so recognised, although it was perhaps other subsequent reports about the incident that were rather more astonishing.

It was the account of the German crew opening fire on the advancing soldiers, of course, and the ensuing fire-fight that was the remarkable element of this story. Getting to the truth of it all has, perhaps, rather taken the gloss from a story that has frequently been billed as 'The Battle of Graveney Marshes'. In any event, what might have been nothing more than a skirmish could hardly be described as a 'battle'. But could it have even have been a skirmish? Certainly, no mention is made of such an event in the RAF A.I.1(g) report although this is perhaps not surprising since these reports were generally of a purely technical detail. Nonetheless, as a contemporary record of the event and the specific Junkers 88 it included as follows:

'Junkers 88 A-1. Crashed on 27.9.40 at 17.45 hours at Graveney Marshes near Faversham. Map reference R5082. Markings 3Z + EL (E in yellow).[4] Airframe built by Siebel Flugzeugwerke, Halle. Acceptance date 28.7.40. Tail and elevators made by Allgemeine Transportanlage GmbH Leipzig.

'Engines two Jumo 211. Plates not found. Aircraft made forced landing following fighter action. Several .303 strikes through starboard air cooler and port wing petrol tank.

'Crew four, all prisoners. One wounded.[5] Armament cannot be ascertained as all guns removed before arrival of intelligence officer.

'Armour; pilot's seat armour but headpiece increased in size to 17" deep, thus reaching the roof of the cockpit. Seven 5" strips, 5mm thick, running fore and aft fitted to full length of under-door of cockpit. Usual external bomb racks under wings, two each side of fuselage. Kuvi bomb sight fitted.

'Pilot has Revi sight for dive-bomb aiming, with bomb release handle on control column. Second bomb release handle near Kuvi sight in front position.'

---

4 The individual aircraft letter 'E' resulted in the aircraft being named 'E fur Eule', or 'E for Owl' and this was painted on the fuselage under the cockpit.

5 The figure of one wounded is at odds with the testimony of the crew and other contemporary records.

Once again, Flt Lt Laurence Irving, the army's XII Corps RAF intelligence officer, had found himself caught up in this episode and recorded the detail in his diary, thus:

'27 September
'In the evening I got a message from 1 London Divn. Junkers 88 A-1 No 088 8099 landed fairly intact near the Sportsman Inn. Crew of four. Three wounded. London Irish reported this to A.I.1(g) and A.I.1(k) at Barnet.

'28 September
'Went off early to see about the Junkers 88. At scene of crash met Col Macnamara and divisional commander. The former told me that he happened to be near the platoon quartered at the Sportsman Inn. The crew of the enemy aircraft got out and opened fire on his platoon with two machine guns and a sub-machine gun.

Here the aircraft's individual call-sign 'E' for Eule (or Owl) is painted in yellow above the squadron emblem below the cockpit.

'The platoon were preparing to take charge of the aircraft. Colonel Macnamara deployed his men and advanced across 300 yards of absolutely flat country, cut up with dykes. When they were within 100 yards of the enemy aircraft the crew waved a white rag. As the troops approached, however, one of them made a dart for the aircraft whereupon the sergeant dashed in, loosing off his revolver. In this melee three of the crew were slightly wounded but the aircraft was not fired upon.

'I lunched with the London Irish and later saw the German crew. All except one (a very poor type) were tough enough in the gangster manner.'

So, here in a contemporary document we have perhaps the first written account of the alleged exchange of fire albeit that it differs very substantially from other accounts given by those who were there. Most particularly, we have Col Macnamara allegedly leading the action to 'capture' the aircraft and crew but, by all other accounts, he was not actually present at all! And it certainly seems that he wasn't. This, though, isn't the only discrepancy we find and, in fact, the subsequent testimonies of two of the captured Luftwaffe crew rather flies in the face of any 'battle' or 'skirmish' story.

In 1987 the author contacted the wireless operator/air gunner of the Junkers 88, Uffz Erwin Richter. His account of the action that day was clear, but made absolutely no mention of any 'skirmish', as such, but confirmed that one of the crew *was* indeed shot on the ground:

The badge and the name 'Eule' made for attractive souvenirs that were salvaged from the wreck by the London Irish Regiment. These trophies currently form part of the London Irish Regimental Museum.

"During an anti-aircraft engagement over London one engine failed. As a result we were separated from our unit and immediately attacked by three fighters. Ruhlandt [Uffz Fritz Ruhlandt, the pilot] dived at once and as he neared the ground he found that the second engine had failed as the result of fighter fire. There was no longer any opportunity to bale out as we were so near to the ground and we had to make an emergency landing.

"During the fighter attack I was wounded in both eyes by glass splinters. Uffz Ruhlandt was wounded by a shot through the ankle on the ground. The other crew members

Uffz Erwin Richter on his wedding day.

Uffz Fritz Ruhlandt.

remained unwounded. A detachment arrested us and took us into custody and we were very well treated. After interrogation I was taken to hospital and operated on in both eyes."

Less forthcoming was Uffz Ruhlandt, who in 1987 simply stated this was the first mission he had flown with this crew but was at pains to point out, like Richter, that treatment throughout his captivity was good. Again, he made no direct mention of any engagement with ground troops, albeit that we know he was shot through the ankle by soldiers of the London Irish.

Further to all of this, we have a discrepancy with Flt Lt Laurence Irving's account of three crew members being wounded; Richter stating that only two were wounded, himself included. Compounding this with more confusion, we have the MOD's Air Historical Branch stating in 1986 that three of the crew were hurt in the engagement with the London Irish Regiment, but rather confusingly stating that Richter was the only unwounded member of the crew. What the Air Historical Branch further said of the episode, though, is worthy of comment.

The original A.I.1(k) report states:

'The crew are also said to have fired at people trying to prevent them from destroying their aircraft and coming to arrest them; this, however, cannot be confirmed and is completely denied by the crew. During this engagement, three of the crew were wounded.'

The Air Historical Branch also went on to further comment:

'The crew were as follows:
Pilot – Uffz Fritz Ruhlandt
Observer – Uffz Gotthard Richter
Wireless Op/Air Gunner – Uffz Erwin Richter
Air Gunner – Gefr Jakob Reiner
It would appear from the above that some sort of fight took place, but it is far from clear that the crew fired at anything but their own aircraft. It may therefore be that to characterise this skirmish as a battle would be something of an exaggeration.'

However, might it even be a stretch to characterise it as a skirmish? Perhaps it is.

Constructing a rational explanation as to what really occurred that day on Graveney Marshes, and subsequently, is perhaps not too difficult. It also helps us to look objectively at the 'battle' or 'skirmish' label that has long been attached to this event. However, and albeit that such can only be speculation or conjecture, the reader will hopefully concur that what I offer here is the most logical of explanations.

There would seem to be little doubt that once the aircraft had landed it was approached by unarmed troopers from the London Irish Regiment and, as they did so, the crew emerged from the relatively undamaged Junkers 88 and tried to destroy it in line with their standing instructions. This they attempted to achieve with gunfire, which was not an entirely unusual set of circumstances in such cases.

As a consequence, the unarmed troops thought they were coming under fire and judiciously took cover as another section of their comrades, armed this time, came to their aid and approached the bomber, firing as they did so. During that fusillade, in which the London Irish discharged between forty-eight and fifty-three rounds of .303 rifle ammunition, Fritz Ruhlandt, the pilot, was hit and wounded in the heel. None of the other crew members were wounded in the firing by the British troops, with Erwin Richter certainly having been hurt in the fighter attack, and not on the ground.

The action to take the Junkers 88 and its crew was led by Capt Cantopher, Lt Yeardsley and Sgt Allworth. Despite his somewhat vicarious claims otherwise (to Flt Lt Irving) Col Macnamara was not involved in the action on that day.

Of course, and as we have seen, Irving's diary written on the 28th might well be the first documentary evidence of any engagement taking place, although this could owe more to the enthusiastic re-telling of the tale by officers of the London Irish over lunch that day rather than having any real basis in fact.

It is not difficult to image the scene at The Sportsman Inn that night where it is more than likely that the enthusiastically celebrating soldiery downed a few pints of Guinness. No doubt, in the telling and re-telling of the tale, the events got a little more embellished.

Wide-eyed locals, agog at all the excitement, probably also recounted the story of the German bomber crew who took on the might of the London Irish. Some local versions of the story even have the Germans 'holding out for hours' and 'taking over a sandbagged emplacement'. All is palpable nonsense, of course. But a ripping good yarn, all the same. And why spoil such a wonderful 'Boy's Own' type story with the rather less exciting facts? In next to no time, the 'facts' of the story, though, were very firmly established in local lore and the 'Battle of Graveney Marshes' legend was born.

More recently, some written accounts of the event would have us believe that this was the first exchange of fire between British troops and a foreign 'invader' on British soil since the Battle of Fishguard on 23 February 1797, when 1,200 French soldiers were evidently routed. However, on that occasion history records that the invaders apparently did not fire a single shot. Thus, any supposed precedent may have been far more distant.

Given the extraordinary events that are supposed to have surrounded the arrival of this particular eagle at Graveney Marshes during the Battle of Britain, an examination in this book of the real circumstances of that event was essential. Unfortunately, however, the truth of the matter is almost certainly rather less dramatic than the myth and legend would have us believe.

CHAPTER 6

An Edelweiss in the Clover

S HORTLY AFTER FIVE O'CLOCK ON the morning of Sunday 28 July 1940, farmer Charles Gillingham was getting ready for his daily round of chores at Buckholt Farm just to the north of Bexhill on the outskirts of Sidley in East Sussex. Although the war had not greatly touched these parts thus far, the sound of a circling aircraft did not particularly attract Charles Gillingham's attention; at least, not initially. Increasingly, aircraft overhead were all part and parcel of daily life but thus far no German raiders had really made their presence felt in the area. Although there had been one or two air raid alerts, and odd German aircraft up and down the Channel, the Battle of Britain had not yet got into its stride. In any event, the local air raid warning hadn't been sounded today, either, and there was no reason to suppose that this was anything other than a circling British aircraft.

Glancing skywards, and out towards the sea, Charles could glimpse the aircraft and reckoned it must be a RAF Blenheim; twin engines, high tail and a glazed nose. However, just a few moments later it had disappeared into the mist over the English Channel. Then, out to sea, there were four distinct and very loud 'crumps'; what he took to be the explosions of four bombs.

Moments later, the engine sounds were again getting closer and ever louder and Charles now took a keener interest. Then, out of the rolling bank of sea mist, the aircraft headed straight towards the farm, descending rapidly and clearly on an approach to land. As it got closer to the astonished farmer, a rattle of Lewis gun fire from a nearby army post startled Charles and set off the farm dogs and the geese in a frantic cacophony of barking and screeching. Above all the racket he watched as something spiralled up and away from the descending aircraft as the machine skimmed hedges and trees, lower and lower, before slithering wheels-up across the clover field and finally coming to rest not many yards from Buckholt Farmhouse.

When the dust kicked up by the crash-landing aircraft had settled he could clearly see the German crosses on the dull green fuselage as four figures emerged cautiously from the open back of the cockpit. Locally-stationed soldiers raced and whooped across the field towards the bomber and Charles stood rooted to the spot – transfixed by the drama of his own personal little bit of the war that had suddenly and so unexpectedly arrived on his doorstep. For now, however, there were farm chores to be getting on with. They couldn't wait while he gaped at the bomber or its dishevelled and disconsolate occupants. That could come later.

The bomber that had so dramatically arrived in the meadow off Watermill Lane was a Junkers 88 A-1 of the 3rd Staffel KG51 (the *Edelweiss* Geschwader), Werke Nummer 7036, carrying the fuselage codes 9K + HL. It had taken off from its Melun base to the south of Paris at around 22.30 hours with the important railway town of Crewe being the target for its four under-wing-stowed 250kg bombs. However, things started to go awry with the sortie almost immediately after take-off as the direction-finding apparatus failed and left the observer, Ltn Wilhelm

Soldiers from the 302 Searchlight Battery, Royal Engineers, pose with 'their' Junkers 88 at Buckholt Farm, Sidley, on 28 July 1940.

Ruckdeschel, to grapple with maps and compass headings above a blacked out countryside.

Suddenly, ahead of them, the crew could see a large town or city with no blackout and to their alarm realised that they had crossed the Irish Sea and were looking at Dublin in neutral Eire! A rapid turn-about took them back over mainland Britain. The question was; where were they? Having headed east back out of Eire and across Wales and the West Country, and then due south, they finally found themselves over central London at 3,000ft but managed to convince themselves that the city must in fact be Paris, because no anti-aircraft fire had engaged them. At least, they reasoned, they must be near their Melun base. Or so they thought.

Still heading south as it got progressively lighter, the crew struggled to find their home airfield. Or any airfield! Presuming they had overshot Melun they turned northwards again on a reciprocal course, until they once more found themselves over London but this time down to 1,500ft. Turning about, and again heading south, they finally found themselves over the mist-covered South Downs where three fighters approached in the distance but left them alone which led the crew to conclude they must have been friendly Me 109s.

Now, a coastline appeared. Given the position of the rising sun off to their left there could be no doubting whether or not their compass was playing tricks on them; this was the English Channel and this was the south coast of England. However, their meanderings now meant that fuel was too critical to even make it back across the Channel, let alone all the way to Melun.

Reluctantly, Lt Ruckdeschel ordered the four bombs to be ditched and for the pilot, Ofw Josef Bier, to turn back in over the coast to make a forced-landing at the earliest opportunity. As they re-crossed the shoreline at Bexhill-on-Sea, Ofw Bier had already picked out a long flat field ahead of him that would suit his purpose, and as he settled down for what would be an exacting gear-up forced-landing he ordered the canopy to be jettisoned so that the crew could exit as soon as possible after coming to a halt.

At the very moment the canopy top tumbled up and away (the object seen by Charles Gillingham) the Junkers 88 was struck on its port side by a number of bullets. One of them smashed through the nose glazing, went through the sole of one of Bier's flying boots and kicked his foot off the rudder pedal as it ricocheted out of the cockpit without injuring him.

Sapper Harry Wilde (centre) points out one of the bullet holes he put into the Junkers 88.

Sapper Harry Wilde, manning the Lewis gun of the 302 RE searchlight battery, was sure the Junkers 88 was coming in to attack them and saw his short burst hit home on the bomber which he later stated had 'wobbled' distinctly under his hits. Not only that, but the crew had immediately thrown off the cockpit roof as soon as he had fired at them! Then, in front of Wilde's astonished eyes, the Ju 88 skidded and bumped across the fields and screeched to a jarring halt amongst the clover. There was no doubt about it. As far as Wilde was concerned he had downed the German bomber and the cock-a-hoop searchlight battery crew later posed with their 'prize', pointing out the bullet strikes for the benefit of the camera.

Little did they know the true story behind the arrival of the Junkers 88, or that their bullets that had remarkably missed injuring Josef Bier had been the only bit of luck that the crew had had since leaving Melun several hours earlier. For Bier and Ruckdeschel, and their radio operator Uffz Heinz Ohls and flight mechanic Uffz Martin

Ofw Josef Bier.

Multhammer, they would face a long captivity. Taken into custody by the soldiers of the searchlight battery, the four were later interviewed by Intelligence Officer Fg Off C. M. D. Eales from RAF Hawkinge before being taken away under escort by the 8th Batt. Devonshire Regiment (based at nearby Battle Abbey) to Cockfosters during the early afternoon. Although the war was over for the four hapless Luftwaffe airmen, the same could not be said for their aircraft.

Recognising that the aircraft was in excellent condition RAF intelligence officers from the A.I.(g) technical intelligence department ordered that the aircraft be carefully dismantled and taken to the Royal Aircraft Establishment, Farnborough, for detailed examination. By 30 July the dismantling process was well underway and by 31 August the aircraft was officially taken on charge by the RAE who had established that not only was the aircraft in exceptionally good order but that it could be made airworthy.

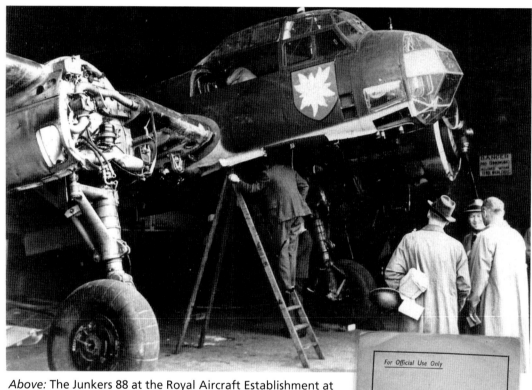

Above: The Junkers 88 at the Royal Aircraft Establishment at Farnborough where it was re-assembled and repaired.

Right: Pilot's handling notes for the various examples of enemy aircraft operated by the RAF were published by the Air Ministry, this being the set of operating instructions for the Junkers 88.

For Official Use Only

INSTRUCTIONS
FOR FLYING
THE
JUNKERS 88

A.M. Pamphlet 114D.

Accordingly, the underside damage occasioned in the belly-landing was repaired, a new canopy cover acquired and the aircraft re-painted in British camouflage and markings and allocated the RAF serial number AX919. Fully restored and overhauled, the Junkers was ready for its first flight in the hands of Sqn Ldr L. D. Wilson on 3 April 1941. During that month it flew a total of three flights with a combined duration of one hour forty minutes for air tests and handling evaluation. It did not fly again until June of that year when it undertook a thirty-minute performance test flight but it would appear that W.Nr 7036 (aka AX919) was proving difficult to keep airworthy. It stayed grounded until June 1942 when it was taken by road to RAF Duxford for delivery to 1426 Enemy Aircraft Flight and used as a spares ship for other airworthy Junkers 88 aircraft that were now on strength and in a better state. Whilst the ultimate fate of 7036/AX919 is unknown it may be safely concluded that it was broken up for scrap at RAF Duxford, an ignominious end once its usefulness had been exhausted. Although other earlier Luftwaffe arrivals in the UK had also been earmarked for flying duties, this Junkers 88 was among the first of its type to be returned to the air by the British.

Repaired and made airworthy, the Junkers 88 was test flown in RAF markings.

Although 7036/AX919 has long gone, at least one relic of the first Junkers 88 flown by the RAF has survived. When researching the incident in 1971 the author visited Buckholt Farm and met Charles Gillingham who was, then, still resident in the farmhouse. His recollection was vivid, and he duly produced original photographs of the downed Junkers 88 along with one of the flexible ball-and-socket gun mounts that had been smashed from the broken cockpit.

More interestingly, he left a record of the event through his eye-witness recollections of what had happened that day. Locally, around the towns of Bexhill and Sidley, there was also quite a profusion of Perspex rings, crosses and small model aeroplanes made from broken bits of the smashed canopy glazing and, from time to time, more than seventy years later, examples of these little souvenirs still turn up in the area. Much of the raw material (apart from the Perspex) was spirited away, long before the dismantling process began, by local boy Jim Spandley and his pals who hid in adjacent hedgerows waiting to pounce when the eyes of the soldiers, Home Guard or police guarding the aircraft were diverted.

An interesting element of the landing of this aircraft in Britain is the fact that it had become lost due to the 'failure' of its direction-finding equipment. Although the crew could not possibly have known it, that failure may well have had much more to do with British subterfuge than to a simple technical failure of the on-board equipment.

Already at this relatively early stage of the Battle of Britain, and a period of increased German air activity over the British Isles, the RAF had begun to introduce electronic countermeasures designed to confuse Luftwaffe raiders through interference with their direction-finding system. As we will see in the next chapter, a highly-specialised RAF signals unit was set up for this very purpose and achieved some notable successes. The loss of this particular Junkers 88 may well have been one of the very first to fall victim to a clandestine RAF operation.

Today, at Buckholt Farm, all trace of the event and most memories have long since passed, although an otherwise unremarkable gap in a hedgerow marked the spot through which the bomber was dragged away and was, until very recently, still visible; a far from obvious, but still extant trace of a drama that had taken place here during the Battle of Britain. Those who now attend the regular point-to-point and gymkhana events in the field where the Junkers 88 landed will have not the slightest inkling of the episode that once took place on that same spot. Clover still flowers here. But there is no longer any trace of the Edelweiss.

The unit emblem of KG51, a large Edelweiss flower on a blue shield. Here, the insignia is shown in detail in this close-up shot taken at RAE Farnborough before the bomber was re-painted in British markings.

CHAPTER 7

'Bale Out!'

THE TERM 'PILOTLESS AIRCRAFT' IN relation to German air activity against the British Isles might be more usually associated with the description that was somewhat euphemistically applied to the V1 flying bomb during the early stages of the 'Doodlebug' attacks of 1944. However, much earlier in the war there had been at least three instances of Luftwaffe bombers landing in Britain with nobody on board and where absolutely no sign could be found of the crews who had flown them. To all intents and purposes these were pilotless aircraft.

Although two of these cases were ultimately solved by the RAF's A.I.1(k) intelligence officers, one other case remained a mystery until long after the war. It is appropriate at this stage to introduce here the RAF's 80 (Signals) Wing whose operations would have an impact on Luftwaffe losses detailed later in this volume and who may well have played a part in some of the incidents covered in this chapter, as well as possibly having led to the downing of the Junkers 88 as detailed in the previous chapter.

Formed during June 1940, 80 Wing came into being at what was the lowest point in Britain's war fortunes and, as intended, its prosaic title conveyed nothing of the unit's true role which was to carry the struggle into an entirely new dimension; electronic countermeasures. As we have seen, British intelligence services had learnt that German bomber crews, using completely new radio devices, could bomb with a fair degree of accuracy at night or in bad weather. It was a discomfiting revelation. The early-warning chain home (CH) and chain home low (CHL) radar stations that surrounded Britain's coastline largely enabled RAF Fighter Command to intercept any attacks launched during the hours of daylight. But there was no corresponding degree of success to be expected from the night defences.

The hope had always been that the cloak of invisibility which had obscured the bombers from the ground and air defences would also hide the intended targets from enemy bombers, especially with a comprehensive and nationwide blackout scheme. Now, it seemed that the Luftwaffe could operate effectively in the dark and that British cities lay naked and exposed to attack, with the existing defences relatively impotent to deal with such assaults.

Heading up the clandestine 80 Wing was Gp Capt E. B. Addison. His brief: to organise and equip a unit to neutralise the German devices,

Group Captain E. B. Addison, head of 80 (Signals) Wing, RAF.

and with the utmost despatch. In this task he would receive the fullest support from Prime Minister Winston Churchill down and within two months a makeshift radio-jamming organisation was in existence in the form of 80 (Signals) Wing. The wing increased in effectiveness almost daily until May 1941 when the Luftwaffe drew a halt to its night Blitz against Britain.

For the most part, the family of gadgets at Addison's disposal were designed to emit strong jamming signals to blot out completely the navigational radio beams that were being radiated from France. However, there was one notable exception to the jamming approach; the so-called Meacon or masking beacon. The Meacon not only prevented Luftwaffe aircrew from getting good bearings on their beacons back in France but actually presented an erroneous bearing in its place. The system was ingenious, yet actually quite simple.

The German navigational beacons in France would each radiate their own two-letter Morse recognition signals followed by a fifty-second-long dash during which aircraft navigators could use their direction finders to determine the relative bearing of the beacon.

The corresponding British Meacon was created to mimic the German system and comprised a transmitter and receiver. The receiver was fitted with a directional aerial which was set up in such a way that the equipment only picked up those radio beacons coming from the specific German beacon it was intended to mimic. When these emissions were taken in at the Meacon receiver they were immediately amplified and passed by landline to the Meacon transmitter. The latter then re-radiated the same identification letters and dashes, exactly in step with the German transmissions and if that beacon's call sign happened to be changed when transmitting then the Meacon would perfectly and automatically respond.

The effect of this piece of clever chicanery was interesting; if the German bomber was nearer to the beacon than the Meacon its direction-finding equipment would give true bearings on the real beacon. Generally, this would be when the enemy aircraft was near or over its own territory but, of course, it was really the raiders already overhead or nearing British soil that 80 Wing wanted to confuse.

If the bomber was mid-way between the beacon and Meacon, the bearing needle would waver between both, causing concern and confusion to the Luftwaffe crew. However, and as was the case when German bombers were actually attacking Britain, the aircraft would be nearer to the Meacon and the direction finder would be drawn inexorably to that signal. In these instances the Meacon gave a beautifully steady but extremely misleading bearing and the German crew would have absolutely no way of knowing that this was the case. Time and again the Meacon stations were able to seduce German bombers away from their intended flight paths leaving them hopelessly disorientated. Some plots revealed aircraft leaving the country in a north-easterly direction when their route home was clearly south-easterly. Quite likely a good number of German bombers that had failed to return to their airfields were simply sent to their night-time doom far up into the North Sea when they should have been making the short hop southwards across the English Channel. Others may have simply become lost due to electronic jamming by 80 Group.

At around quarter to midnight on 21 October 1940, a Dornier 17 Z-3 of the 1./Küstenfliegergruppe 606, sporting the code letters 7T + AH, Werke Nummer 2783, lifted off from its base at Lanvéoc-Poulmic near Brest briefed to attack Liverpool in another of the raids that comprised the ever-continuing tempo of the night Blitz. Already, Liverpool and its docks had become a relatively regular target for aircraft of the 1./Ku.Fl.Gr 606, the unit having returned to the city several times in previous weeks.

In many respects, the operation on 21 October was a relatively 'routine' night-bombing sortie and the Luftwaffe bomber crews at this time knew that survivability rates had increased significantly since daylight bombing raids on any scale had all but ceased. Sure, night flying on operational sorties over enemy territory was still a risky business, but far less so than it had been. It was a fact that British night-fighter defences were minimal and not yet particularly effective but anti-aircraft fire could still be a problem and, of course, there was always the danger from barrage balloon cables. However, a bomber crew's chances of getting through a sortie unscathed were much higher than they had been during the daylight raids of the summer, although a daylight sortie to Liverpool by three Dornier 17s of the same unit on 11 October had resulted in the loss of one of the raiders in the Irish Sea, shot down by Spitfires.

Quite what went wrong for Lt Walter Stirnat and his crew that night is a little unclear, but it would seem that the aircraft ran into a severe electrical storm near Shrewsbury which had damaged the aircraft's electrical and navigational equipment and resulted in the pilot deciding to return to base. Flying south, a further storm aggravated the situation and although they had in fact reached France the navigational equipment indicated otherwise.

Turning about, the Dornier 17 flew back to England where, running short on fuel, the crew baled-out over Salisbury Plain. Whilst the electrical storm may well have been a contributory factor, the possibility cannot be excluded that the real reason for the electrical disturbances in the navigational system was that the RAF's 80 (Signals) Wing was operating its box of tricks and perhaps this is really what confused the German crew. Either way, the four crew members were now drifting down on their parachutes over Wiltshire. Expecting to hear the 'crump' as their Dornier crashed to earth, and to have seen the likely flash of an impact explosion when it hit the ground, they instead could hear the bomber flying off north-eastwards.

Landing respectively at Chilmark, East Knoyle, Hindon and Wylye (near Old Sarum) the crew comprising Lt Walter Stirnant, Lt zur See Heinrich Würdermann, Uffz Fritz Schörnisch and Uffz Martin Küttner were very quickly rounded up and taken POW, but not before one of the crew had seen a notice in English and realised with horror the truth of their collective predicament.

The Dornier 17 Z-3 on mud flats at Ness Point, Ewarton, 21 October 1940.

Meanwhile, their abandoned Dornier, still trimmed for level flight, continued on without them on its north-easterly heading gently descending although otherwise flying perfectly normally. Onwards towards London, and then directly over the centre of the capital, this *Marie Celeste* of the skies continued on its almost ghostly flight. En-route, it was engaged by anti-aircraft guns across no fewer than five counties but with the engines finally using their last drops of petrol, the bomber made an absolutely perfect and utterly remarkable landing on the tidal mud flats at Ness Point, Ewarton, close by HMS *Ganges*.

The tide was out and the gently wind-milling propellers curled and stopped as they hit the mud as the Dornier slid gently along to halt near the water's edge at 01.04 hours on Tuesday 22 October. The fuselage had gouged out a lengthy trench and the rudders' long grooves were witness marks of what was seemingly a perfectly-controlled landing conducted by the pilot on the very edge of the River Stour; but it was a landing some 130 miles from where the entire crew had abandoned their aircraft.

In far-away Wiltshire, the police and military authorities were hunting for the aircraft the four Germans had baled out of but could find nothing in the area, and nothing had been reported. Doubtless, they felt, it had disappeared somewhere into the vastness of the military training area of nearby Salisbury Plain and would probably be discovered there by the army when daylight came. At the same time, and over 100 miles away, Suffolk police were mounting a manhunt for the absent Luftwaffe airmen. Clearly, they must be somewhere on the run. However, something was very strange; there was no sign of any footprints away from the bomber in the deep glutinous mud.

As RAF intelligence officers from A.I.1(k) took charge of the four prisoners, other RAF officers from the technical intelligence department of A.I.1(g) struggled out across the deep mud to the Dornier 17 and clambered aboard to complete their investigations. In the written summary, and on behalf of Wg Cdr J. A. Easton, the report writer noted *inter alia*:

'...the cause of the crash is unknown, but two bullet strikes passed through the fuselage from below. Crest: eagle holding British Isles map in its claws. The number of crew and their fate are unknown but windows are broken and bloodstains are in the aircraft.'

The presence of both bullet holes and bloodstains is something of a mystery, as none of the crew had been reported as injured and neither did they mention to their captors that the aircraft had been shot at. There are, though, some possible and quite rational explanations for these two apparent anomalies. First, we know that persons accessed the cockpit before the arrival of Air Intelligence officers and it is quite likely that these individuals may have cut themselves on the broken Perspex or on pieces of jagged metal when helping themselves to 'souvenirs'.

As to the bullet holes, there might be two explanations for this. Either the aircraft had been shot at whilst the crew were still on board and they remained completely unaware of the fact (which is a distinct possibility), or else the un-manned aircraft was fired on as it descended, lower and lower, towards its final resting place. Eventually, however, and despite the uncertainty of the air A.I.1(g) officers in determining where the crew had gone to, a connection was finally made between the prisoners collected from the Wiltshire countryside and the empty Dornier 17 near Harwich. However, the *East Anglian Daily Times* reported on 22 October 1940:

'A search is still being made for the crew of a Nazi bomber brought down at Ewarton in case any of them have survived, stated the Ministry of Home Security last night. Members of the public are asked to keep a look out for these German airmen and to report anything suspicious to the chief constable of Suffolk.'

Such was the obvious concern in the area where the supposed Luftwaffe airmen were thought to be at large that the censors had taken the unusual step of actually allowing the crash location to be identified. Under normal circumstances, such events would be described vaguely in such terms as 'an east-coast town'. However, once the connection with the captives in Wiltshire had been established the search was immediately abandoned, but not before the authorities in Suffolk had expended a great deal of effort looking for them.

As to the Dornier itself, after examination by the RAF intelligence officers it was said to have been towed or dragged off the mud out into deep water and sunk as the easiest means of disposal.

Although the actual reason for the navigational problems that had beset the crew cannot be confirmed it was an interesting coincidence that exactly one week later, on 29 October, the crew of a 9./KG53 Heinkel 111 H-2 baled out nearby after they lost their bearings following a complete failure of their direction-finding equipment during a night bombing sortie to Gravesend.

Just like the crew of the Dornier 17, who had believed they were over German-occupied territory, these airmen had been fooled into thinking they were over the Netherlands, their bomber crashing into mudflats on the other side of the River Stour at Parkestone Quay. Under the circumstances it is difficult to think anything other than that these crews were all falling prey to the electronic countermeasures of the RAF's 80 (Signals) Group. But these were not the only examples of Luftwaffe bomber losses in 1940 that managed to fly on, un-manned, for very long distances before finally crashing.

Just over a month after the Dornier 17 had come to grief alongside the River Stour, a Junkers 88 A-5 made an uncontrolled descent into the terrain at Blindley Heath, Surrey, during the very early hours of 28 November 1940. The aircraft was a machine belonging to 6./KG77, 3Z + EP, Werke Nummer 7116, and it hit power cables at around 01.35 hours before crashing nearby and breaking into several large sections.

The wreckage of the Junkers 88 that arrived on Blindley Heath, Surrey.

Local residents reported seeing parachutes before the crash, but as things transpired this can only have been a figment of their imagination. Nevertheless, a manhunt was initiated for what were supposed to be four Luftwaffe airmen who were at large somewhere in the Surrey countryside. However, when investigators examined the wreckage in the light of dawn there was no trace of any casualties in the remains of the cockpit and the search for the survivors was consequently widened with break of day. It turned out to be a fruitless task.

Meanwhile, somewhere near Reims, France, four Luftwaffe fliers were probably settling down to a restorative coffee, or perhaps something a little stronger, all four completely unaware that a huge hunt was going on for them across on the other side of the English Channel. The hunt, however, was growing more urgent with the discovery of items in the cockpit that, if anything, indicated that the crew must surely be hiding up somewhere locally. Rummaging amongst the strewn and scattered maps and documents the RAF intelligence officer found a notebook which had some obviously hastily-written sentences written on its cover. Translated, the text read: 'I must have a DF (direction-finding) bearing' and then, on another, the message: 'Pass around. Bale out.'

Another view of the wreckage as police and soldiers puzzle over what might have become of the non-existent crew.

Exactly what had gone wrong on 3Z + EP's final flight is difficult to establish precisely. Since 3./KG77 do not seem to have been rostered for any sorties over Britain that night it may well have been simply the case that the crew had become lost on an internal flight. Certainly, bad weather with poor visibility, including some fog, had been a problem over parts of Europe on this particular night and thus may have been a factor.

On the other hand, the possibility that it had been on an operational flight against the British Isles cannot be entirely excluded. It is tempting to put two and two together in respect of this loss and to suggest that the note demanding a DF 'fix' might be indicative of further deliberate electronic interference with German navigational systems. There is no evidence of this. But it is an interesting coincidence, all the same.

History does not record the names of these four airmen, but if they had fallen into the RAF's dastardly electronic countermeasures trap they had been exceedingly lucky to somehow find themselves back over friendly territory before jumping out of their aircraft. Back in Britain, the search for them continued over a considerable period of time and employed soldiers, Home Guard and the police as well, allegedly, as the local hunt riding to hounds. Eventually, the search was wound down, it being concluded that the crew must have fallen dead at remote locations and had just not yet been located.

As the war progressed there was at least one other similar odd occurrence involving a pilotless German aircraft carrying on for a long distance to make a near-perfect landing, and although it is way out of the general chronological order of other cases in this book, and was not brought down through electronic wizardry, mention must be made here of the Dornier 217 which arrived in Cambridge on 23 February 1944.

During the winter of 1943 code-breakers at Station 'X', the Bletchley Park 'Enigma' intelligence-gathering station, had picked up detailed information that the Luftwaffe was preparing for a major new operation against British cities. In what became known as 'The Little Blitz', the Germans launched Operation Steinbock on the evening of 21 January 1944 with 227 bombers sent out to London. For the Luftwaffe, this was a maximum effort and although nowhere near matching the RAF or USAAF raids of the period against German territory it was certainly a significant escalation of German air operations.

On return to base from the raid, the bombers were re-fuelled and re-armed and sent off for a repeat attack and for the next four months these assaults continued against London, Hull, Bristol and other major cities and targets. To most people, of course, the Blitz-proper had lasted from September 1940 through to May 1941 but the smaller 1944 offensive killed 1,556 civilians with another 2,916 seriously wounded. On the debit side, the Luftwaffe lost 330 aircraft and their crews over the duration of these attacks; one bomber with its crew killed or captured for every five people killed on the ground.

With Operation Steinbock just entering its second month, yet another air attack against London was ordered for the night of 23/24 February with the aircraft of KG2, KG6, KG54 and KG66 amongst those participating. Although it was but a month in to the assault, serviceability levels and aircraft losses were already affecting the numbers of sorties that could now be flown and the night in question would see a further five bomber aircraft lost or damaged in these attacks. It was a severe attrition rate that was already becoming difficult to sustain, especially with Germany's reduced ability to replace aircraft or crews.

There was also a marked nervousness amongst Luftwaffe bomber crews operating against Britain at this time, especially with the much-improved British defences that included radar controlled and efficient night fighters and equally much-improved anti-aircraft gun defences, not to mention the continuing electronic warfare that was being waged against the raiders. It was against this background, then, that we can view the unusual circumstances of loss of the Dornier 217 M-1 at Cambridge on that night.

At 20.20, aircraft of 2./KG2 took off from their base at Orléans to bomb targets in the Millwall and Isle of Dogs area, taking a route via St Valéry-en-Coux to Eastbourne where the bombers had climbed to 16,500ft before entering a shallow descent to 13,000ft over London. Amongst the formation was the Dornier 217 M-1, U5 + DK, Werke Nummer 56501, which had arrived early in the target area with the crew deciding to 'loiter' over the north London district to wait for the white target markers to go down from the aircraft of I./KG66.

Unfortunately, hanging around in the London area was never a wise course of action for Luftwaffe bombers with the ever-present danger from flak and prowling Mosquito night fighters. Nevertheless, the pilot of U5 + DK, Ofw H. Stenmann, had been orbiting the Wembley area when his aircraft was singled out for attention by the anti-aircraft batteries below, including the 'Z' (Rocket) AA Battery at Ealing with its frightening but not always desperately effective three-inch projectiles. However, some hits were registered by either rocket fragments or AA shell shrapnel from the 3.7 inch guns and damage was apparently sustained to the fuselage, starboard engine and wing.

The hits, and the close proximity of other defensive fire, had evidently shaken Stenmann sufficiently for him to believe that the situation was critical and he ordered the crew to bale out. Very soon, Stenmann was drifting down over Wembley along with his crew, comprising Uffz W. Rosendahl, Uffz Behrens and Uffz Schwarzmüller. As they descended, and just like the crew of the Dornier 17 abandoned over Wiltshire in October 1940, the crew of U5 + DK quite expected to see their bomber plunge into the blacked-out city below them and detonate violently. Still on board was a full bomb load of incendiaries. Puzzled that there was no eruption of fire among the huddled rooftops below, the four men drifted down toward the city as anti-aircraft fire crashed noisily nearby and, off to the east, the white target markers released by I./KG66 now illuminated the horizon, a horizon that was soon flecked with the vivid orange flashes of bomb detonations and the repeated 'crump-crump' of heavy explosions.

Meanwhile, they thought they could hear the sound of their Dornier flying away northwards, quite normally, and perhaps three of the airmen wondered if their pilot had regained control and was flying on without them. In fact, Stenmann, the last man out, was drifting down with them in the dark while the Dornier carried on, albeit in a gradual descent. It was a flight that continued onwards for some sixty miles, until the bomber was on the outskirts of Cambridge.

In Cambridge, the 'all-clear' had already sounded when the head air raid warden for the East Chesterton district of the city, Mr J. B. Collins, called in a message to the ARP central control at Cambridge Guildhall at around 22.40 to report: "A German bomber is down at Milton Road allotments." Initially, Collins' report was treated with considerable scepticism: "Are you sure about that? The all clear has already sounded. There are no German aircraft reported in the vicinity!" Collins emphatically insisted to control that there was, most assuredly, a big German bomber in the vicinity and it was currently sitting among the potatoes and cabbages at Milton Road. Frustrated that he was struggling to get control to believe it he hurried off to deal with the incident on-site. There, he met with Lawrence Tilley, a RAF armourer on home leave, and the pair helped to clear the scores of people now swarming to the crash site and trampling across the allotments.

Rather more worrying than the squashed vegetables, it was soon discovered that a trail of incendiary bombs lay scattered in the wake of the German bomber and nobody knew what might be on board that could possibly explode. In fact, recalled Lawrence "....there was a ticking sound coming from the aircraft and at first it was thought this might be a bomb of some kind. Investigating, and with my heart in my mouth, I found it was nothing more sinister than a still spinning and unsettled gyro-compass." More puzzling, though, was the whereabouts of the crew. To all intents and purposes the Dornier had been landed very skilfully and the crew must surely be at large. In echoes of Ewarton a search was mounted for the missing crew, until a link was eventually established with the men who had parachuted into Wembley.

Certainly, the landing of the bomber was more than miraculous. Not only had it come down

The un-manned Dornier 217 M-1 which made a near perfect landing in some Cambridge allotments.

on open ground amongst a mass of housing but it had done so with no crew on board and had literally skimmed the rooftops along Milton Road before settling into the vegetable plots beyond, from where it had slid alarmingly towards the rows of houses in Warren Road. At the very last moment the Dornier was stopped in its tracks when one wing struck a substantial concrete post, bringing it to rest.

RAF intelligence investigators did, in fact, have another prize; the first relatively intact Dornier 217 M-1 aircraft to fall into their hands. Maybe, and given the condition of the aircraft and the fact that 600 gallons of fuel and forty gallons of oil remained on board, it might yet have been possible to get this aircraft back to France. It is clear from RAF intelligence reports that it was felt the pilot had been somewhat hasty in giving the bale-out order. Perhaps, with luck and a fair wind, Stenmann might have got his crew safely back home. Here, and perhaps through an awareness that homebound navigation was sometimes a problem, the Luftwaffe had organised the firing of star shells to mark the route home from the French coast but, unfortunately, such rudimentary navigational aids were not going to be needed for the crew of U5 + DK.

Fairly intact though it was, the Dornier was too badly damaged to be considered for return to flight and was subsequently quite roughly dismantled and taken to the RAE at Farnborough on 29 February. In the week whilst it sat at Milton Road it was visited by large numbers of eager sightseers. How many visitors were attracted to the site can be judged from the fact that an impromptu collection for the Red Cross was set up and a quite astonishing £100.00 was raised from the 6d viewing fee being charged by the enterprising local residents.

Before it was taken away, though, Warden Collins decided to have something for his trouble, and also for the 6d he had to drop into the Red Cross collecting tin. Grabbing a piece of the wing structure for himself, he broke all the rules in the book, but then this German bomber had caused him more work than he had undertaken during the entirety of all his warden duties throughout the war. And he decided he was going to have something to show for it.

The Dornier, minus Warden Collins' chunk of wing, underwent its usual dissection at Farnborough and the standard technical report ensued. Amongst the details noted was that a plate on one of the fins was marked Werke Nummer 5574, and that same number was painted in yellow on the tops of both fins. Ordinarily, this would be clear indication of the aircraft Werke Nummer, or construction serial number, although Luftwaffe records show the aircraft as actually having the Werke Nummer 56051.

That little mystery aside, one of the notable comments in the report tells how the FuG 214 tail-warning radar (to warn of the approach of night fighters from astern) was missing with only the bracketry in place. By implication, it reads that the radar was not fitted and, unless it had been taken by a souvenir hunter a tad more ambitious than Warden Collins, it might well be indicative of German equipment shortages by this stage of the war.

By the time this Dornier 217 M-1 and its four crew members had all found their way into British hands, however, the most significant German prisoner taken from an aircraft that fell over the British Isles had already been captive for nearly three years. Had things gone how that particular prisoner had apparently anticipated, the war would have been over long before the incident at Milton Road, Cambridge.

CHAPTER 8

The Strange Case of Albert Horn

L ATE ON THE NIGHT OF Saturday 10 May 1941 a German aircraft was reported as having crashed at Bonnyton Moor near Eaglesham, a few miles south of Glasgow. On the face of it, this was a less than remarkable event throughout the British Isles at this stage of the war. The aircraft had been tracked across Scotland by the Observer Corps and the assistant director of the Corps' 34 Group was a Major Graham Donald. Puzzled by unlikely reports that the aircraft had been a Messerschmitt 110, Donald set out to view the wreckage and was also directed to the local Home Guard HQ where the single occupant of the aircraft was being held. Major Donald takes up the story:

"I found the pilot at the Home Guard HQ. He simply stated that he had not been hit, was in no trouble, and had landed deliberately. I managed to dig up enough German to get a bit more out of him. He said he had left solo that evening from Munich. I pointed out that, even with extra tanks, he could not have got back after starting right in South Germany. He agreed, and repeated that he was on a special mission and had not intended to get back.

"He gave his name as Hauptmann Alfred Horn, aged forty-two. His face was very familiar to me and we discussed Munich, where he was from, and which I have visited. I studied his face while conversing for a few minutes. I then remembered it. I am not expecting to be believed immediately that our prisoner was actually number three in the Nazi hierarchy. The name he gave may well be Alfred Horn. But the face was that of Rudolf Hess."

Truly, this was the most remarkable of all the stories involving the arrival in Britain of German aircraft and their various occupants. Quite possibly more has been written about Rudolf Hess, his strange arrival in Britain and subsequent events related to this man, Hitler's deputy, than could fill an entire library. However a great deal of mystery surrounds this event which has inevitably led to a huge amount of speculation and a whole raft of varied and sometimes wild conspiracy theories.

There is no merit or purpose in further examining any such angles of the Rudolf Hess story here or any technical, political or military analysis of his defection or the flight itself. That has been done by other authors before me, including some excellent work on the generalities and specifics of it all, particularly a technical analysis of the flight itself, as well as looking at some of the enduring myths and legends that have subsequently grown up. Rather, it is the author's intention here to look solely at the factual circumstances surrounding Hess's actual arrival at Bonnyton Moor and, in particular, the close role played in this entire event by the Royal Observer Corps and of the part played, too, by the RAF in tracking and trying to intercept the Messerschmitt 110.

Rudolf Hess, the deputy Führer, photographed here with Adolf Hitler.

Of itself, this entire story is certainly more than extraordinary. As we have seen from Major Donald's initial recognition of a man who would become Britain's most infamous prisoner of war, the appearance of Rudolf Hess in Britain was met with understandable and astonished incredulity.

At around 22.10 on 10 May 1941 the RAF's chain home radar system had tracked an incoming raid heading for the Northumberland coast at a height of around 12,000ft. It was hardly an unusual event for this period and the plot was designated 'Raid 42' by the RAF and was passed, as a matter of routine, to 13 Group of RAF Fighter Command via the command's HQ at Bentley Priory in far-away Middlesex.

It was also picked up by a post of the Royal Observer Corps, 30 Group (Durham), at a point seven miles north east of Alnwick when it had been re-designated 'Raid 42J' (possibly because of some confusion as to whether the raid had split into two) but what was unusual was that the aircraft had lost height very rapidly and crossed the coast at very low altitude and perhaps, now, at around 100 down to fifty feet.

Of course, once the aircraft had crossed the coastline it became invisible to the radar system, anyway, as the radar only looked to seaward and there was consequently a total reliance upon the Observer Corps to plot and report its inland track. Once it had been picked up by post A2 of 30 Group it was subsequently tracked by post A3, who were then led to suggest that the unidentified aircraft might well be a Messerschmitt 110, partly given its speed, as it was continuously tracked across the group's plotting table. However, Observer Green at Post A3 is also said to have identified the aircraft visually in silhouette as it roared past at low altitude.

At about 22.30 hours it was seen by post F2 in 31 Group. Onwards across Scotland the speeding Raid 42J was plotted until visual or sound plots of it were lost by post G1 at 22.36 in what was now the area of 31 Group, ROC. By now, the aircraft had climbed up to around 5,000 feet and pretty much maintained that altitude for the major part of its transit across Scotland.

When the plot had been lost to G1 it was headed on a WNW track towards the ground of 34 Group but for a considerable distance, though, any actual track of the aircraft was lost as it crossed the Forest of Ettrick where there were no observer posts. Handing the plot on to 34 Group, post G1 in 31 Group was able to report the heading of the aircraft when it was lost to them. Thus, the assumed track across the large expanse of the forest could be calculated. Sure enough, it re-appeared at 22.45 hours, still on the same heading, but now in 34 Group's ground. However, accurate sound plotting was now getting confused by the noise of an RAF Defiant flying in the same area, an aircraft that was actually up looking for the lone hostile machine.

Shortly before 23.00 the 'hostile' was plotted, briefly, crossing the west coast (where it was recorded as 'low') but once over the sea the aircraft turned back inland on an almost reciprocal course before heading north east, now at about 4,000ft before post H2 at Eaglesham were able to report that it had crashed at 23.09 hours at Bonnyton Moor. It was in the Glasgow operations room of 34 Group that Major Graham Donald had been monitoring the course of the raid. Puzzled about this aircraft, Donald jumped into his car and drove to the crash site, intent on solving the mystery.

As we already know, Donald would ultimately be introduced to the mysterious 'Hptm Alfred Horn' but before being taken to meet the prisoner he first wanted to have a look at the wreckage of the aircraft and he found it spread across about an acre-and-a-half at Floors Farm. There had been a small fire, but the fact that only a small amount of petrol was left on board meant that the fire had not been great and despite its condition Donald was easily able to identify the smashed up aircraft as once having been a Messerschmitt 110. Later, he reported: 'It had no guns[6] [sic], bomb racks or reconnaissance camera.'

However, Donald would later write to the head of the Royal Observer Corps, Air Cdr Warrington Morris, on 14 May 1941:

6 The aircraft was indeed fitted with guns, some of which appeared in later photographs of the wreckage. However, no ammunition was actually carried on board the Messerschmitt 110 at the time of the defection flight.

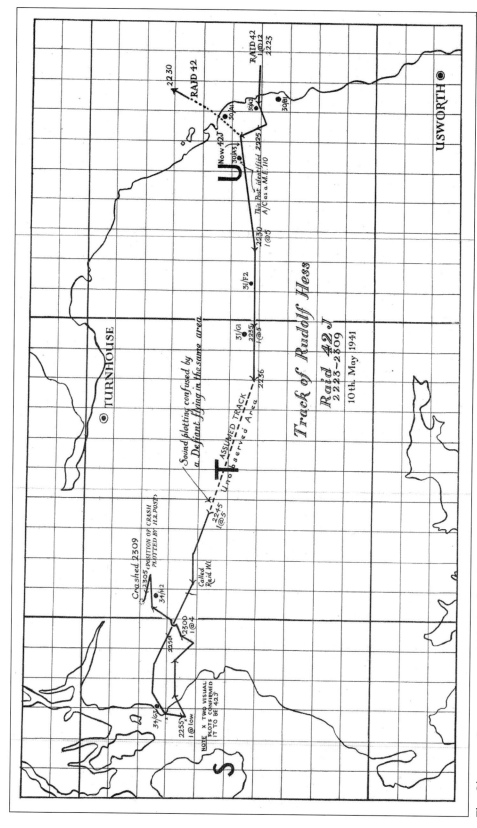

The Observer Corps map on which the detailed track of the Messerschmitt 110 flown by Rudolf Hess was plotted.

The Messerschmitt 110 abandoned by Rudolf Hess. It was photographed at the crash site and, later, at a nearby railway yard before taken south by the RAF for exhibition. In one of the photographs, RAF men display three of the Messerschmitt's 7.92mm MG17 machine guns in a 'H' for Hess configuration.

'Dear Air Commodore Warrington Morris

'Probably you will have read my report upon the tracking, reporting and identifying of both the German 'plane and pilot between 23.00 hours and 24.00 hours on Saturday night, the 10th instant, by 34 Observer Group of the Royal Observer Corps.

'As this flight of Rudolf Hess to Scotland may well prove to be a turning point in the war, I feel that the honour of being the first group to identify the 'plane correctly as a Me 110, and the pilot as Rudolf Hess, should be clearly acknowledged as being to the credit of 34 Group.

'I want you to regard this letter as being entirely personal and confidential to yourself, as it is merely intended to amplify the brief report which I made on Sunday 11th, immediately after the event.

'The point which I could not tactfully embody in an official report was that after I definitely identified "Captain Alfred Horn" my remarks to the assembled police and Home Guard were simply greeted with hoots of derision. I solemnly assured them that our prisoner had escaped from Germany, that his remarks indicated there was a "split" in the Nazi party, that he personally knew the Duke of Hamilton, and that he was definitely Rudolf Hess, the deputy Führer of the German Reich. The amusement was terrific. George Robey never aroused more!

'I finally asked the police, Home Guard etc to take good care of our very special prisoner, and said that I would endeavour to pass his message to the Duke of Hamilton immediately.

'I immediately went back to our Glasgow centre. There, I am glad to say, our duty controller, Mr W. Paisley, and the crew, all gave credence to my report. I then telephoned Turnhouse aerodrome where the Duke of Hamilton is a wing commander. I spoke to the duty controller, told him the 'plane was a Me 110 (stripped), that the pilot came over meaning to surrender, that he had a message for the duke, and that he knew him. I also told him that if the name Alfred Horn meant nothing to the duke he could say on my authority that the pilot's real name was Rudolf Hess. I am afraid that the duty controller began to find the story funny, also. I did my best to convince him I was in dead earnest and that the duke should be notified at the earliest possible moment. Whether this was done or not, I cannot tell.

The Duke of Hamilton, a group captain in the RAF, and whom Hess claimed to have once met at the 1936 Berlin Olympic Games.

'I knew only too well that if Hess was to be induced to "come clean" (in film language) and to be really helpful, then it was essential to treat him especially well from the start. I fear he was treated as a very ordinary prisoner for the first twenty-four hours or so.

'On Sunday, I heard unofficially from the police that the whole story was looked upon as balderdash. My OGO (Lt Col Kennedy) and our DAC (Air Cdre Gordon) were both inaccessible over in the Isle of Arran and I was seriously considering telegraphing Mr Churchill about the whole show. On Monday, however, I managed to contact the DAC and the OGO and showed them my written report which has been forwarded to you. The whole thing, of course, is now history.

'I do feel, however, that the Air Council, or our grand prime minister, should be informed that one efficient unit of Britain's defence at least was aware that a Messerschmitt 110 was over Scotland (all other reports said a Dornier 215), reported to police and Home Guard where it crashed, and also reported that the pilot was Rudolf Hess. That one efficient unit, I am proud to say, is 34 Observer Group of the Royal Observer Corps. An observer's primary duty is to be observant, and to be good at "identification". The Rudolf Hess show seems to come under the heading of "identification", I think!

'Please believe me, I am not anxious for my own name to come into this. The work was team work between posts, centre and AOGO and a pat on the back for 34 Group would buck up the esprit de corps greatly.

'I hope I have not done anything unduly unorthodox in writing to you personally like this. I merely wish to amplify my official report a bit. In any case, please regard this rather diffuse "amplification" as being confidential to yourself. I would not like to cause any offence, if my writing direct to you should not be correct procedure.

'One other point. There was one young officer present in the Home Guard HQ who actually backed up my recognition of Hess as being reasonable. His name is:

Pilot Officer F. J. Malcolm
RAF Army Co-Operation Squadron
Westonzoyland
Somerset

If contacted he will undoubtedly bear out my account of the events.

'I think it would be very gratifying to the Royal Observer Corps as a whole to be so clearly connected with such a historic event.

Yours faithfully
Graham Donald
Major
AOGO 34 Observer Group'

To an extent, Donald may well have been seeking some personal recognition for his part in events, albeit that he went to some pains to stress he didn't and that the whole episode was down to a team effort. Either way, he was surely proud of his and 34 Group's involvement and thus he must have felt, ever so slightly, that somebody had rained on his parade when the reply came through. In his letter of 18 May 1941, Warrington Morris was mildly congratulatory but wasn't, perhaps, quite so effusively laudatory as Donald might have hoped:

'Thank you for your very interesting letter regarding Rudolf Hess. I congratulate you on being able to suggest to some of the posts that the aircraft might be a Me 110 due to its high speed, and your subsequent "recognition" of the pilot. It is, of course, quite understandable that, at first, such recognition should be received with incredulity and that it required a great deal of perseverance on your part to persuade anyone to accept it as a possibility and to report the matter to higher authority.

'I now have sufficient information to write an official report. The aircraft was first recognised as a Me 110 when seen by a post in Northumberland, and again by two posts in 31 Group, but both the fighter group and sector insisted that it must be a Dornier 215. I have nothing to indicate any post in 34 Group gave a definite recognition and it was only when you suggested that the enemy aircraft might be a Me 110 that one of the 'H' Posts thought this likely.'

To an extent, Warrington Morris had rather rubbished Donald's claim to have been first to identify the aircraft as a Me 110. In fact, credit for the initial correct identification of the Messerschmitt 110 went to Observer George W. Green in post A3 near Chatton, Northumberland. What Warrington Morris couldn't challenge, though, was Donald's claim to have been first to identify Hess, but even in this respect there was an element of mild rebuke in Warrington Morris's tone as he went on:

'There is only one point that Air Intelligence have spoken to me about, i.e. that it appears from your report that after Hess had informed you that he had landed deliberately, you had enough German to get a bit more out of him. As you are probably aware there is a special organisation of officers to interrogate prisoners as soon as possible after capture and they are anxious that no one else should do so before their arrival as it tends to make the prisoner more careful in what he says.'

By the time that Donald had got to this part of the letter he must have been somewhat crestfallen. If he had not been overtly seeking personal thanks he was certainly seeking it for his group. Clearly, that wasn't going to be forthcoming. Moreover, he was now getting a ticking off for talking to Hess and, to an extent, the hoped for accolades had rather turned to brickbats.

Donald had rather been put in his place, but his excitement at becoming involved in arguably one of the most notable events in the entire war can surely be excused. Understandably, he wanted to stake his place in the whole Hess defection circus. However, quite apart from the role played by the Royal Observer Corps in the saga, the RAF had also played its part, too.

The initial indication of an incoming 'raid' had, as we have already seen, been picked up by the RAF radar system and it was the chain home stations at Danby Beacon, Douglas Wood and the chain home low stations at Bamburgh and Cresswell that all reported the raid as a single aircraft, although the chain home station at Ottercops Moss reported it as three aircraft. However, all of this information coupled with that which was coming in in real time from the observer posts, was fed ultimately to RAF Fighter Command's filter room at Bentley Priory who passed instructions to 13 Group to intercept the raid.

Sgt Maurice Pocock, a pilot with 72 Squadron.

Already airborne on routine patrol over the Farne Islands were two Spitfires of 72 Squadron from RAF Acklington, Northumberland, and these were vectored to try to find and destroy the raider. However, the patrolling Spitfires were unable to locate it and, instead, another Spitfire of 72 Sqn was ordered off at 22.20 hours as Sgt Maurice Pocock in P8042 was sent on what turned out to be yet another fruitless hunt. Thirty-five minutes later he had returned to base, having seen nothing.

However, RAF Fighter Command were committed to the hunt and ahead of the relatively unwavering track of the enemy aircraft, Defiant T4040 of 141 Sqn from RAF Ayr had been scrambled to intercept and was expertly vectored onto Hess's track. Certainly, Plt Off William Cuddie and his gunner, Sgt John Hodge, came very close to the Messerschmitt and, in actual fact, the sound plotting of Hess's aircraft was hampered by the merging sound of the Defiant as the two aircraft, in close proximity with each other, exited the Ettrick Forest area. Indeed, and although the Defiant crew saw no aircraft, theirs on the other hand was spotted by a vigilant Hess who identified it as a 'Hurricane'. It was the moment on the whole extraordinary flight that Hess came the closest to disaster and the Canadian pilot, Cuddie, with his air gunner, Hodge, came equally close to making the most extraordinary air combat 'kill' of the war.

Also searching for the enemy aircraft as it crossed Scotland towards Glasgow was a Defiant of 141 Sqn, flown by Plt Off Cuddie with his gunner, Sgt J Hodge.

Given that, according to the 3rd Bn. Renfrewshire Home Guard, Hess carried no identification, wore the uniform of a Luftwaffe Hauptmann and the borrowed flying kit marked to its owner Helmut Kaden it is interesting to speculate; what if Hess had been killed? British intelligence authorities would have had quite a job in finding out who this mystery lone flier actually was. How long would it have been, one wonders, before the pieces of the puzzle would have been put together? As it was, Hess baled out of the Messerschmitt 110 and we at least know some detail of those last moments of his very strange and not wholly explained adventure.

After turning back inland from the west coast, Hess climbed to an altitude of around 4,000ft but with Cuddie still in pursuit and fuel running low he began to make preparations to bale out. He switched off both engines and feathered the propellers, although the starboard engine refused to stop and continued to run until he throttled it right back. Opening the cockpit roof and unfastening the two side windows, Hess undid the straps and tried to stand up to abandon the aircraft. However, the slipstream simply pushed him back into the seat and with the aircraft in a rapid descent he had to get out, and quickly, if he was to survive and so he pulled back on the control column to try to turn the aircraft on its back. Instead, he blacked out when the Messerschmitt responded to his violent control input although the aircraft had now entered a steep climb and was on the point of stall.

At this moment, Hess came to, pushed with both feet and managed to get clear of the aircraft as it finally stalled and fell away beneath him. Pulling his D-Ring the parachute billowed open as the Messerschmitt dived to its fiery destruction beneath him at 23.09 hours. Moments later, Hess hit the ground in a meadow on Floors Farm, Eaglesham.

Initially, Hess passed out again on hitting the ground but he soon came round and was apprehended by ploughman David McLean whose house Hess had landed immediately alongside. McLean, asking if the parachutist was German, was astonished to get a reply in good English and in the affirmative with the airman going on to identify himself as Alfred Horn.

The reason for Hess's choice of assumed name, or even the reason for any assumed name, remains something of a mystery – although those trying to unravel the whole conundrum have pointed to the fact that Hess's brother was called Alfred and that Horn was the name of his wife's stepfather, Karl Horn. The multitude of conspiracy theorists who have taken an interest in the case also often point to the fact that the initials A. H. were also those of Adolf Hitler.

As we know from the testimony of Major Graham Donald, he had seen Hess at the Home Guard HQ at Busby but from here he was shunted around different locations, from barracks to Buchanan Castle to the Tower of London and to Mytchett Place in Surrey. In Germany, Hitler and his cohorts reacted with perplexed rage over Hess absconding and put out statements talking of his mental state and the 'hallucinations' leading to actions that had arisen wholly out of his 'mental disturbances'. In the context of his mental condition, the German high command may well have been pretty much on the mark.

David McLean, the astonished farm-hand who first apprehended Hess at Eaglesham.

Certainly, Hess had set off on his risky long distance flight from Augsburg with the hare-brained plan to fly to the Dungavel home of the Duke of Hamilton, to meet with him and try to negotiate peace with the British. Although there is perhaps more mystery than established fact about much of the whole saga, the complex events have been dissected and pored over in many publications to date. To reiterate, there is no point or merit in rehearsing them again here save to say that after conviction at the Nuremberg War Crimes Tribunal Hess was sentenced to life imprisonment by the Allies.

To the Russians, life meant life and they would not consider early release. Instead, as Prisoner No. 7, Hess remained incarcerated in the notorious Spandau Prison, Berlin, as its only prisoner and guarded in turn by the Russians, Americans, French and British on a rotating basis. During his imprisonment, there were even bizarre claims that the prisoner was not really Rudolf Hess at all, but an imposter.

Rudolf Hess, with his head in his hands, at the Nuremberg War Crimes Tribunal.

It is true to say that controversy and mystery surrounded Rudolf Hess from the moment he took off from Augsburg right up until the moment of his death. That moment came on 17 August 1987 when Hess supposedly committed suicide in a hut inside the grounds of the prison by strangulation using a piece of electric flex. However, even his death was mired in controversy with unproven suggestions that the ninety-three-year-old was far too frail to have committed suicide in this way and that he must have been murdered.

When Major Donald had first identified Alfred Horn as none other than Rudolf Hess he could barely have imagined the wild and tortuous course of events that would follow Hess over the coming years, but it is true to say that it was surely the strangest tale of all those to emerge from the various German aircraft to have arrived in Britain. Perhaps, though, it wouldn't be strictly true to say that the Rudolf Hess affair was stranger than fiction but more accurate, perhaps, to describe it as being just as strange as fiction. A popular novel of the period was *The Flying Visit* by Peter Fleming, a book in which we find Adolf Hitler parachuting into England to try to make peace. Such a notion, or anything remotely like it, was just the thing of fantasists. And yet, for all of that, Hitler's own deputy really did do pretty much the same thing.

CHAPTER 9 Turncoat Messerschmitt

ETTING HOLD OF THE LATEST Luftwaffe technology whether actual aircraft or associated aeronautical equipment, or even related information, was always a perpetual quest for the RAF's Air Intelligence officers during World War Two. With the Messerschmitt 109 being the most widely used of all Luftwaffe fighters throughout the war it was inevitable that the RAF would want to seek to learn all it could about every development of the type and every modification.

As the war progressed the RAF managed to secure an airworthy example of pretty much every model and variant of the Messerschmitt 109 in front-line service, and that line began with the Me 109 E model. The first of these to fall into Allied hands was a Messerschmitt 109 E-3 of II./JG54 that made a wheels-down landing in an orchard at Wœrth, Bas-Rhine, on 22 November 1939 when its pilot, Fw Paul Hier[7], became disorientated by fog and poor visibility.

Captured by the French, the aircraft was transferred to the Centre d'Essais en Vol (CEV) which was the flight test centre roughly equivalent to the Royal Aircraft Establishment, Farnborough, and situated at Bricy, near Orléans. Here, the aircraft was flight tested by the French but handed over to the RAF at Amiens on 2 May 1940 and flown to England. Given the RAF serial AE479 it became the first of what was a long line of Messerschmitt 109s evaluated for the RAF. Although this particular aircraft loss is outside the remit of this book, suffice to say that by the end of 1940 the Me 109 E was already being superseded by the new Me 109 F.

When the Luftwaffe began to replace the tried and trusted Messerschmitt 109 E the RAF were, naturally, very keen to know more about what was clearly a formidable new opponent. Although the type had been active over southern England from as early as 25 October 1940 the Luftwaffe's replacement programme ran on into the first few months of 1941. It was not really until the spring and early summer that German fighter units on the French coast were becoming fully re-equipped although, for a while, both the E and F types were in service side-by-side.

By early 1941, of course, the tempo and nature of the air war had changed. No longer were large formations of bombers venturing over the UK with covering fighter escorts. Instead, the RAF were pressing into northern France on daylight 'Circus' operations – heavily-escorted daylight attacks by RAF bombers on a variety of different targets. It was almost a mini re-run of the Battle of Britain – but in reverse. The escorting fighters, mostly Spitfires, were regularly engaging with the new Me 109 F although the technical secrets of the Luftwaffe's latest weapon so far eluded the intelligence officers of the RAF. Only smashed-up remnants of shot-down wrecks had yet fallen on British soil, and so there were just meager scraps to examine and assess. This was destined to change, however, on 10 July 1941.

---

7 Fw Paul Hier was released from captivity as a POW when France capitulated to the Germans and he returned to operational duty. On 15 November 1940, whilst flying with 4./JG54, he was lost over England and is believed to have crashed into the sea off Shoeburyness flying Me 109 E, Werke Nummer 1501, at around 11.00 hours.

B

The first Messerschmitt 109 E to fall into RAF hands was this aircraft of II./JG54 that landed at Wœrth, Bas-Rhine, on 22 November 1939.

The aircraft, a Me 109 E-3, was first test-flown by the French before transfer to the RAF in May 1940.

On this particular day three Short Stirling bombers of 7 Squadron, led by Flying Officer Witt, were tasked to carry out 'Circus 42' which was to be a heavily-escorted attack on industrial installations at Chocques, near Béthune. Over the French coast, however, the formation was engaged by intense anti-aircraft fire. One of the Stirlings, flown by Flying Officer C. V. Fraser, took a direct hit on its port inner engine. Almost immediately the Stirling was ablaze and went down with the loss of all seven crew members.

Witt pressed on his attack with the other Stirling (flown by Pilot Officer Roach) and both crews reported direct hits on the target area. However, a hornets' nest had now been stirred up and having run the gauntlet of the coastal flak batteries the Stirlings and their escorting fighters were further troubled by sporadic anti-aircraft fire on the run to and from the target area. This did, of course, also have the effect of disrupting any interception by the German fighter force which had to wait until the formation was on its way back out and homewards before attempting to engage.

Short Stirling bomber.

Leading the fighter onslaught, when it came, was the Kommodore of I./JG26, Hauptmann Rolf Pingel, who swept into the British formation with a scything attack from his mixed force of Messerschmitt 109 Es and Fs. Several of the escorting Spitfires were dispatched, although not without cost when Uffz Erich Hammon was sent flaming into the sea in his Messerschmitt. Pingel, in his almost-new Me 109 F-2, Werke Nummer 12764, was keen to get at the bombers. Indeed, standing orders for the Luftwaffe fighter pilots at the time were to ignore the fighters if possible and go, instead, for the bombers. After all, it was they who could inflict the real damage.

By now, the chase had extended way out across the English Channel and Pingel, exasperated by the return fire from 'his' Stirling, made swift in and out attacks on the bomber managing to badly pepper its tail section. (Later, Pingel would tell how the Stirling was "pouring fire from every orifice".) Distracted by his attacks on the bomber, and by a number of hits by return fire from the surprisingly-challenging Stirling, Pingel apparently failed to see the Spitfire closing on him as he crossed in over the English coast. From almost dead astern, Sgt Jan Smigielski in a Spitfire of 306 (Polish) Squadron engaged Pingel's aeroplane.

Writing to the author of this event in 1979, Pingel explained that all of a sudden he found that coolant and oil temperatures were rising and the engine began to fail. He had no idea if this was the result of fire from the bomber or the English fighter, or whether the engine had just failed by itself. 'Maybe,' he went on, 'it was a combination of all three events.' Either way, he had no option open to him. He was over the English coast and there was no hope, now, of getting back to France or even very far out into the English Channel. He was also far too close to the ground to bale out, and with a badly-faltering engine Rolf Pingel bellied his Messerschmitt into a field of standing cereal crops at St Margaret's Bay in Kent.

So quickly was it all over that he did not even have the chance to jettison the cockpit canopy – standard practice in the event of such emergency landings in order to facilitate a quick exit in case of fire. Badly shaken, Pingel gingerly raised the cockpit

Hptm Rolf Pingel, a leading Luftwaffe ace.

Rolf Pingel's aircraft after a wheels-up forced landing in a field at St Margaret's Bay, Kent.

Taken to the Royal Aircraft
Establishment at Farnborough, Rolf
Pingel's Me 109 F-2 was photographed
from every angle before its repair and
return to flying condition for
evaluation purposes.

canopy to get out. As he did so, he woefully reflected that his mechanic would normally jump onto the wing and open it for him. Right now he should have been back at his Clairmarais base celebrating his twenty-third victory with a champagne toast. Snapping out of his dejected musings, Pingel then thought better of just walking away from the aeroplane and standing on the seat he prepared to set fire to it.

A sudden burst of Bren gun fire over his head from an army detachment who had just rushed into the field dissuaded him from his intent and he sheepishly raised his hands high above his head hoping that the warning shots would stop. They did, but it was not quite the reception he had hoped for at the end of his flight. Fortunately for the RAF the army gunners had fired over rather than at the precious Messerschmitt 109 F. For Rolf Pingel, and to coin a phrase, the war was over. But it was far from over, just yet, for his aircraft.

Here, in a Kent field and in almost pristine condition, sat the latest example of Messerschmitt's feared fighter and, before very long, RAF intelligence officers were swarming all over it. Clearly, it would take little to get this aeroplane back into the air and, consequently, it was dismantled with great care and transported directly to the Royal Aircraft Establishment at Farnborough. Here, it was minutely examined by engine, airframe, instrument, fuel and armament experts and carefully photographed from all angles.

It was also discovered during examination at Farnborough that there were no bullet holes anywhere in the machine. Rolf Pingel had been mistaken; he had taken no hits from either the Stirling or the 306 Squadron Spitfire and, as a result, the 'claim' made by Jan Smigielski was disallowed. Whilst the Pole had most likely shot at Pingel's Messerschmitt his bullets had all gone wide of the mark and the unfortunate pilot had simply suffered a major coolant system failure or leak.

Included in the suite of official RAE photographs was this image of the cockpit in which the gun-breech aperture left by the removal of the MG 151 cannon can be seen clearly.

Also at Farnborough, and crucially as it later turned out, the engine-mounted MG 151 cannon was stripped out for a detailed look at this newly-encountered weapon. As a result, a large aperture between the engine bay and cockpit was left by the removal of the gun due to the fact that the breech end of the cannon protruded into the cockpit well. Compensating ballast in the form of lead shot sewn into long canvas sleeves was added in its place and some effort was made to blank off the opening into the engine bay but sealing gaskets and bulkheads were left out. Otherwise, the Messerschmitt's damaged coolant system was repaired and the radiators overhauled and pressure tested.

What the Royal Aircraft Establishment now had was an airworthy Messerschmitt 109 F and what the Royal Air Force wanted was to know how it performed in the air against the Spitfire. It was essential, therefore, to assess its combat strengths and weaknesses. Repainted in RAF markings and given the serial number ES906, the Messerschmitt was test flown at RAE Farnborough on 19 September 1941 before it was delivered on 11 October to the Air Fighting Development Unit at RAF Duxford for comparative tests against the latest marks of Spitfire. So much, though, for obvious RAF interest in the Messerschmitt 109, but what about the intelligence value of its pilot, a relatively high-ranking Luftwaffe fighter leader and a high-scoring pilot?

Rolf Pingel's Messerschmitt 109 F, now RAF serial number ES906, at Duxford during the autumn of 1941 whilst undergoing flight evaluation tests.

Although the value of captured airframes was considerable, and especially so when they could be repaired and flown, it was often what the captured aircrew themselves could reveal of the Luftwaffe's operations and equipment that would be the real nugget of gold. In the case of Hptm Rolf Pingel, RAF intelligence had secured not only a valuable prize in the form of an important aircraft but also information secured during the interrogation of Pingel himself.

In some cases it is clear that Luftwaffe POWs revealed little or nothing of any particular merit. Especially the more lowly-ranked individuals, and while that may have been more to do with the fact that they had fewer beans to spill it was equally the case that they were frequently very security conscious and would only give up their name, rank and number – all that was required under the Geneva Convention. Equally, many captured Luftwaffe officers didn't give much away either, although it seems that others were more than garrulous in what they were willing to tell. A case in point was certainly Hptm Rolf Pingel who had merited a nine-page report of closely-typed revelations.

Covering topics such as bases, fighter strength, daylight raids, the Messerschmitt 109 F, camouflage and markings, the new Focke Wulf 190, German fighter tactics, British tactics, replacements, losses and personnel the document contained a treasure trove of useful information. Much of the report by Squadron Leader S. D. Felkin, dated 20 July 1941, is likely to have been built up from already-sourced knowledge and intelligence, but it is also clear that Pingel either filled in some of the missing detail or else confirmed what had already been surmised from other sources.

Sqn Ldr Joe Kayll being decorated with the DSO and DFC by HM the King at RAF Kenley on 27 June 1940, his trusty service revolver at his side!

For example, Pingel was able to talk about Wing Commander Joe Kayll of 54 Squadron who had been shot down and taken POW on 25 June 1941, just two weeks before Rolf Pingel's own incarceration. Quite likely this was the earliest confirmation of Kayll's capture that had reached the Air Ministry's ears, and with RAF intelligence officers doubtless much amused by Pingel's account of how Kayll had threatened all and sundry with his revolver before he could be disarmed. As a consequence of this behaviour, Pingel related, Joe Kayll was not invited for the traditional drink at the St Omer mess.

However, it was the technical information that was of more value and Pingel talked freely of the Me 109 F including its operational limitations and related concerns about the aeroplane's wings and their lack of stability. He told how two pilots (including Hptm Balthasar) had been killed during the previous three weeks by tearing the wings off their Me 109 Fs trying to follow Spitfires in snaking dives. (However, despite Pingel's conviction that Balthasar's wings had come off in a dive there is, in fact, compelling subsequent evidence that he was shot down by an RAF fighter.)

Pingel further went on to divulge useful information as to operational limitations; combat ceilings, endurance, rated altitude and weaponry. All of this would be useful in the proposed air-testing of the Messerschmitt 109 F, especially in the absence of any set of official pilot's notes. Additionally, the minutiae of day-to-day life in the Luftwaffe always proved useful if it could be obtained. Such information, when thrown into the mix, could surprise subsequent prisoners during interrogation and an already unsettled and perhaps frightened prisoner could then be leaned upon to divulge rather more than he otherwise might. For this same reason, of course, it is likely that the mail bags found in Leonhard Buckle's Gotha 145 (Chapter 3) were of considerable value as raw material for this rather nefarious purpose.

Sometimes the subjects of interrogation concluded that their interrogators knew it all, anyway, and so what was the point of not talking or adding or correcting information? An example of such idle chatter came from Pingel, with the revelation that a certain Major von Osterroth had been killed in a crash, with a Major Kuscher having to deliver the graveside oration. In it, Kuscher became confused with Generalmajor Theo Osterkamp, commander of the fighter arm of Luftflotte 2. "And now, dear Theo, happy landings in Valhalla" he intoned, much to the consternation and stifled amusement of the assembled officers of the funeral party.

Pingel also went on to reveal that Osterkamp was currently seeking a divorce and it was certainly information such as this, along with the funeral story, that would cause serious unease amongst subsequent POWs. It could understandably be a disconcerting puzzle; how on earth did their captors know this sort of detailed knowledge? We return, though, to the Messerschmitt 109 F itself.

The aircraft was by now in the hands of the Air Fighting Development Unit where it was to undergo a whole programme of evaluation and flight testing. On 20 October 1941 it was being flown by a Polish pilot, Fg Off Marian J. Skalski, who took the Me 109 up to high altitude above nearby RAF Fowlmere to perform pre-arranged comparative diving trials against a Spitfire. The plan was for a dive at fifty degrees and heading towards Duxford airfield in company with the test Spitfire. Quite likely, Skalski would have been appraised as to the potential for structural failure of the wings during pull-out from the dive and would have been sufficiently alert for such a risk arising. But it was not the wings, on this occasion, that were the problem.

Suddenly, observers on the ground noticed that something was going wrong as the Messerschmitt's speed increased dramatically and the dive steepened into the near vertical. He clearly needed to pull out if disaster was to be averted. The accompanying Spitfire's somewhat alarmed pilot had long pulled out of

Fg Off Marian Skalski.

the dive and watched helplessly as ES906 still screamed earthwards at full throttle. With an earth-shaking thud the fighter finally struck the ground in a smallholding near Green Lane in Fowlmere village, driving the wreckage and body of the unfortunate pilot deep underground upon impact with the soft soil.

Although they were quickly on the spot, the RAF personnel arriving from Duxford and Fowlmere found there was very little left for them to salvage although the remains of the unfortunate pilot were carefully extricated from the buried wreckage of the cockpit. Arriving on the grisly scene, the Duxford medical officer managed to secure tissue and blood samples which later revealed Skalski to have been poisoned, with at least 30% carbon monoxide being found in his blood. The MO was thereby able to conclude that the pilot was either unconscious or not fully functional at the time of impact. In other words, he had been overcome by engine exhaust fumes and had suffered carbon monoxide poisoning. The supposition was made that exhaust gases had escaped into the engine bay and then percolated through into the cockpit due to the removal of the MG 151 gun which had left an ineffective seal between the engine bay and cockpit.

With Skalski's body removed from the scene and the cause of death already ascertained by the medics there was no merit in recovering what little remained of the Messerschmitt. For the sake of expediency, the engine was left embedded in the loamy soil and the rear fuselage and tail wreckage simply thrown into the crater before it was filled in. On 24 October a Polish chaplain officiated as Skalski was laid to rest in nearby Whittlesford parish church. To all intents and purposes the saga of Rolf Pingel and his Messerschmitt 109 F was over.

By 1979, however, the author and others became interested in examining the crash site of this Messerschmitt and unearthing both tangible remains of the aeroplane and its unusual history. In September of that year a major excavation of the site was undertaken and the engine, propeller blades, cockpit parts, the tail unit and tail wheel were all recovered from a depth of around twelve to fourteen feet.

Amongst the wreckage, still visible, were traces of RAF camouflage paint (dark earth/dark green) and the re-painted bright yellow of the undersurfaces and even remnants of the RAF serial, ES906. On the tail could be clearly seen a red white and blue fin flash with a swastika showing through underneath; a truly fascinating find. More unusual, though, was the discovery of a brass plate from one of the repaired radiators clearly marked up with the letters RAE (Royal Aircraft Establishment) and stamped with test pressures details.

Not only had the wreckage of an unusual aeroplane been unearthed, but so had its remarkable history. Rolf Pingel, still living at the time of the recovery, was fascinated to learn of the find but expressed his regret at the fatality

Skalski was buried a short distance from the place where he was killed.

that had occurred with the final loss of his Messerschmitt. All the same, he accepted gratefully a scale model of a Messerschmitt 109 F cast from scrap alloy that had been collected from the wrecked aircraft. This model, in 1/72nd scale, took pride of place on his study desk until his death in more recent years.

Uffz Oswald Fischer's Me 109 F-4 at Beachy Head. RAF personnel are seen here examining the aircraft.

Although the RAF had lost its important evaluation example of the Messerschmitt 109 F, much had already been learned about the capabilities and limitations of the new fighter although it is true to say that almost as much information had been gleaned from its pilot, than it had from any technical examination or test flying.

His openness about fighting tactics in the Messerschmitt 109 F, too, must have been an extremely useful insight for the RAF as to how the aircraft was utilised, most especially the knowledge gleaned that pilots of the new aircraft had to be particularly careful when pulling out of a fast and steep dive in order to avoid catastrophic failure of the wings. Such information as this could usually only realistically be known from operational experience of the type.

Although no further examples of the Messerschmitt 109 F were obtained for test flying until an F-4/B example was captured on 20 May 1942, the overall knowledge already gained had surely been invaluable, especially with the aircraft type now widely entering service on all fronts and replacing the Messerschmitt 109 E variants. The evaluation was a clear reminder, if one were needed, that there was an on-going requirement to keep pace with German aeronautical developments if the air war was to be conducted on anything like equal terms.

The RAF were not long in acquiring another airworthy Me 109 F, this time an F-4 version, when Uffz Oswald Fischer's aircraft of 10.(Jabo)/JG26, Werke Nummer 7232, was hit by machine-gun fire during a shipping strike off Newhaven on 20 May 1942. Just like Pingel, and with an overheating engine and no hope of a return flight across the English Channel, Fischer made an emergency wheels-up landing near Beachy Head and thus provided the RAF with their replacement.

Despite the useful data established on the type, a newer and rather more menacing German fighter was just coming into front-line service and was a far greater worry for the RAF. In his interrogation, Pingel had commented on this aircraft, stating that " ... a great deal is expected of it". The subject of British concern and confident German expectation was the Focke Wulf 190.

The Messerschmitt 109 F proved to be a formidable opponent for RAF Fighter Command and the capture and test flying of a pristine example had proved invaluable in gathering intelligence, particularly as regards to how the fighter could best be countered. After the loss of that aircraft on 20 October 1941 it would be a while before another airworthy Me 109 F fell into British hands. Meanwhile, the type continued to serve with the Luftwaffe on all fronts with this Messerschmitt 109 F-4 of 7./JG53 being shot down by Flak near Mechili, Libya, on 16 December 1941 its pilot, Oblt Heinz Altendorf, being captured. An impressive tally of the pilot's twenty-three victories marked on the rudder bears testimony, if any were needed, to the fighting ability of the Me 109 F and the need for detailed intelligence to counter it.

CHAPTER 10   To Get a Butcher Bird

WHEN HPTM WALTER ADOLPH'S II Gruppe of JG26 took delivery of its first Focke Wulf 190 on or around 7 August 1941 the aircraft over which RAF intelligence had fretted for some while was finally in service. Once any initial glitches were sorted, and the Gruppe's pilots had become more familiarised with operating the type, it didn't take long for them to be declared operational and by mid-September of that year they were at last in action. And the RAF's desire to get their hands on an example for evaluation was surely intensified.

Apocryphal though it might possibly be, the story goes that one of the RAF's first encounters with the Fw 190 was entered into with considerable naïve enthusiasm as the British fighter leader involved called to his pilots something to the effect of: "Tally ho! This will be easy, chaps. They're using captured Curtiss Hawks!"

It was from a flight line like this that it was planned to steal a Focke Wulf 190 from a Luftwaffe fighter airfield in France.

94

Whilst this may not be a wholly factual account of what actually occurred it certainly was the case that there was a degree of shock amongst many RAF pilots who first encountered the Fw 190 in action. And if the tale is true, then of course the pilots involved were very quickly disabused of any such notion when battle was joined and the German fighters began to run rings around them. Certainly in the case of at least one RAF fighter pilot, there exists clear evidence that he thought he may have been up against a Hawk. In his combat report of 18 September 1941, Plt Off Cyril Babbage DFM, 41 Squadron, stated:

'We intercepted several enemy aircraft one of which fired ineffectively at my No. 2 after the squadron had broken up. This aircraft appeared to be very similar to a Curtiss 75A but with a slimmer fuselage. It then turned south at high speed and I followed with 12¼ pounds boost and 2,800 revs with the result that I was overhauling slowly, indicated air speed 350 mph at sea level. I got within range just off Ostend and fired a five-second burst with cannon and machine guns from dead astern. The enemy aircraft broke up and crashed into the sea.'

By coincidence, the suspected 'Curtiss' that Babbage had destroyed was flown by none other than Hptm Walter Adolph, a twenty-four-kill Ritterkreuz-holder and Kommandeur of the first Focke Wulf 190-equipped unit on the Channel front. His body was washed ashore the following month. From its performance (which Babbage was at pains to emphasise) it was very clear that this was most certainly no Curtiss Hawk!

Steadily, and against a background of the growing realisation by RAF fighter pilots that they were dealing with something altogether more potent, British losses to the Fw 190 began to mount during the late summer and autumn of 1941. One such was Sgt J. G. West DFM of 616 Sqn who fell into the 'Curtiss Hawk' trap and paid the price on 27 September.

Limping back across the English Channel in his crippled Spitfire he was lucky to have survived the encounter and finally baled out just offshore at Bexhill-on-Sea in East Sussex. As with the majority of Fighter Command engagements against the Fw 190 at this time, West was flying a Spitfire Vb and it quickly became apparent that this mark of Spitfire was not really up to taking on the '190 on anything like equal terms. There, were, though successes like that enjoyed by Babbage. But a captive Fw 190 would at least enable the RAF to better assess the strengths and weaknesses of the type.

The new Fw 190 was referred to in the intelligence report relating to the capture of Rolf Pingel (Chapter 9) from which it is clear that the RAF were anxious to learn all they could about the new type. It was just a case of getting hold of one, although the acquisition of an example of this the latest enemy fighter in an undamaged condition was a requirement far easier to state than to achieve.

Jeffery Quill had been a test pilot pre-war but flew operationally as a Spitfire pilot with 65 Sqn during the Battle of Britain.

Given that the RAF had still failed to secure one by the early summer of the following year, Captain Philip Pinckney, a commando officer who was undeterred by the many obvious difficulties, put forward a plan to snatch a Fw 190 from under the very noses of the Luftwaffe. His audacious proposal was for two men to attempt to achieve by stealth what a battalion would not achieve by force: to steal one of the new German fighters and fly it back to England. For sheer effrontery, the plan, which is reproduced in full below, can have few equals in military history. And it might just have succeeded.

Captain Philip Pinckney.

'MOST SECRET AND URGENT
To: Officer Commanding No 12 Commando
From: Captain Pinckney, E Troop, No 12 Commando

'Sir,
I understand that as a matter of great urgency and importance a specimen Focke Wulf 190 is required in this country. I attach a proposal for procuring one of these aircraft.

'I have the honour to request that this, my application to be allowed to undertake the operation described, may be forwarded as rapidly as possible through the correct channels to the chief of combined operations. I further propose that the pilot to accompany me should be Mr Jeffery Quill who is a close friend of mine, and as a well-known test pilot of fighter aircraft he is well qualified to bring back the plane. He is also young, active, a yachtsman, and a man in every way suitable to carry out the preliminary approach by land and sea.

'If Mr. Quill cannot be allowed to undertake this operation, then perhaps a substitute could be made available from the Free French Forces? I am most anxious to be allowed to volunteer for this operation.
I have the honour to be, Sir
Your obedient servant
(signed) P. H. Pinckney'

23 June 1942

1) Object: to bring back to this country undamaged a Focke Wulf 190
2) Forces required:
    One MGB [motor gunboat] equipped with DF [direction-finding radio] apparatus, to carry a Folbot [collapsible canoe] to within two miles of the coast of France.
    One Folbot equipped with wireless transmitter.
    One officer of a commando.
    One specially selected pilot.

Method
3) **Day 1**

a) On the night of D1, the MGB, carrying the officers and Folbot, will leave England after dark and proceed at best speed to within two miles of the French coast off a selected beach.
b) On reaching the beach the Folbot will be carried inland and hidden in a wood or buried in the dunes. The officers will lie up during the following day.

4) **Day 2**
After laying up all day the officers will move inland until they are within observation range of a fighter aerodrome.

5) **Day 3**
a) On D3, the officers will keep the aerodrome under observation and plan the attack for the start of nautical twilight (i.e., just before sunrise) on D4.
b) During the night of D3, the officers will penetrate the aerodrome defences by stealth and will conceal themselves as near as possible to a selected Focke Wulf aircraft.

6) **Day 4**
a) At the start of nautical twilight on D4, when the aircraft are warmed up by the ground mechanics, the two officers will take the first opportunity to shoot the ground mechanics of the selected plane as soon as it has been started up. The pilot officer will take off in the machine and return to England. The commando officer will first ensure the safe departure of the aircraft and will then withdraw to a previously reconnoitred hide-up. Should no opportunity to seize the aircraft have presented itself, the officers will withdraw to a hide-up and make another attempt the next morning.
b) During the night of D4, the commando officer will return to the concealed Folbot.

7) **Day 5**
a) After nautical twilight of D5, or during the succeeding night, this officer will launch the Folbot and be picked up by an MGB.
b) The MGB should be off the coast for two hours before nautical twilight on D5, D6 or D7 providing the weather is calm. If the weather is unsuitable, the MGB should come on the first suitable morning. The officer after launching the Folbot will paddle to a pre-arranged bearing. The MGB, making due allowance for the day and consequent set of the tide, will proceed on a course to intercept the Folbot. In addition the officer will make wireless signals, which will be picked up by the MGB using DF gear.

Notes
Selected Aerodrome:
a) The selection of an aerodrome will be dependent on intelligence not at present available to me. The requirements are:

1) Within twenty miles of a landing beach which is not too strongly defended, and which has a hinterland of dunes or woods offering a hiding place for the Folbot.
2) Within observation range or a few miles of a covered approach or a wood or place of concealment.
b) It is thought that possibly Abbeville aerodrome might be suitable with a landing made on the Somme estuary. The Cherbourg peninsula, entailing a cliff-climbing on landing,

might give a good chance of making an undiscovered landing, providing a suitable aerodrome is nearby.

9) Return of the Plane:

Arrangements must be made with Fighter Command to ensure that the pilot officer is not shot down by our fighters on returning with the captured aircraft. It is suggested that these arrangements should not be dependent upon wireless or on the officers taking distinctive markings or signalling apparatus with them. Possibly RAF Fighter Command could be instructed not to shoot down any enemy Focke Wulf 190 appearing over the coast during specified times on selected days. In addition, the undercarriage could be lowered for identification. If a Focke Wulf 190 after all is unprocurable on the aerodrome, a Messerschmitt 109F could be brought back instead. I understand that its acquisition would also be valuable.

10) Date:

The landing should be made on a rising tide to cover footprints and also on a dark night to achieve surprise.

11) Alternative Return of Commando Officer:

If it is considered an unacceptable naval risk to bring back an MGB to pick up the commando officer, this officer could either paddle on a course pre-arranged by Fighter Command and eventually be picked up by an RAF rescue launch or, as a third alternative method of withdrawal, he could be instructed to make his way back through occupied France.

12) Other Considerations:

a) Food. The officers will be equipped with ten day's compressed rations.
b) Preparation. The officers should have ample time to train together for a period which need not exceed 10 days. Training should also be carried out on the MGB.
c) Security. The officers suggested in the covering letter accompanying this proposal are both at present stationed at Bursledon, where they frequently go sailing together; the commando officer owns a double Folbot which is used daily; there are MGBs stationed at Bursledon; training could therefore be started without delay and without arousing any suspicions that an operation was under rehearsal.

Pinckney's bold and ambitious proposal was allocated the rather un-imaginative operational code-name 'Airthief' and detailed planning began; the airfield at Cherbourg-Maupertus was considered suitable for such an enterprise. Yet while still in the embryo stage, Airthief was overtaken by a coincidence more bizarre than any fiction writer would devise. (However, as the reader delves further into the stories contained within this book they might well be inclined to the view that many of the accounts here are, in any case, better suited to fiction – one way or another!) In the case of Airthief, and on the very evening after Pinckney submitted his proposal, 23 June 1942, a German pilot actually landed his Fw 190 at RAF Pembrey in South Wales.

Captain Philip Hugh Pinckney did not survive the war and was killed in action with 2nd Regt of the Special Air Service in Italy on 7 September 1943[8]. Of the chances of success of Airthief, Jeffery Quill subsequently commented:

8 Captain Philip Pinckney's brother, Flt Lt Colin Pinckney DFC, had served as a fighter pilot during the Battle of Britain with 603 Squadron and was later killed on active service against Japanese forces on 6 June 1941.

"Provided we could get to the aircraft with its engine running, get the German airman out of the cockpit dead or alive and get me into it, I thought I had a 50-50 chance of getting back to England. As to the early part of the operation I was not qualified to have a view and I was guided entirely by Philip who seemed very confident. I would just have done what he said. He was obviously relying on stealth – and perhaps we might just have got away with it. Philip was always evasive about his own plans for getting back. I had a splendid way of getting back by air, but it was a very different kettle of fish for him. But he was very resourceful and might well have made it, one way or another, provided I had got the aircraft off the airfield without too much of a hue and cry.

"Anyway it was all a non-event, as it turned out. Philip Pinckney was the inspiration behind the whole thing. Had it succeeded it would have been 90% due to him and the balance of danger would have been heavily against him. I think he was bitterly disappointed when it was called off and he was quite cross about the German pilot landing in Wales. I am afraid that I have to confess to a certain easing of tension within my guts!"

Whilst the proposals might on the face of it seem hare-brained they may well have been partly influenced by the earlier successful raid against a radar station at Bruneval on the French coast by a party of commandos. This had been carried out on 27/28 February 1942, and during this operation key pieces of a German Wurzburg radar set were dismantled and seized and a German radar technician taken POW. Thus, there was at least some favourable precedent for audacious operations of the kind proposed in the Airthief plan.

However, if Pinckney was 'quite cross' about the unexpected arrival in Britain of a Fw 190 it would surely be no exaggeration at all to say that the Air Ministry (not to mention Jeffery Quill) must have been 'quite pleased'. The pilot who had delivered it was twenty-five-year-old Oblt Armin Faber.

Oblt Armin Faber had arrived with JG2 during the summer of 1941 and although the unit was not equipped with the Fw 190 until April 1942 Faber had already claimed to have shot down four RAF aircraft between November 1941 and 3 June 1942. He had just seventeen operational flights to his name at this time, although post-war research cannot substantiate the claims that Faber made. At the end of May 1942 he was made Gruppen Adjutant of III./JG2 on 1 June 1942 as a replacement for Oblt Werner Stöckelmann who had been killed in a flying accident on 27 May 1942. Armin Faber would get another kill to his name on 23 June 1942, but would end up that day being taken prisoner and presenting the RAF with an immaculate Fw 190.

Early in the evening of 23 June 1942 six Bostons of 107 Sqn, led by Wg Cdr Lewis Lynn,

Oblt Arnim Faber, III./JG2, summer 1942.

took off from RAF Exeter to attack Morlaix on Ramrod 23 with fighter escort provided by the Perranporth and Exeter Spitfire wings. At Cherbourg-Maupertus, the base of 7./JG2, the unit was on standby and many of the pilots were relaxing by playing handball on the runway. Suddenly, the alarm was sounded and one of the pilots, Uffz Willi 'Bill' Reuschling, wearing just his shirt, shorts and sports shoes raced to his aircraft donning lifejacket and flying helmet and having strapped in to await the order to start engines:

> "We did not have to wait long. Fighter-escorted bombers were north of Brest. We took off after the Staffelkapitän and turned south west, passing between Jersey and Guernsey and heading for Brest. After a few minutes we were told that the bombers had turned and were now headed back for England. So, the Staffel turned north and followed them and after a short time the English coast could be seen. We were flying at 9,000ft and were scanning below for any signs of RAF aircraft.
>
> "I spotted about twenty Spitfires flying very low but could not see the bombers. I told Oblt Mayer who gave the order to attack but we dived far too quickly and were closing too fast and in danger of over shooting."

What Reuschling had spotted were the Spitfires from the Exeter wing, led by Wg Cdr Alois Vašátko DFC flying in a Spitfire of 310 (Czech) Sqn. His wingman was Sgt Vaclav Ruprecht who apparently was Reuschling's intended target:

> "Suddenly a Spitfire appeared in front of me, only about fifty metres away, and I managed to get in a very quick shot before pulling back hard to avoid collision. Suddenly, my head hit the canopy and my aircraft started to cartwheel. The controls had all gone slack and looking behind I could see my tail was missing."

Closing on the enemy fighter threatening Ruprecht, Alois Vašátko's Spitfire had collided with Reuschling's Fw 190, completely slicing off the tail whilst the German aircraft's propeller had in turn scythed into the Spitfire and almost certainly killed the Czech wing leader instantly. 'Bill' Reuschling later recounted his terrifying experience. He was certainly very lucky to escape with his life:

> "Bale out! Bale out, I thought! Immediately my training came back to me and knowing that I was only 100 metres above the sea I quickly jettisoned the cockpit canopy, released the seat straps and was thrown out. I waited a few seconds before opening my parachute, felt a slight jerk and immediately hit the water."

Following the loss of the Czech wing leader, chaos reigned as the Fw 190s swept amongst the wheeling, diving and scattering Spitfire formation and it is fair to say that a somewhat confused dogfight ensued. During this furious but short engagement one further Spitfire of 19 Squadron (W3644) was lost, along with its pilot, Sgt A. L. Ridings. Another two Spitfires were damaged, with one pilot wounded in the leg, although, while all of this was occurring, a lone Fw 190 was heading north.

Armin Faber had joined up with the 7th Staffel of JG2, taking off shortly after they had. He had later become separated from the Staffel and after witnessing Reuschling's collision he spotted two Spitfires that were headed towards him. Sgt Frantisek Trejtnar of 310 Sqn wrote of what had happened in his diary:

'23 Tuesday: All day on duty. Afternoon on patrol. I caught a Fw 190 over Exeter. After a twenty-minute chase it turned on me. We both shot but I was the one to get it. Jumped by parachute from damaged Spitfire and on landing I broke my right leg. After four hours, I was taken to Exeter hospital. They mended my leg immediately but left two splinters in my arm. I woke from the anaesthetic at six in the morning. Hurt nicely all day.'

Apart from accounting for Trejtnar, Faber also claimed to have damaged another Spitfire which he saw crash-land (possibly an aircraft of 19 Sqn) before spotting a lone Spitfire (Frantisek Trejtnar) upon which he opened fire and then saw the pilot bale out.

What exactly happened next cannot be said for certain. Faber must certainly have been low on fuel and was also possibly disorientated as a result of the two combats. For whatever reason, instead of flying south he flew north. He then saw an airfield which he couldn't correctly identify but this turned out to be RAF Pembrey, near Swansea, in South Wales.

Faber lowered his undercarriage, landed, taxied over to the watch office and surrendered to an amazed duty pilot. 'Bill' Reuschling had been rescued after a short swim in his sports kit and was duly taken prisoner. When told about what had happened to Oblt Armin Faber he said to his interrogators that the III Gruppe Adjutant was "…just the sort of bloody fool one would expect to do a thing like that".

Whilst Ruprecht's Fw 190 was scattered in

Uffz Willi 'Bill' Reuschling.

pieces across the floor of the English Channel some six miles off Bolt Head, and beyond the reach of RAF intelligence, Faber had certainly delivered them the ultimate prize. According to a flight data card in the cockpit, what they specifically had was a Fw 190 A-3, Werke Nummer 313, with a build date of 21 March 1942. The RAF was now in possession of a fully-serviceable Focke Wulf 190, brand-new and just about factory-fresh.

It wasn't long before curious RAF officers flocked to RAF Pembrey to look at the new acquisition there, although by 29 June Werke Nummer 313 had been allocated the RAF serial number MP499 and had been dismantled and taken by road to the Royal Aircraft Establishment at Farnborough. Here, it was repainted in the standard RAF markings for 'prototype' aircraft; dark earth and dark green upper-surface camouflage, with yellow under surfaces and a yellow 'P' in a circle on the fuselage to denote its prototype status on the RAF's Air Ministry inventory. For a

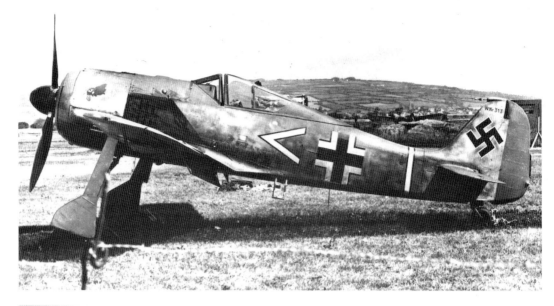

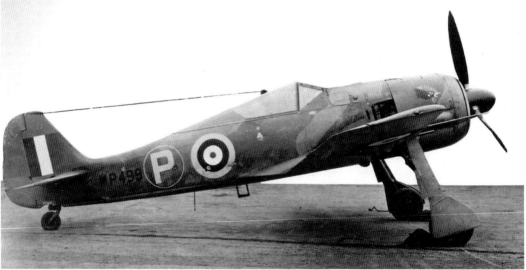

This was Oblt Arnim Faber's Focke Wulf 190 A-3, WNr 313, after he had landed it at RAF Pembrey, and then in RAF markings.

while at least the III./JG2 cockerel's head emblem was retained on the engine cowling and by 3 July 1942 the aircraft had been suitably inspected and prepared for its first flight in RAF hands with Wg Cdr H. J. Wilson at the controls.

All of the early test flights were flown by Wilson, during which time it was pitched intensively in comparative trials against other Allied types. Whilst the 'competing' types were all flown by pilots of the Air Fighting Development Unit at RAF Duxford the trials were actually all carried out at Farnborough. The reason for this was simply that Duxford then had a grass-only runway and it was thought too risky to operate the Fw 190 from grass.

Part of the trials programme included a flight which was effectively a speed-trial against a Rolls-Royce Griffon-engined Spitfire, a standard Spitfire Mk IX and a Hawker Typhoon. This was carried out in front of an official delegation on 22 July 1942 (not quite a month since the arrival of the Fw 190 in Britain) and was won by the Griffon-fitted Spitfire. It is said that this demonstration largely influenced the placing of large orders for the Griffon-engine Spitfire.

For a while, and as Armin Faber languished as a POW, his captive Fw 190 proved to be an extremely useful flight evaluation tool and was also examined in great detail from a technical point of view. This included a forensic examination of the BMW 801-D fourteen-cylinder radial engine, its weaponry, armour and the general construction of the airframe. In the later report it was noted, *inter alia*, that:

The BMW 801 engine is examined and photographically recorded.

'The workmanship on the aeroplane examined shows a definite deterioration from the standard found on the German aircraft of various types previously seen. In particular, in many places countersunk rivets were found only partly filling the countersink or eccentrically hammered down. In one or two instances rivets were found to be almost touching one another and the edges of several sheets had been cut away to avoid rivets. In several cases rivets had been left out in the main spar where the rivet holes were fouled by overlapping sheets.'

Aside from this black mark against the build standard, and perhaps related issues with factory quality control efficiency, there was very little that the RAE investigators, technicians and scientists could find to say in any negative manner. In many respects, it impressed those who flew it, too, especially with its well laid out cockpit and excellent visibility. However, the questions as to any identifiable areas of vulnerability were of paramount importance in terms of how the Fw 190 might best be engaged by Allied pilots. Again, there was little that could be found as truly susceptible or that might have been regarded as anything out of the ordinary for fighter aircraft, generally, of that period. However, in its report of October 1942, RAE assessed that:

'The pilot will, in all probability, become vulnerable through the windscreen in the 10 degrees above attack with the larger calibres and through the side screens and side of the cockpit in the 10 degrees off attack from either port or starboard. It is also possible that 0.5" armour piercing, 20mm ball and 20mm armour piercing would penetrate to the pilot through his instrument panel from 10 degrees above. On the result of the tests carried out he is vulnerable only through the side screens to the larger calibres in the direct ahead attack and even in this case the damage he sustains will probably only be from fragments of glass and may not therefore be serious.'

Clearly, the flight testing and ground evaluation had confirmed what the RAF already knew; that the Fw 190 was the most formidable of opponents against the fighter aircraft currently then in service. Only, now, the RAF knew the detail of its potency and its multifarious technical intricacies.

MP499, formerly Werke Nummer 313, continued to be flight tested and evaluated until 29 January 1943 but after completing twelve hours and fifteen minutes of test flying it was eventually relegated for further ground testing; the fuselage for live firing tests, the wings for destructive testing in a rig and the engine for bench tests.

It was finally struck off charge as an airframe on 18 September 1943, its purpose well served and with new Allied types now coming on stream that could finally get the edge against the Fw 190. By now, and in any case, the RAF had obtained pristine examples of the newer Fw 190 A-4/U8, one of which had landed at RAF West Malling on 17 April 1943 and the other at RAF Manston on 20 May 1943 (See Chapter 9) and also another Fw 190 A-5/U8 which had landed at RAF Manston on 20 June 1943.

Armin Faber had set a bit of a trend when it came to landing the very latest examples of perfectly serviceable Focke Wulf 190 aeroplanes at RAF airfields. However, and notwithstanding the later arrivals, the landing of Werke Nummer 313 on 23 June 1942 at RAF Pembrey was more than a landmark in view of the fact that all other examples of the type that had arrived in the British Isles up until 17 April 1943 had been badly smashed-up wrecks.

There was no doubting that, in deference to its killing ability, the aircraft more than lived up to its nickname of the *Würger* or Butcher Bird. However, by late 1942, the introduction of the Spitfire IX had widened the performance gap between the Spitfire and Me 109 and had become more than a match for the Fw 190. That said, however, the *Würger* remained a most formidable opponent.

CHAPTER 11 Caught in the Meacon's Trap

T HE SUCCESSES ACHIEVED BY THE Dornier 17 in both its Z and P variants during the campaigns against Poland, the West and over Britain between 1939 and early 1941 had shown the design to be a reliable workhorse and an effective weapons delivery asset. That said, it had already been recognised in 1937 that there was a need to up-grade the existing design and, to this end, the Dornier Flugzeuge company submitted a proposal to the technical branch of the RLM (Reichsluftfahrtministerium, or Air Ministry) for what was a scaled-up development of the basic Dornier 17 design.

This was to meet the Luftwaffe's requirements for a longer ranging, heavier and more versatile warplane that needed to be capable of lifting substantially heavier offensive loads and delivering them in either level or diving flight, albeit that the requirement for a dive-bombing capability with the aircraft was later abandoned. Classified as a heavy bomber, the project received the designation Dornier 217 and by the end of 1938 the first prototypes had been constructed.

By 1940 flight testing and development was well advanced with early production models being delivered later that year. They were operational with 2.(F)/11 in Romania by January 1941 employed on clandestine photographic reconnaissance over the Soviet Union in preparation for Operation Barbarossa. By mid-1941 the BMW 801 engine-equipped Dornier 217 E-1 was finally being issued to two front-line units operating against mainland Britain and its surrounding coastal waters, KG2 and KG40.

Although Dornier 217s had already been engaged and shot down by British defences from the summer of that year onwards, all of them had thus far fallen into the sea. The RAF had still to examine one up-close, and although it was only a matter of time before one fell over land there was a high probability that such a victim, when it arrived, would be largely smashed up. For now, A.I.1(g) watched, waited

Oblt Günther Dolenga, 5./KG2, autumn 1941.

and hoped. Also watching and waiting, but not specifically for the Dornier 217, was the RAF's 80 (Signals) Wing who we have already met in Chapter 7. Appropriately, the unit's motto was: 'Confusion To Our Enemies'.

As one Luftwaffe pilot later observed of his Meacon misadventure on a night in October 1941 when writing to the author in 1975, 80 Group had certainly lived up to its motto: "I hadn't exactly been caught," he observed "but I was already in the trap as soon as I neared Britain." That flier was Oblt Günther Dolenga, a pilot with 5./KG2.

It was at around midnight on 11 October 1941 that Oblt Dolenga and his three crew members (Uffz Walter Trompeter [observer], Uffz Willi Sprink [wireless operator] and Uffz Konrad Friederich [flight engineer]) took off from their base at Evreux and headed out westwards towards the Scilly Isles for an armed shipping reconnaissance in their Dornier 217 E-1. This was familiar hunting territory for Dolenga and his crew and already emblazoned on the fin of the Dornier 217 was the white outline of a British 20,000-ton ship, claimed as damaged during July.

Given luck, Dolenga reckoned that this war flight, his fiftieth, would see a British ship sunk. As it happened, though, many of Dolenga's recent war flights had hardly been crowning successes.

For instance, on 10 August 1941, U5 + DN had made a day flight into the Atlantic looking for an aircraft and carrying four 500kg bombs but nothing could be seen in the mist and the bombs were jettisoned in the sea. On 18 August U5 + DN had reverted to a land target and took another four 500kg bombs to Birmingham but was unable to find the target in 10/10 cloud and dropped the bombs randomly. On 1 September, another four 500kg bombs were jettisoned during an intended attack on Newcastle when heavy AA fire and night-fighter action caused the mission to be aborted. Again, on 16 September, another sortie had to be abandoned due to British night-fighter attacks during a dusk shipping reconnaissance off the east coast. Altogether, U5 + DN and her crew had been having a run of bad luck. Maybe the fiftieth war flight would see better fortunes.

To celebrate, a bottle of sparkling French wine was on board to be drunk on return to Evreux. Hopefully, after a run of misfortune, it would be a case of this time having something to actually celebrate, although quite apart from toasting this milestone, next week would also see his twenty-sixth birthday. Additionally, he had also been promoted to Staffelkäpitan to replace Hptm Lienemann who had recently suffered a broken leg.

A horseshoe was also hanging in the cockpit, a good luck charm from his ground crew. As things would turn out, the celebratory sparkling wine would go undrunk and the lucky horseshoe clearly needed a little more magic power in order to overcome the RAF's electronic counter-measures.

Dolenga's Dornier 217 was an E-1 variant and one of the tranche of the first 100 production models delivered to the Luftwaffe and its Werke Nummer (0069) confirmed that it was the sixty-ninth off the production line. Already, though, the type was being superseded by the E-2 version although these were only coming into service to replace E-1s when these were lost or damaged beyond repair. Given his status as Staffelkäpitan-in-waiting, Dolenga could doubtless have demanded that he be allocated an E-2, but as it was he preferred his faithful Do 217 E-1, U5 + DN. For one thing, the E-1 was marginally faster than the E-2 version due to the fact that it had no gun turret behind the cockpit and was therefore somewhat better streamlined. Additionally, the lack of turret on the E-1 made for a rather more spacious cockpit and Dolenga felt altogether more comfortable in his 'D' for Dora.

As he set course towards the western approaches of the English Channel, and despite the clear danger of any operational sortie, Dolenga still had good cause to feel confident and quietly satisfied with his war thus far. Equally content was Gp Capt Addison with his box of electronic tricks at 80 (Signals) Group.

Dolenga's shipping reconnaissance west of the Scilly Isles was completed without incident or the hoped-for contact with British shipping and soon after 02.00 hours on the morning of 12 October the Dornier 217 was headed eastwards back towards its base. However, and unknown to Dolenga, the winds encountered over the Atlantic had not been as forecast and, as a consequence, the Dornier was already somewhat off-track for its return to Evreux.

Moreover, the north coast of France had not appeared in front of the aircraft as had been expected. Scanning the gloom below them the crew could make out only the white-crested waves in the sea below and far ahead. Dolenga, somewhat confused, nevertheless assumed that he was somewhere over the western reaches of the English Channel and duly turned northwards in the hope that his navigator could get a fix on the south coast of Cornwall which he expected to appear shortly.

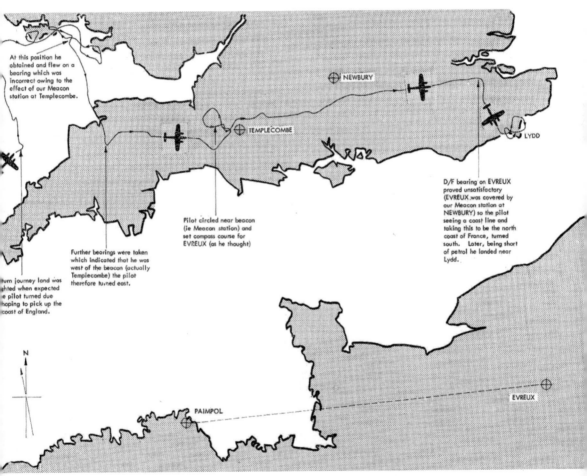

Map showing the erratic course of Dolenga's Dornier 217 on 11/12 October 1941.

About half-an-hour later, and when a line of breakers obligingly appeared along a coastline, the Dornier flew up and down the shore for some while as the frustrated crew tried to match the coast to their flying maps. Giving up in the darkness, and with partial cloud cover further impairing the quest, Dolenga decided to head southwards towards the French coast.

Unfortunately, what he had assumed to be the south coast of Cornwall had, in fact, been the south coast of Wales and what he now assumed to be the English Channel was, in fact, the Bristol Channel. He would neither be the first nor would he be the last German aviator to fall into that geographical trap as we have seen. Of course, it wasn't the only trap that Dolenga was going to fall into on that sortie.

Thus far, Dolenga and his crew had been the victims of wind speeds and had then made a simple navigational error. However, such glitches were not going to mislead them for long, they confidently believed. Now, as they flew across what they assumed to be northern France and Brittany, the navigator tuned in his radio direction finder to the beacon at Paimpol and Tocqueville and was comforted to receive strong and clear signals.

Under normal circumstances the considerable difference between the expected and the actual bearings would have immediately been apparent. However the crew had now been unsure of their position for some considerable time and were quite content to grasp without question the apparent lifeline that the beacon signal was throwing them. For now, at least. However, the signals in which they trusted didn't come from the Paimpol beacon at all but, instead, the 80 Wing Meacon at Templecombe near Yeovil, Somerset.

Unaware that the trap had now been sprung, Dolenga continued in blissful ignorance until he reached the location of what he thought to be either the Paimpol or Tocqueville beacon at around 04.00 hours. The problem was that Paimpol was positioned on the French coast, and below was nothing but land. And if it were Tocqueville then he ought to be able to see the Channel Islands.

For a while, the Dornier circled waveringly to the west of the Meacon, but there was no sign of a coastline anywhere nearby and the collective consternation on board was becoming considerably heightened by the minute. However, as Dolenga headed from the Meacon on a course of zero-eight-zero, which should have taken him directly to Evreux from Paimpol, there was more cause for anxiety; now, they should be picking up the Evreux beacon. Instead, they were getting signals from the Newbury Meacon and their direction-finder needle began to sway hopelessly as the Dornier passed to the south of it.

Nevertheless, Dolenga continued steadfastly along his established course believing that it must surely bring them, eventually, to Evreux. Instead, they were on a heading for Rochester and as they neared the north Kent coast the Thames estuary and Isle of Sheppey loomed in the early morning light at around 04.45 hours. Plausibly, this could be the north coast of France and so Dolenga turned southwards on a track that he yet hoped would take him to Evreux, although the crew now realised that they were certainly very thoroughly lost. But at least there was the comfort of knowing they were over German-held territory. Or so they thought. Imagine, then, the confusion on board the Dornier 217 when yet another coastline loomed up ahead. Where on earth were they?

Puzzled by this further navigational headache and geographical mystery, Dolenga concluded that, after all, they must have wandered down across north-western France and ended up either somewhere on the Biscay coast or near Granville on the Normandy coast. None of it made much sense, though, but that was the only logical explanation and since fuel was getting low there was little choice but to make a wheels-up forced landing in the first available field.

Firing a number of red Verey cartridges to announce his emergency arrival, Dolenga lined the Dornier 217 up for its enforced landing and as it slid across the grass the bomber finally came to rest half-in and half-out of a small watercourse. Its back was broken, propellers splintered and the cockpit wrenched sideways. As it came in for its landing a number of anti-glider-landing poles had been swept aside, but the crew were still certain they were in France.

Dolenga landed his Dornier 217 on the Kent/Sussex border near Lydd where it careered across a field and ended up on the bank of a drainage channel.

Dolenga himself had been slightly injured in the crash but sent two of his crew off to reconnoitre and get assistance. It was only when they saw the outline of a British soldier with his distinctive tin hat that the truth dawned on them and the pair hastened back to the aircraft. Here, the crew tried unsuccessfully to set off demolition charges and to remove wireless equipment but were prevented from doing so by the timely arrival of locally-stationed troops. It didn't get any worse than this. Clearly, Dolenga's run of bad luck remained unbroken. Unbroken, too, was that celebratory bottle of sparkling wine that RAF investigators found in the cockpit.

The Dornier 217 had in fact come down on the bank of Jury's Gap sewer, a drainage ditch that runs across Broomhill Level at Camber, East Sussex, and very close to the county border with Kent. Interestingly, the RAF's A.I.1(k) intelligence report noted: 'Dolenga was an experienced pilot, who had been a blind flying instructor for seven months in 1940, and it is therefore surprising that he should have become lost in this way.' In its commentary, here, the report rather suggests that A.I.1(k) did not have any inkling, at this stage, of the part played by 80 (Signals) Wing in the demise of U5 + DN.

The secrets of the Dornier 217 were now about to be laid bare as the wreck was dismantled into manageable sections on-site and transported to the Royal Aircraft Establishment at Farnborough for a detailed technical evaluation. Here, and although the Dornier 217 was far too badly damaged to repair for flight evaluation, a comprehensive report was assembled on the BMW 801 A/1 engines, airframe and equipment.

As for the Meacon system, the apparatus continued to claim successes. Some of them may have been 'unknown' in that victims might well have crashed in the seas around Britain or failed to return home due to navigational confusion caused by the Meacons, with the cause of such losses remaining a mystery to either friend or foe. However, a little over a month after Dolenga's downfall, and on 26 November 1941, a Junkers 88 A-5 of 1./Küstenfliegergruppe 106 became disorientated during an armed shipping reconnaissance of the Irish Sea between Bardney Island and Wicklow.

Turning for home at the end of the sortie, the crew then thought they had been subject to a miscalculation of wind strengths but had, in fact, been 'Meaconed'. Finding themselves over Cardigan, the navigator mistook that town for Plymouth and headed south. As they crossed North Devon, and eventually did find themselves over Plymouth, the crew reasoned that they had crossed the English Channel, flown across part of Brittany and were now over the Bay of Biscay and that Plymouth, below them, was an unidentified French coastal port.

These were states of confusion that were something of a pattern amongst Luftwaffe crews who were caught in the Meacon trap over the west of England. Turning back inland, the Junkers 88 crew then found themselves over RAF Chivenor,

A. Rear of Port engine nacelle.
B. Dinghy recess.
C. Port engine cowling.
D. Port cabin gun position (firing forward).

E. Fin slots.
F. Removable fuselage tip.

G. Port Cabin gun position (firing forward).
H. " " " " (firing rearward).
J. Dinghy recess.
K. Exhausts.
L. Wooden V.P. airscrew.

The Dornier 217 photographed *in situ* by the Royal Aircraft Establishment as part of the technical evaluation of the aircraft.

North Devon, where they fired a red and white flare and landed, wheels down, at 21.15 hours. The startled aerodrome defence company were concerned that the Junkers 88 might be about to take off again and fired a 'precautionary' burst of automatic fire into the cockpit. The gunfire slightly wounded the observer, Ogefr Erich Kurz, although the others, Uffz Erwin Herms (the pilot), Gefr Heinrich Klein and Ogefr Friedrich Krautler were unharmed. Herms immediately shut down his engines and the startled crew were taken POW by an equally-surprised RAF ground party.

Again, the Meacon had chalked up a success although this time the aircraft was in pristine and airworthy condition and was subsequently operated by the RAF wearing British markings and the serial number HM509. During its time in RAF service it ended up having a part in the wartime film In Which We Serve when the aircraft was temporarily returned to the livery of its former owners.

The former Junkers 88 A-5 of 1./Kustenfliegergruppe 106 now test flown by the RAF in British markings and with the serial number HM509.

The same night that Uffz Erwin Herms' crew had been 'Meaconed', and again most likely due to the influence of the same electronic countermeasures system, another Junkers 88, this time an A-4 of 2./Küstenfliegergruppe 106 was lost in the sea off Lands End with all four crew in what remain unexplained circumstances. However much German aircrews might have become aware of the Meacon's confusing influence on accurate navigation and geographical positioning, they would still continue to fall victim to its siren lure or simply become lost when signals were either confused or jammed.

Meanwhile, Günter Dolenga's bottle of wine hadn't gone to waste. Instead of being quaffed to celebrate a successful German sortie it was auctioned to raise funds for the RAF Benevolent Fund and was no doubt drunk, instead, to toast the successful capture of the Luftwaffe's latest bomber. Such were the fortunes and misfortunes of war.

12 Thieves, Defectors and Others

A LMOST EXCLUSIVELY, AND QUITE UNDERSTANDABLY, the majority of Luftwaffe aircraft that had been lost over the British Isles had come down with German pilots or crews on board. There was, however, a remarkable and most unusual exception; the arrival of a Bücker Bü 131B Jungmann bi-plane at RAF Christchurch on 29 April 1941.

Before the war, Frenchmen Jean Hebert and Denys Boudard had taken initial flying lessons with the national Aviation Populaire scheme and, with their aviation background, had subsequently joined the Armée de l'Air from which they had been formally discharged in March 1941. Despite the difficulties and dangers the pair wanted to escape from occupied France to Britain in order to join the Free French Air Force and continue the fight against Germany. In order to do so they hatched an ambitious but risky plan.

Cannily gaining employment with a French construction company laying concrete taxiways at German airfields in northern France the pair were intent on stealing an aeroplane that was within their capability to fly and to then escape with it across the Channel to Britain. Watching and observing how the Luftwaffe operated its aircraft, where they were parked and what types might

The Bücker Bü 131B Jungmann flown from Caen-Carpiquet aerodrome.

be available to steal the pair had spied out a Bücker Jungmann that was used as a runabout by the station commander at Caen-Carpiquet airfield where they were then working. For them, it fitted the bill. It was a two-seat training aircraft and, they reasoned, well within their capabilities to fly. It was just a case of getting their hands on it. That opportunity, however, finally came on 29 April 1941.

Although the weather conditions were not ideal, the aircraft had been parked in a position that allowed the two young Frenchmen to clamber aboard, un-noticed, start the aircraft and taxi out to take off before anybody had a chance to realise what was happening or was able to stop them.

Heading out over the French coast the pair quite expected at any time to be pursued and shot down by scrambled Messerschmitt 109 fighters, but if any pursuit was even ordered the fighters didn't find them in the heavy rain that now lashed across the Channel. Flying at low level all the way, and struggling with unfamiliar controls in the troublesome weather, the plucky Frenchmen finally made landfall on the Dorset-Hampshire border and immediately set about finding somewhere to land. Then, looming ahead of them, the airfield of RAF Christchurch appeared and, low on fuel, they made a straight-in approach and landing.

Loitering in the circuit was, perhaps, unwise whatever their fuel state, arriving as they were in an aircraft that would be unfamiliar to the British and which was also marked somewhat conspicuously with German crosses. After all, there had been no prior knowledge of the pair's arrival and, to all intents and purposes, this was a hostile aeroplane. By great good fortune, though, and notwithstanding the fact that RAF Christchurch was then occupied by a Special Duties (Airfield Defence) Flight of three Hurricanes, the Bücker had managed to escape

Jean Hebert (left) and Denys Boudard (right), photographed here with Flt Sgt Pritchard shortly after their dramatic arrival at Christchurch.

interception by either German or British fighters and, elated, Hebert and Boudard pulled off a perfect three-point landing.

Of course, any such arrival was greeted with initial suspicion until the stories and identities of the two men could be established. However, once the intelligence services were happy that everything stacked up, Hebert and Boudard were enlisted into the Free French Air Force and underwent formal pilot training in preparation for transfer to their respective squadrons.

As to their rather pretty little aircraft, Werke Nummer 4477, CD + EG, it was initially taken to London on 22 May by road for display in War Weapons Exhibition Week, where it was photographed with Colonel Valin, the C-in-C of the Free French Air Force in Britain. Rather strangely, it was displayed with a placard that highlighted the exploits of Hebert and Boudard but incorrectly described the event as having taken place on 21 May, the day before the exhibition was mounted. The intention was that, on return from exhibition, the aeroplane should be placed on the strength of the station defence flight at RAF Christchurch and it was allocated the RAF serial, DR626. Unfortunately, it turned out that the aircraft had been so badly damaged by souvenir hunters whilst on display in London that it was no longer in airworthy condition. With spares not available, and repair impractical, the Bücker was finally struck off charge on 5 November 1941.

The stolen German bi-plane is photographed here with an officer of the Free French Air Force and the placard detailing the escape.

As for the two Frenchmen, unfortunately Flt Sgt Jean Hebert lost his life in a flying accident on 9 June 1943 in Miles Master DL412 when he flew into fog off Filey and crashed into the North Sea. At around 15.00 hours that day the coastguard reported that an aeroplane had crashed into the water off Reighton Gap and the RNLI lifeboat *The Cuttle* was launched but only succeeded in finding a wheel and pieces of smashed aircraft. There was no trace of any survivors and it was concluded that Hebert had been killed when he deviated from the agreed exercise, descended to check his position and then struck the sea. It was a sad end for a young man who had risked so much to escape to Britain in order to continue the fight.

Denys Boudard, however, survived the war and had gone on to fly Spitfires with 340 (Ile de France) Sqn and participated in providing fighter cover for the Normandy landings in June 1944. It was during this period of operating over France, and once the Caen district had fallen to the Allies, that Boudard feigned engine problems in his Spitfire and landed at Caen-Carpiquet in order to become the last Frenchman to fly out of there and the first to return. It was, perhaps, just a further manifestation of the man's irrepressible flair and spirit that had led him to steal the German bi-plane from that very airfield in the first place. However, in considering their daring escape from France, it wasn't always the case that such bold and impetuous adventures ended quite the same way. Sometimes, it was Germans escaping from the Germans. And it didn't always go according to plan.

As the war drew towards its conclusion it had already long been clear to many Germans that the struggle was lost. For some, disaffected with the Nazi regime or unwilling any longer to risk their lives in what they saw as a futile struggle they no longer believed in, defection was always an option. Of course, the possible consequences for loved ones left behind might have been a serious disincentive to many. In other instances, a potential defector possibly had nobody left in Germany when families and kin had been lost in the bombing offensive or through other war causes. In such cases there was nothing left for them to lose.

Of course, defection was much more prevalent towards the war's end and especially so as the Red Army advanced inexorably from the east. That alone was sometimes an incentive to defect towards the west before it was too late. After all, it was clearly going to be better for a German serviceman to be in British or US hands than in the hands of the Russians. As the war drew into what were obviously its closing stages, so it was that such defections became rather more frequent.

However, it was certainly relatively unusual for a defection to be enacted as early as 1943 and one of the first cases of Luftwaffe airmen flying to Britain to give themselves up occurred on 10 September of that year. Leading Aircraftman S. C. Pemberton, of 2767 Sqn (Light Anti-Aircraft Sqn) RAF Regiment, had a grandstand view of the whole episode when a Messerschmitt 108 'Taifun' came down at RAF Ford in West Sussex:

"In the late summer of 1943 whilst billeted in the barrack block at RAF Ford I was awakened at around 7 am by the sound of cannon fire. Looking out of the window I saw a circling Mosquito over the airfield forcing down a German monoplane which then made a crash landing. It was an unarmed observation [sic] plane which held two Germans who had apparently flown across the Channel to surrender.

"It appears that the warning shots of the Mosquito panicked the German pilot into a crash landing and, in doing so, both men on board were injured and taken to our sick quarters. I was told later that both men had civilian clothes and cutlery in suitcases with them.

"Apparently, one of the two died of his injuries but the other one survived. The intelligence officer was very disappointed with this outcome as the dead man could have apparently furnished us with so much more information than his companion. The whole episode was kept a closely-guarded secret."

What Pemberton had seen was the arrival of a Messerschmitt 108 B-1, a light communications aircraft, that had belonged to Stab./KG40 and had been stolen by Uffz Jonni Suppinger and Uffz Viktor Packer from its Châteaudun base at 06.00 that morning. (KG40 was, at that time, a Focke Wulf 200 Condor-equipped unit operating on long-range maritime reconnaissance and anti-shipping strikes over the Bay of Biscay and Atlantic Ocean.)

A restored Me 108 still airworthy in Germany today.

The aircraft, Werke Nummer 2014, F8 + CA, had crossed the English coast at Selsey Bill, the nearest point on the British shoreline after the flight from France, and where the two occupants furiously fired red and white Verey cartridges which they had hoped would indicate they had no hostile intentions. Turning eastwards, the track took them either by accident or design to RAF Ford where the Me 108 prepared to land and, again, fired off red and white signal pistol flares.

Unfortunately for Suppinger and Packer, however, a 29 Sqn Mosquito piloted by Flt Lt Read of A Flight had already been sent off to investigate what were reported as two hostiles approaching from the sea and Read was understandably not in a compromising mood when he saw a German-marked aircraft approaching his home airfield. To him, the red and white signal cartridges were of no consequence. The enemy aircraft represented a potential threat.

That said, as the Messerschmitt 108 lowered its landing gear and was clearly on a final approach to land, Read was prepared to adopt a rather less belligerent attitude. Instead, he followed the Me 108 into the circuit and then fired 'past' rather that 'at' the enemy machine; firing according to the RAF Ford operations record book '…not, it is believed, with lethal intent'. Clearly, if the Me 108 had selected gear-up and headed back to sea the powerful Mosquito could easily have blasted the slow, diminutive and unarmed Me 108 from the sky.

Lethal intent or not, the landing executed by the Messerschmitt 108 was extremely ponderous. What exactly occurred is uncertain, but either the landing was sufficiently heavy to collapse the landing gear or the gear was not properly locked down and the Messerschmitt screeched to a halt on its belly, badly damaged, and with its two occupants injured. Again, we turn to the RAF Ford operations record book for a contemporary account of the episode:

' ... It turned out to be a Me 108 with two German under-officers (with, rumour says, a suitcase and English money). They were fired at by Flt Lt Read and also by two Typhoons and the ground gunners. The result was that they did a wheels-up belly-flop with accent on both the belly and the flop. The 'plane became Cat. B[9] and both under-officers were removed to hospital, Cat. unknown.'

Extricated from the wreckage, Suppinger and Packer were rushed off to the RAF Ford sick bay at nearby Tortington Hall where Suppinger subsequently succumbed to his injuries the next day. Packer was reported to have only been slightly hurt and he later recovered. Initially, twenty-six-year-old Uffz Jonni Suppinger was buried at Chichester cemetery but was later re-buried in Block 1, Grave 100, of the German military cemetery, Cannock Chase.

Quite what the real truth might have been behind this supposed defection is unknown, but it would appear that the Luftwaffe, initially at least, believed that the Messerschmitt 108 had been stolen and flown to either Spain or Portugal. Although it cannot be substantiated, other RAF personnel present at Ford at the time later told how they had 'heard' that the two airmen were about to be transferred to the Eastern Front and defected out of fear.

However, if reports about the subsequent broadcasts to Germany by defecting crew members on board the Dyce Junkers 88 (Chapter 13) are accurate, the possibility cannot be excluded, either, that both men were encouraged to defect by those broadcasts. In the absence of any information to substantiate things, however, this may only be viewed as speculation albeit such reasons might well be more than credible.

As for the aeroplane they arrived in, although numerous captured examples of the Messerschmitt 108 were used by the RAF in Europe and Britain at the end of the war this, not surprisingly, was the only example of its type to end up in Britain under 'war conditions' during the 1939-1945 period, even though the badly damaged hulk was subsequently scrapped.

Unfortunately it was of limited technical value to the RAF not only by virtue of its insignificance militarily but also because at least three of the type were already in Britain at the commencement of war; one that was seized at Croydon airport in September 1939, one that had been Messerschmitt's demonstrator aircraft for its UK agents in 1938/39 and one that had been imported to Britain by AFN Ltd. All three were used by the RAF, but after the write-off of one of them (Werke Nummer 2039/DK280) in September 1942 it may well have been reprieved by the arrival of the aircraft at Ford. Previously recorded as struck off charge, the aircraft was then reprieved and brought back on charge in November 1943, apparently the result of spares being sourced. The arrival of W.Nr 2014 in the September of that year cannot have been entirely coincidental in the sourcing of spare parts for 2039.

Apart from the arrival of Rudolf Hess (Chapter 8) another unusual Messerschmitt aircraft arrival brought a further defector the year after the landing of the Messerschmitt 108 at RAF Ford. Like the Ford episode, this was a two-seat aircraft but in the form of the trainer version of the Messerschmitt 109 fighter. This time, however, there was only one person on board.

Mrs Kathleen Bell was in her cottage at East View in Herringfleet, Suffolk, during the early evening of 15 May 1944 when she heard the sound of a low-flying aircraft approaching. At first,

---

9 Cat B was Category B damage. Category A, B and C was used to classify airframe damage by the RAF. Cat A was repairable on unit, Cat B would need repair at a factory or a maintenance unit and Cat C was a write off. In this case, the aircraft was ultimately not deemed repairable. Clearly, it had limited operational significance as an aircraft for RAF intelligence or evaluation purposes. In this instance, then, the information potentially brought by Suppinger and Packer about KG40 would have been the greater prize.

she took relatively little notice. The abundance of USAAF airfields of the 8th Air Force in the region meant that there were almost always American aircraft in the area, particularly P-47 Thunderbolts and P-51 Mustangs. But something about this sound was different. This didn't make quite the same noise and she gazed skywards to spot a single-engine aeroplane painted in an unusual camouflage scheme.

As it flashed past, descending lower in the direction of Herringfleet Common, the sight of the German black crosses stopped her in her tracks and she watched as the aircraft disappeared from view, getting lower and lower. Hearing the muffled sound of a distant crash at the same time that the engine noise stopped, she

The Messerschmitt 109 G-12 two-seat training aircraft of 1./Jagdfliegerschule. It was photographed here in a hangar at the Royal Aircraft Establishment, Farnborough, where it had been taken for examination.

rushed indoors to tell her husband, Harry, what she had just seen. Harry was a sergeant in the local Home Guard and he ran to the area of the crash that his wife had indicated as Kathleen jumped on her bicycle and pedalled to Somerleyton police station to raise the alarm.

Arriving on the scene more than a little breathless, Sgt Harry Bell found that the Messerschmitt 109 had come to rest after smashing through the top branches of a tree and was now on the uphill incline of a small valley beyond the landing point the pilot had clearly been aiming for on Herringfleet Common itself.

The aircraft was smashed into three distinct sections; the engine nacelle, the fuselage with its cockpit, and, in one complete section, the wings, inverted and with one wheel pointing skywards. The fuselage, with its cockpit canopies still closed, was lying partly on its port side.

Initially, it seemed to Bell that this was perhaps not a survivable crash given the condition of what was left. At the very least, any occupant would likely be quite badly injured. Approaching the wreckage with cautious trepidation, he peered amongst the bashed-up sections of Messerschmitt and realised there was some movement inside. Then, sticking through a jagged tear in the fuselage structure, he could see a pair of wriggling feet.

By now, a soldier who had also witnessed the crash was on the scene and the pair heaved open the canopy cover and managed, with some difficulty, to haul the still conscious pilot from the cockpit. In broken English he asked anxiously where he was. "England," he was told. A mumbled but clearly enthusiastic, "good" somewhat threw his two rescuers, who rather imagined that the German pilot would be less than pleased to have arrived in Britain. Perhaps he was dazed and just didn't understand what he was being told, the two men thought. However, they could not yet have known anything of the reasons for his crash landing and were making entirely reasonable assumptions given the circumstances.

As Sgt Bell tended the rescued pilot, the German pointed to his left leg and it later turned out that it was very badly broken. However, the pilot had a very visible and badly-bleeding injury in the form of a serious cut to his left wrist. In order to dress the wound, Bell removed the pilot's

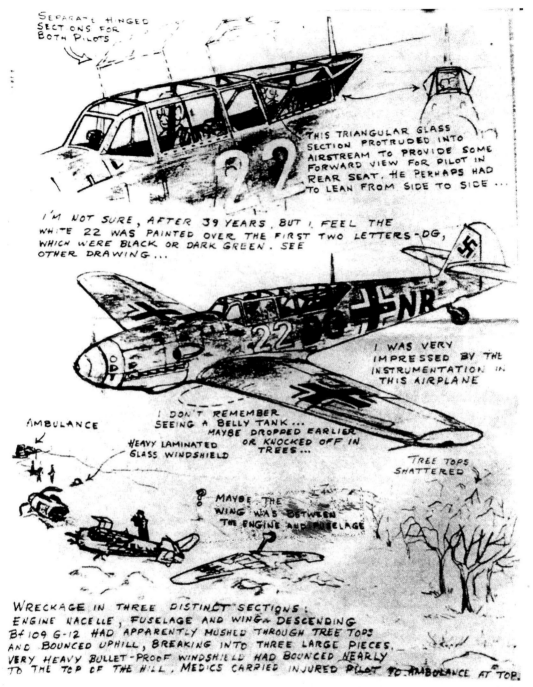

SEPARATE HINGED SECTIONS FOR BOTH PILOTS

THIS TRIANGULAR GLASS SECTION PROTRUDED INTO AIRSTREAM TO PROVIDE SOME FORWARD VIEW FOR PILOT IN REAR SEAT. HE PERHAPS HAD TO LEAN FROM SIDE TO SIDE ...

I'M NOT SURE, AFTER 39 YEARS, BUT I FEEL THE WHITE 22 WAS PAINTED OVER THE FIRST TWO LETTERS - DG, WHICH WERE BLACK OR DARK GREEN. SEE OTHER DRAWING ...

I WAS VERY IMPRESSED BY THE INSTRUMENTATION IN THIS AIRPLANE

AMBULANCE

I DON'T REMEMBER SEEING A BELLY TANK ... MAYBE DROPPED EARLIER OR KNOCKED OFF IN TREES ...

HEAVY LAMINATED GLASS WINDSHIELD

TREE TOPS SHATTERED

MAYBE THE WING WAS BETWEEN THE ENGINE AND FUSELAGE

WRECKAGE IN THREE DISTINCT SECTIONS: ENGINE NACELLE, FUSELAGE AND WING. DESCENDING Bf 109 G-12 HAD APPARENTLY MUSHED THROUGH TREE TOPS AND BOUNCED UPHILL, BREAKING INTO THREE LARGE PIECES. VERY HEAVY BULLET-PROOF WINDSHIELD HAD BOUNCED NEARLY TO THE TOP OF THE HILL, MEDICS CARRIED INJURED PILOT TO AMBULANCE AT TOP.

Although no photographs of the Messerschmitt 109 *in situ* at Herringfleet have been traced, the aircraft was drawn by a locally-based USAAF officer, 2nd Lt Bob Harper, who later supplied these copies of his drawings to the aviation historian and author, Dr Alfred Price.

watch but the injured German made it plain that he wanted it returned. Unable to put it back onto the bandaged wrist, Bell slipped it into the leg pocket of the pilot's flying overalls and indicated to the German what he had done. Later, however, there was considerable fuss about the apparently missing watch, with Bell implicated in its disappearance, until it was finally located in the trouser pocket of the flying overalls where he had carefully left it.

After she had left Harry racing to the crash, an equally breathless Mrs Bell arrived at the Somerleyton police house at around 19.12, pretty much at exactly the same time that her husband was hauling the German pilot from the cockpit of the wrecked Messerschmitt. After Kathleen had gabbled her message, PC Heard set off on his bicycle for the downed aircraft with all due haste, his tin hat rattling on the handlebars and cycle bell ringing furiously.

Meanwhile, Inspector Read and Sgt Ellis from Lowestoft police station set out by car and got to the scene shortly after PC Heard. By now, more and more people were arriving on the spot, including civilians and assorted military personnel. As civilians were shooed away, the pilot was carefully carried to the police car and taken to Lowestoft hospital. Officially detained, the prisoner was searched and his identity confirmed as Obfw Karl Wimberger. It was quickly established that he was, indeed, glad to be in England and was certainly a defector.

The Lowestoft police were later able to report: 'It is understood that this prisoner arrived in the nature of an escapee, that he wishes to be of assistance to the British authorities and that he travelled the 400 miles in two hours.'

Wimberger, an Austrian, was immediately subjected to detailed interrogation by officers of the RAF's A.I.1(k) department who learnt that the pilot had long-held anti-Nazi convictions and claimed never to have made any oath of allegiance to the Nazi party. Before the Austrian Anschluss, Wimberger had joined the Austrian air force in 1937 and had been training as an observer when he was discharged by the Germans after they took control of Austria.

Later, on the outbreak of hostilities, Wimberger was recalled to service and posted to the Vienna-based Luftzeuggruppe and pilot training. From the outset, it appears that Karl Wimberger might not have been made of 'the right stuff' for a combat flier although, given subsequent events and his claims during interrogation, the possibility that his apparent disdain for the Nazis might well have impacted upon his Luftwaffe career cannot be discounted.

After completion of pilot training, Wimberger found himself posted to a target-towing unit at Celle, and later on in Norway. At the beginning of August 1942 he was sent for Zerstörer (Messerschmitt 110) training at Dęblin although by October of 1943 he had been posted for night-fighter pilot training with 2./JG110 at Altenburg.

Although speculation, one cannot help but wonder if any perceived 'weak' political allegiances that might previously have hampered sought-after postings were now being overlooked in the desperate need to find new pilots for the defence of the Reich. Whatever the facts of the matter, Wimberger found himself posted to a night-fighter school at Vienna although told his interrogators that he was posted back to Altenburg after a short while due to his lack of experience. Throughout, according to Wimberger, he harboured anti-Nazi feelings but in January 1944 he was injured when crash-landing a Messerschmitt 109 at night. This resulted in a spell in hospital and when he was discharged he discovered that he had been declared unsuitable night-fighter pilot material. Now, he found himself posted for day-fighter training at Zerbst, near Innsbruck, with 1./Jagdfliegerschule on 8 May 1944.

With an Allied invasion clearly imminent in the West, a dire and worsening situation on the Eastern Front and the aerial home defence of Germany an ever more desperate affair it didn't take very long for Wimberger to consider his options and make a plan; if a moment presented itself, he would defect. Very soon, a perfect opportunity arose.

On the afternoon of 15 May, Wimberger had been carrying out circuits and bumps at Zerbst in Messerschmitt 109 G-12, White '22', DG + NR, Werke Nummer 15110, when his instructor climbed out of the cockpit and ordered Wimberger off on a one-hour cross-country flight. With the aircraft fully refuelled, including a full sixty-six-gallon drop tank, Wimberger took off at around 17.10 and put his plan into operation. Already, he had memorised the course from Zerbst that would take him to the nearest point on the east coast of England; steering 284 would ensure landfall on the Norfolk coastline.

As it happened, the meteorological conditions that day perfectly suited his plans; 10/10 cloud at 6,500ft would be the ideal cover from any Allied fighters. Proficient on instrument flying, all Wimberger had to do was to maintain his heading and stay in the clouds out of potential trouble. Briefly, as he crossed out over The Netherlands, he glimpsed the Zuider Zee, then, he was over the North Sea.

Calculating the time of his journey he estimated when he should be near the English coast and at that point came out of cloud and down to very low altitude. Dropping his landing gear as a signal of intent to surrender, Wimberger was now down to thirty or forty feet as he crossed in near Hopton-on-Sea before climbing again slightly and tucking up the wheels.

Luckily, he hadn't been detected by either the chain home or chain home low radar stations. Or, if he had, no raid warning had been flashed to towns in his path and no RAF Fighter Command interception had been ordered – leastways, not up until 18.57 when Wimberger was on 'finals' above Herringfleet. Luckily for him, too, any coastal defence anti-aircraft guns had failed to identify or engage the Messerschmitt and it was only in his rather botched forced landing that Wimberger's luck had slightly failed him.

All the same, perhaps he can be excused for misjudging his wheels-up landing given his gruelling and mentally challenging flight of almost two hours that had required precision, focus and concentration. All the while, of course, was the nagging worry that he might encounter Allied fighters if the cloud cover broke. And he was utterly defenceless if that should occur.

As it turned out, Karl Wimberger's defection flight had been a fairly skilful piece of precise navigation and 'evasion' with landfall being made almost precisely at the point intended when he left Zerbst. Although a great deal of detail may be gleaned from RAF Air Intelligence reports on the incident we cannot really second guess all of the reasons that may have driven him to his defection. Whatever his motivation his flight had had a relatively lucky end and had not been the disaster suffered by Suppinger and Packer in their Messerschmitt 108 defection. Interestingly, the Herringfleet Me 109 incident was not the only arrival of a Me 109 'G' model in the British Isles that summer.

By July 1944 the German military situation was critical; things were as bad as they could be on the Eastern Front, the Allies had landed in Normandy and were pushing inland across France and the round-the-clock USAAF and RAF bombing campaign was shattering the heartland of Germany. Only the commencement of the V1 flying-bomb campaign, and shortly the V2 rocket assault, gave any measure of renewed hope for the German military machine – albeit that such hope was short lived when both of these missile assaults faltered and failed as the launch bases for the weapons were steadily over-run or bombed out of operational existence.

It was against this background, then, that a Messerschmitt 109 G-6/U2 Gustav arrived intact in Britain on 21 July 1944 at a time when the pace of Luftwaffe air operations against the country, and hence 'arrivals', had markedly slowed.

With the large-scale bombing of German cities being one of the Third Reich's major defence headaches, all conceivable measures were employed to counter the relentless tide of attacks. One of those measures was the formation of Wilde Sau (Wild Boar) units by the Luftwaffe under Jagddivision 30, comprising three single-engine day-fighter units (JG300, 301 and 302) that were tasked with the interception of night bombers through the visual acquisition of enemy raiders, either by their shadows being cast on the clouds when illuminated from below by burning targets, when illuminated by searchlights or when the fighter pilots were attracted to the bomber streams by anti-aircraft fire.

It was all part of the desperate attempt to stop the un-stoppable, and in the early hours of 21 July 1944, I./JG301 was operating its Messerschmitt 109 G-6 aircraft from St Dizier in eastern France looking for enemy bomber streams. Somehow during that operation two of JG301's fighters found themselves lost and a long way from home over the Kent coast. Orbiting RAF Manston, the two aircraft flashed their downward identification lights and landed at around 02.40.

Perhaps unsure of himself at this unfamiliar aerodrome, Fw Manfred Gromill executed a wheels-up landing in his aircraft (Werke Nummer 163240) although his comrade, Lt H. Prenzel, was a little more confident and carried out a perfect wheels-down landing and thus presented the RAF with a fully airworthy Me 109 G-6/U2 aircraft, Werke Nummer 412951. As it happened, the arrival of multiples of Luftwaffe fighter types landing together at British airfields during World War Two was not without precedent. Also, and by coincidence, RAF Manston had been the airfield of arrival for Lt Wolfgang Teumer of 2./JG51 who had belly-landed his battle-damaged Messerschmitt 109 E-3 (Werke Nummer 4101) here on 27 November 1940.

Lt H. Prenzel's Messerschmitt 109 G-6/U2.

Repaired, that aircraft was test flown by the RAF as DG200 and although not the first Messerschmitt 109 E to be flight evaluated by the RAF it was one of the longest-serving examples of the 'E' variant to have been operated by them. So far, and throughout the entirety of the war, the British had been able to keep track of successive developments of the Messerschmitt 109 marque, through the E, F and now the G models. Messerschmitt 109 E-3, W.Nr 4101, ended up surviving the war and can be seen today as part of the Royal Air Force Museum collection at Hendon. Such longevity was not on the cards for the newly-arrived Me 109 G-6/U2, however.

Werke Nummer 412951 needed little more than a top-up of fuel before it could be test flown

Flt Lt Len Thorne poses with the rather forlorn wreck of what had been Lt Prenzel's aircraft.

by the RAF who simply had to paint roundels over the crosses, fin flashes over the swastikas and the serial number TP184 onto the red fuselage band that denoted this to be a 'Defence of The Reich' aircraft. To all intents and purposes, 412951 was ready to go and one of those who flew it was Captain Eric 'Winkle' Brown. Of this particular Messerschmitt 109 G-6/U2 he said:

"The Me 109 always brought to my mind the adjective 'sinister'. It has been suggested that it evinced characteristics associated with the nation that conceived it, and to me it looked lethal from any angle; on the ground or in the air. Once I had climbed into its claustrophobic cockpit it felt lethal! The cockpit was small and narrow and was enclosed by a cumbersome hood that was difficult to open from the inside and incorporated rather primitive sliding side panels. Space was so confined that movement of the head was difficult for even a pilot of my limited stature."

Captain Brown goes on to talk of the challenging landing characteristics of the type and with its narrow-track undercarriage, minimal forward view and a tendency to swing it could be quite a handful to get down, and ballooning or bouncing could be a problem on rough ground. Perhaps it was for these very reasons that Fw Manfred Gromill decided to land wheels-up at RAF Manston rather than risk a night landing on an unknown airfield. However, Lt Prenzel's former mount enabled a qualified assessment of the type to be made by Eric Brown. In summary, he was able to say:

"By the time the evolution of Willy Messerschmitt's basic design had reached the G-series it was no longer a great fighter, but it was still a sound all-rounder and the Me 109 G had greater flexibility from some aspects than preceding sub-types. Allied bomber formations were certainly finding the Gustav a formidable antagonist for it had heavy firepower, a reasonable overtaking speed and it presented a very small target profile to the gunners. If the Me 109 G could no longer take on the later Allied fighters on even terms during the last year of the war, this reflected no discredit on the design team that had conceived it."

Captain Eric Brown went on to comment on the aircraft's poor ground handling characteristics, and it was on the ground, ultimately, that Lt Prenzel's Me 109 G-6/U2 (TP814) ended up being written off on 22 November 1944 at the Air Fighting Development Unit, albeit not directly due to the aeroplane's challenging handling. The accident happened whilst the Me 109 G-6/U2 was in the hands of an AFDU pilot. Flt Lt Len Thorne takes up the story:

"Great care had to be taken when taking off and landing due to the Me 109 G Gustav's inclination to swing and ground-loop at the slightest provocation.

"When taking off at Wittering on the grass I avoided such trouble, but could do nothing when the port oleo strut fractured as the aircraft was about to unstick. The port wing tip struck the ground and TP184 carried out a complete cartwheel. It came to rest the right way up but was rather badly bent. As other Me 109s were then available it was decided not to undertake repairs."

If nothing else, the accident illustrated the hazards often faced by Allied pilots testing enemy aircraft. Flt Lt Thorne had been lucky, but already there had been a number of injuries and fatalities caused through such flight testing. Although often dangerous, it was necessary work. Of course, and until large numbers of German aircraft were captured intact at the end of the war, the vitally important testing and evaluation of Luftwaffe aircraft types by men like Captain Brown could only be carried out on examples downed over the British Isles, or Allied-held territory, and that were either pristine and intact or else were easily repairable. Those delivered intact like Lt Prenzel's Messerschmitt 109 G-6/U2 were top prizes in the intelligence war and the race to understand enemy equipment and to devise tactics for countering them.

CHAPTER 13 The Grey War

ON THE AFTERNOON OF SUNDAY 9 May 1943 a message was received by a German radio station from a Junkers 88 on patrol from Denmark to the effect that one of the aircraft's engines was on fire and that he was going to ditch into the North Sea. But events were not quite as they might have initially seemed to the German wireless operator transcribing the distress message. In fact, this seemingly unexceptional incident was far from it and has been the subject of much controversy over the succeeding years since the Ju 88 did not crash but landed instead, entirely intact, in the British Isles.

That afternoon, two Spitfires of 165 (Ceylon) Sqn's Blue Section were scrambled from RAF Dyce to intercept a lone raider that had been plotted heading across the North Sea. Shortly after making landfall some thirteen miles north west of Aberdeen, and in good visibility, the German aircraft encountered the pair of Spitfire Vbs – BN515 flown by American pilot Flt Lt A. F. 'Art' Roscoe DFC (Blue 1) and AB921 with Canadian Sergeant B. R. Scamen (Blue 2). No shots were fired and the two RAF fighters proceeded to escort the aircraft peacefully to RAF Dyce where it landed at 18.20 hours.

The question remains, why did the Spitfires not engage the enemy intruder? And why did the Junkers 88 land apparently voluntarily at an RAF airfield? Possibly it was a case that the crew had become lost, or that the three Germans on board were deserters who felt they could no longer fight for the Third Reich. Or, as some have suggested, was the entire episode in fact a carefully-planned and top-secret British operation?

The aircraft had taken off from Aalborg in Denmark at 15.03 and was flown by Oblt Heinrich Schmitt with Ofw Erich Kantwill, the flight engineer, and Ofw Paul Rosenberger, the wireless operator/air gunner. The Ju 88, from the IV Gruppe of Nachtjagdgeschwader 3 (NJG.3) and coded D5 + EV, landed at Kristiansand in Norway for refuelling exactly one hour later but then took off again at 16.50 for a mission over the Skagerrak. Following the call from the aircraft's wireless operator reporting engine trouble, nothing more was

Ofw Erich Kantwill, flight engineer on board the Junkers 88 R-1.

heard from the crew. It was quite naturally presumed by the Luftwaffe that the aircraft had been lost at sea.

The entry for that day in the 165 Sqn operations record book reads as follows:

'Arthur Roscoe and Ben Scamen were scrambled today to investigate a raider plotted due east of Peterhead. The raider turned south and eventually started to orbit as though lost. The section identified the raider as a Ju 88 and when Arthur approached, the Hun dropped his undercart, shot off Verey lights and waggled his wings. Blue 1 waggled his wings in turn and positioned himself in front of the enemy aircraft. Ben Scamen flew above and behind and the procession moved off to Dyce aerodrome where all landed safely causing a major sensation.'

Flight Lieutenant Roscoe later wrote:

'I was flying Blue 1 when we were scrambled to intercept an "X" raid said to be fifteen miles east of Peterhead travelling west at zero feet. We were vectored 030° and I flew at very high speed in order to intercept before the bandit reached the coast. When about half way to Peterhead, we were told the bandit was flying south about five miles out to sea. We turned east and flew out to sea for a few minutes and then orbited as the bandit was reported due north of us going south. We were then told to come closer in shore and orbit.

'Next we were told the bandit was west of us and orbiting so I flew slightly NNW so I could see to port. I then saw the bandit about a mile inland on my port bow at about 300-400 feet. I approached from his starboard beam and noticed his wheels were down and he fired numerous red Verey lights. He waggled his wings and I answered him back so I presumed he wished to be led to an aerodrome. I positioned myself about

Spitfire pilot Flt Lt 'Art' Roscoe, an American serving with 165 Sqn RAF.

400 yards ahead of him and told Blue 2 to fly above and behind and to one side of the bandit. The Junkers 88 raised his wheels and followed me back to Dyce. Upon reaching the aerodrome he lowered his wheels, fired more red lights, did a short circuit and landed. I followed him around during his complete run-in, just out of range. We then pancaked.'

This certainly does not sound like a pre-arranged event, and yet the aircraft was fitted with the new FuG 202 Lichtenstein radar equipment which RAF intelligence and technical experts were desperate to get their hands on. RAF losses to night fighters over occupied Europe and Germany were reaching unacceptable levels, and much of the German success was due to the effectiveness of its airborne radar. To be handed one of these Lichtenstein sets intact was a welcome bonus to

The captured Junkers 88 R-1 on arrival at RAF Dyce.

the Telecommunications Research Establishment in Malvern and that three Germans had decided to defect with such a valuable gift on board at such a crucial time appeared to be almost too remarkable to be simply good luck. So, was it?

In 1974, the German newspaper *Bild Am Sonntag* investigated the incident in which it alleged that Heinrich Schmitt had been a British agent since 1940. The newspaper claimed that Schmitt had regularly supplied secret information to Britain by way of his father, who sent it from his home in Thüringen via relay radio stations in Portugal and Switzerland. According to the reports Schmitt had flown to the United Kingdom on at least one previous occasion before his arrival at Dyce. He had been chosen to deliver a package to a representative of the British High Command in 1941, landing a Dornier Do 217 at Lincoln during the night of 20/21 May. The landing lights, he claimed, had been turned on to guide him in. Schmitt allegedly handed over the package to a waiting British officer and then immediately took off and returned to Germany.

It is also said that the successful arrival of the Junkers 88 at Dyce was signalled to Schmitt's father via the British propaganda radio station, Gustav Siegfried Eins. The message that was apparently broadcast was 'May has come', which implies that this was a pre-arranged code. To add some possible weight to the theory that Schmitt was working for the British, it was noted by Helmut Fiedler, a former German ground crew on the Junkers 88, that it was most unusual that such a long-serving crew as Schmitt, Rosenberger and Kantwill had never made any interceptions of British aircraft and never shot down any Allied aircraft.

The arrival of the Ju 88 at Dyce certainly did cause a sensation. Hardly had the German aircraft's wheels touched the ground than witnesses were writing or telephoning their friends with the astonishing news.

'A Jerry 'plane landed the other night, surrendered, and I had the job of driving the prisoners to the guardroom', wrote a WAAF called Ethel who worked in the airfield's motor transport section, '….and they were all dressed up in evening dress under their flying kit.' This statement might be worth further commentary since it was a common rumour associated with the arrival of Luftwaffe aircrew in the British Isles[10]. For the most part, German aircrews wore the one-piece combination flying suit over their normal uniform and when the flying overalls were taken off the contrast between the crumpled and oil stained suits against the smart uniform was often markedly noticeable. It is assumed that this is the origin of stories like this which abound in cases of arriving Luftwaffe aircrew, be they POW or deceased.

Another WAAF serving at RAF Dyce, Helen, who worked in the station's met office, wrote:

'I shouldn't be telling you this, so keep your thumb on it or I'll get shot – we were aroused by Florence yelling through the door, "air raid warning red" … we looked out, Maisie said, "Oh, it's only a Mosquito", when off went the ack-ack … shepherded by the new fighter flight, the thing came in and landed … and out stepped three Jerries complete – and I think this is pukka gen – with a despatch case!'

According to another WAAF called Isabel:

'The siren went in camp and we were told that one enemy aircraft was approaching … when to our surprise we saw two fighters coming back escorting another 'plane which was dropping flares … He was directly above us, it was then we saw the black crosses on it … Then another surprise, he put his wheels down to land. Imagine, land on our 'drome! A voice came over the loudspeakers warning the ack-ack batteries not to fire on the 'plane coming in … Anyway we, the three of us, got right up to the kite and three live Jerries got out grinning all over their faces … The excitement was terrific. But after all, it isn't every day a Ju 88 lands on the 'drome, is it?'

To Leading Aircraftwoman K. H. Paterson, also serving in the met office, the incident had all the appearance of a 'planned escape' because 'the Spits did not give a shot and there was nothing wrong with its engines'.

These letters were amongst 2,578 pieces of correspondence checked by a mail and telephone interception team which was quickly established to prevent news of the arrival of the Ju 88 leaking out. Of those communications intercepted more than 400 contained eye-witness accounts of the landing and twenty-four of these were confiscated.

According to the government scientist Prof R. V. Jones, who led the British counter-radar effort, the German crew said that …

"they had little sympathy with the Nazis, and that when they had received orders to shoot down our civil courier flying between Scotland and Stockholm, it was time for them to get out of the war. So, during a normal sortie they signalled that they had an engine failure

10 Rumours and urban myths relating to Luftwaffe aircrew brought down in Britain during the period 1939-1945 are legion. Many have become translated into historical 'fact' in the intervening years although actually without any basis. Common stories are that captured German pilots/crews spoke perfect English and knew exactly where they were because they went to school locally in the 1930s or, another version; that they had previously worked in the area as a hotel waiter. When opportunity subsequently arose to correspond or interview such aircrew during the 1970s and 80s it transpired in such cases that were queried that the former German airman neither spoke English nor had he previously set foot on English soil. Strangely, these urban myths are sometimes a common thread the length and breadth of the British Isles, the author having come across such tales from the Scottish Borders to Cornwall.

and were losing height: in fact they dived down to sea level to get below the German radar cover, and then headed for Aberdeen. They were detected by our radar, and intercepted by two Spitfires from a Canadian squadron who recognised that their intentions were not offensive, and who took the risk of escorting them over Aberdeen and into Dyce.

"Schmitt later confirmed this by declaring that: 'I had seen enough with my own eyes how things stood for us; the oppression, the deaths on the battlefields, the murder of my Jewish fiancée. The country was wading in blood. It was enough.' So he and Rosenberger had decided to defect to Britain. The third member of the crew, Ofw Erich Kantwill, had not wanted to desert to the enemy but the other two gave him no choice, with Rosenberger having held him at gunpoint during the flight to Scotland."

Following his arrival at RAF Dyce to investigate, Jones' immediate concern was that the enemy might learn that the Ju 88 had landed intact and set about trying to destroy it. So, he had the Ju 88 hidden in a hangar out of sight of any German reconnaissance aircraft. Then, to stop the personnel at Dyce from talking openly about the aircraft, Jones decided to give a lecture to everyone on the base about the importance of radar. Though this was a risky strategy, it evidently worked and a degree of secrecy was thus maintained.

The acquisition of the Lichtenstein radar was highly significant in the electronic counter-measures war and the aircraft, Junkers 88 C-6/R1, Werke Nummer 360043, D5 + EV, was quickly repainted in RAF colours and aerial trials with the new radar were conducted by the Telecommunications Research Establishment (TRE), headed by Jones.

The trials noted the radar's effectiveness as well as highlighting its deficiencies as, for example, one subsequent TRE report on the Lichtenstein equipment stated that 'efficient and quick interception is possible only by a fighter which has been vectored to within 30° of its target'.

The evaluation work on the captured radar set also paved the way for 'Window', the anti-radar system which had been developed much earlier but not introduced into the aerial war for the fear that it would soon be copied by the Germans, and in so doing that it would 'blind' Britain's own vital radar network. However, after evaluating the Lichtenstein set an agreement was reached that Window could at last be used.

On the night of 24 July 1943, fifty tons of Window were dropped over a considerable distance from twenty miles west of Heligoland all the way to Hamburg. Altogether, some 112,000 bundles of the aluminium-coated paper slips were dropped which gave the same radar effect as 112,000 aircraft. The Germans had no idea what was happening and, as a result, it proved to be an enormous success and would cut dramatically Allied combat losses.

Schmitt and Rosenberger went on to contribute further to the Allied war effort with the two men apparently being regular broadcasters on Gustav Siegfried Eins which was transmitted to Germany at 16.00 each day. "The war is lost," Schmitt told his countrymen, but under an assumed name, "don't sacrifice your lives for a futile war and incompetent leaders. In England and Sweden there are airfields where you will be welcomed as we were. Remember – waggle the wings of your aircraft, and you will be escorted in to a safe landing."

With Window now proving so effective at jamming the German radar, the Luftwaffe adopted new techniques, such as permitting their night fighters to roam the skies independently and giving their crews a running commentary by radio on where it was thought that the British bombers were heading. To counter this, a high-power ground radio transmitter (known as Corona) was built and was controlled from the British listening station at Kingsdown in Kent.

This operated on the same frequency as the German radio transmitters and Schmitt, Rosenberg, and other German speakers, would communicate their own messages to the German night-fighter crews to confuse them. They would listen to the advice being given to the German pilots and then send contradictory instructions of their own. Naturally, the German pilots did not know who to believe and in one incident, on the night of 17 November 1943, the Corona operator issued a general instruction to all night fighters to land immediately. This they did, despite the protests of the genuine German radio operator!

As for the Ju 88, it left RAF Dyce by air on 14 May 1943, piloted by Sqn Ldr Kalpass and escorted by a force of Beaufighters to the Royal Aircraft Establishment at Farnborough. Given the RAF serial number PJ876 it was used extensively in trials with the Bomber Development Unit and with the RAF's wireless & electrical flight. However, it was delivered to 1426 (Enemy Aircraft) Flight at RAF Collyweston on 6 May 1944 before transfer on 31 January 1945 to the Central Fighter Establishment at RAF Tangmere. Eventually put into store at RAF Sealand it then ended up being allocated for museum purposes and was ultimately transferred to the RAF Museum at Hendon for inclusion in the Battle of Britain Hall which opened in November 1978. It remains on public exhibition to this day.

The Dyce Junkers 88 R-1 photographed here at RAF Biggin Hill, just prior to its transfer to Hendon.

Both Flt Lt Roscoe and Sgt Scamen were acknowledged for their involvement in the safe arrival of the aircraft, thus: 'The pilots are to be congratulated for not opening fire and so bringing home valuable information for the technical branch' noted the 165 Squadron operations record book. Professor R. V. Jones was also aware of the part that these two pilots had played, in stating: 'One of my more diverting efforts on returning to London was to try and get the two Canadians [sic] awarded the Distinguished Flying Cross for *not* shooting the German aircraft down. This was rather too much for the air staff, but they did finally agree that the pilots should be Mentioned in Despatches.'

What, then, are we to make of that mysterious day in May 1943? Well, we do have Schmitt's own words on the subject from the interview he gave to *Bild Am Sontag* but perhaps at least some of that needs to be treated with caution. He explained that his father was a long-standing enemy of National Socialism and had been the secretary to Gustav Stresemann, the foreign minister in the former Weimar Republic and he had kept in touch with the Social Democrats who had escaped to London before the war. Schmitt claimed to have landed at RAF Lincoln in 1941 and the date he gave was just ten days after another mysterious flight over Britain – that which saw Rudolf Hess bale out of his Messerschmitt 110 over Scotland.

Certainly, there were some odd, covert and unexplained things going on in relation to German and Luftwaffe activity at this time, as we shall particularly see in Chapter 16. How much credence, though, may be attached to Schmitt's claims? 'It was all part of the grey war that existed at that time', Schmitt went on to say.

'I wasn't the only German pilot to land by arrangement in Britain, and several British pilots made landings in Germany, which were known to the people who mattered on our side. It was well-known that Hitler was prepared to pay a high price to make peace with Britain, and the secret flights only ended when we attacked Russia, and Britain and Russia became allies.'

According to Schmitt, the landing at Lincoln was on behalf of the Luftwaffe, but what the package was that he claimed to have handed to the waiting British officer, Schmitt said he never knew.

CHAPTER 14
For You, the War is Over

WITH ITS BACK BROKEN, THE Heinkel 111 of Stab./KG26 that been shot down at Humbie on 28 October 1939 (Chapter 1) was of considerable use in technical evaluation of the aircraft type but could not be made airworthy for flight testing. However, on 9 February 1940, another Heinkel 111 of KG26 arrived not all that many miles away in North Berwick where it had been shot down while engaged on an armed shipping reconnaissance, also in the Firth of Forth area. Although damaged, the Heinkel was this time deemed repairable, the first that was capable of being flown after being downed over the British Isles. As ever, the story behind its arrival, and of its subsequent life in RAF hands, was predictably eventful.

At 09.30 on Friday 9 February 1940, Heinkel 111, Werke Nummer 6853, 1H + EN, of 5./KG26 lifted off from its Westerland base and headed out, eastwards, across the North Sea at around 650ft and eventually made landfall just south of the Firth of Forth at May Island when they sighted a ship of around 6,000 tons. Making ready to attack it, they then spotted that it was Danish and was flying seven flags. Breaking away, the Heinkel then came under fire from a cruiser and this led the crew to conclude that the Danish ship was, after all, part of a convoy and turned back in preparation for an attack.

Before they could do so, the wireless operator (also the top gunner) spotted hostile fighters closing in on them and thus the pilot, Uffz Helmut Meyer, broke off his run-in to attack the Danish vessel and instead sought refuge in the clouds. Breaking cover a short while later, Meyer decided to once more try his luck against the Danish ship but it was just a re-run of the previous attempt and they were driven off by the fighters and gunfire from the naval vessel.

Giving up, Meyer headed back eastwards across the North Sea and was left alone by the fighters who were, presumably, content they had driven the raider off and were not prepared to chase it very far out into the inhospitable and wintry sea. Flying towards home for a few minutes, and climbing up to 2,300ft, the crew decided that they would turn about for one last attempt against the merchant ship. Unfortunately, it wasn't a wise decision.

Still lurking over the shipping were the three patrolling Spitfires, and when the Heinkel hove into view once more they were onto it. Flashing into the attack, Sqn Ldr Andrew Farquhar of 602 Sqn, in Spitfire K9962, opened fire and loosed off 625 rounds at the bomber, scoring hits in the fuselage and mortally wounding the wireless operator, Uffz Franz Wieners, at his mid-upper gunner's station.

As it happened, though, it would seem that the majority of Farquhar's 625 bullets went wide of the mark, and despite the wounds to Franz Wieners, there were relatively few overall strikes in the aircraft. A few hits in the oil sumps and radiators of both engines, though, had sealed the bomber's fate and there could now be no return across the North Sea. As a consequence, Meyer ditched his bombs and lowered the undercarriage, indicating surrender, and then banked and turned back towards land with Farquhar on his tail.

Still with its wheels down, the aircraft lost height over the coast until it landed in a field at Heugh Farm, North Berwick. On its landing run, and with both tyres punctured by bullets, it trundled through a hedge and gently tipped forward onto its nose, coming to rest in the tail-up position. Rushing to the scene, farm worker Walter Simpson waved at the swooping Spitfire overhead and remarked: "Our pilot looked that he were making as if to land himself, but then he just dipped low and flew off after waving cheerily from his cockpit." In fact, events involving Farquhar nearly two weeks later might well suggest that perhaps Farquhar was, indeed, 'making as if to land', but had then thought better of it.

Heinkel 111 H-1 of 5./KG26, the first enemy aircraft to arrive in Britain that would subsequently be made airworthy for test flying by the RAF.

First on the scene was a Mr Ian Whitelaw from nearby Rhodes Cottages who nervously stood and watched as the solitary observer while three of the crew members dragged a fourth man from the Heinkel. This man was the injured Franz Wieners who had serious wounds to his legs and back.

Meanwhile Mr W. J. Wright of Heugh Farm, head special constable for North Berwick, was racing to the scene with a posse of farm hands. Still alive when taken from the bomber, Wieners would die later in hospital but Meyer, along with Uffz Josef Sangl and Ogefr Heinz Hegemann, busied themselves around the aircraft and when Special Constable Wright blustered onto the scene, the airmen were prevented from re-entering the aircraft where they were apparently intending to set off two incendiary bombs that RAF Air Intelligence officers later found on board. Thwarted in their intent, the three survivors were officially taken into custody by Special Constable Wright but not before one of the three had purposely dropped his lighted cigarette into a pool of petrol that was now collecting under the bomber. Fortunately, the impulsive plan didn't work and the petrol failed to ignite, leaving the RAF with a relatively intact and easily repairable Heinkel He 111 H-1.

However, and as alluded to above, there is an interesting footnote to the North Berwick Heinkel incident on 9 February 1940 when Sqn Ldr Farquhar downed another Heinkel 111 not too far away at East Coldingham, Berwickshire, on 22 February.

On this occasion, Sqn Ldr Farquhar (again in Spitfire K9962) engaged and shot down a Heinkel 111 P-2 of 1./Aufkl.Gr.Ob.d.L along with Plt Off Victor G. Proudman in Spitfire L1007 of 65 Sqn. The German aircraft, engaged on a photographic reconnaissance of the Firth of Forth area, was attacked by fighters fifteen miles south of Fife Ness. The port engine and wing were damaged, the ventral gunner was injured and the starboard engine began to falter.

Putting the damaged Heinkel down at Lumsdaine, East Coldingham, near St Abb's Head,

A close-up of the KG26 emblem painted on the North Berwick Heinkel 111 with its Latin inscription *'Vestigium Leonis'* (In the Lion's Footprints).

Despite having ended up on its nose during the forced landing on 9 February 1940, the Heinkel was easily repairable and became AW177 on the RAF's inventory. Here, it is seen in a hangar whilst part of 1426 (Enemy Aircraft) Flight.

the crew evacuated the aircraft and dismounted the machine guns in order to keep at bay anyone who might interfere with their intended destruction of the bomber. They successfully achieved this through firing two incendiary devices stowed near the wireless installation. Once the aircraft was alight, they threw the machine guns and all of their papers into the flames. Meanwhile, another drama was about to unfold.

Circling above, Farquhar decided that a superb opportunity had presented itself; he would land adjacent to the crashed Heinkel 111 and take its crew POW and prevent them destroying the aircraft. That, at least, was the plan.

Wheels down, the CO of 602 Sqn landed about 200 yards from the Heinkel but, in doing so, the wheels bogged into the soft ground and the aircraft flipped over onto its back trapping Sqn Ldr Farquhar in the cockpit. Meanwhile, the pilot and radio operator, Lt Erich Grote and Uffz Wilhelm Berger, busied themselves with tending to the wounded flight engineer, Uffz Walter Bachmann while Fw Fritz Springath, the observer, sprinted to the upturned Spitfire and hauled the shame-faced pilot from his cockpit.

Apart from bruised pride at the ignominy of his landing and subsequent rescue by a German, Farquhar was unharmed although the Spitfire was badly damaged. Later, Fw Springath was mentioned in the House of Commons for what was hailed as a commendable humanitarian act. What is particularly interesting, though, is how the episode was reported in the local *Argus* newspaper:

Sqn Ldr Andrew Farquhar, CO of 602 Squadron.

'After a Spitfire pilot brought down a Heinkel bomber yesterday he landed close-in and took the crew of four Germans prisoner. The village postman reported: "I saw a big black machine flying from the sea. It was very low and the Spitfire was almost on top of it. Then I heard a burst of fire and the bomber crashed." A farm worker followed on: "Three Germans climbed out of the bomber and lifted out another man who seemed badly injured. They carried him across the field. Then they went back and got in again. They weren't inside long. They jumped out, and smoke and flames shot up."

'As this happened the Spitfire landed and the pilot clambered out and raced toward the Heinkel, but a few seconds too late. Flames were rising thirty feet from the bomber. The British pilot guarded the Germans until troops arrived and then helped them carry their wounded comrade to a farm close by.'

However, it would seem that the newspaper was being more than a little economical with the facts and no doubt it was felt best not to reveal what actually happened. Either way, the truth of the matter was revealed in a letter from another Spitfire pilot based at RAF Drem, Fg Off Frank Howell of 609 Sqn, writing to his brother Henry. In it, Howell tells how it really was:

'The only thing of interest that has happened up here is that awful show when the Heinkel landed at St Abb's Head. Of course, you must have read about it. The "dashing" pilot landed near the machine and tried to prevent the Jerries firing it, of all the crass stupidity! I have never seen such a miserable attempt at being a hero or something. It was the CO of 602 Squadron. A squadron leader! My my. The field was like a miniature mountain and of course he went ass over tit and landed flat on his back and was firmly stuck in the cockpit, upside down! Of course, the Germans being decent chaps lifted what was left of the tail and got him out, thus saving his life – or if not that, from a nasty headache.

'Actually, the Heinkel was nicely set alight, whilst the wretched squadron leader was on the wrong end of a revolver trying to bluff a bullet-headed German to hand it over! The scream of it all is that the "ace British Spitfire pilot" had not even got a peashooter with him! A silly man. The king is coming to see us all tomorrow and I expect he will get a DFC or something. I know what he really wants!'

Howell pulled no punches in his assessment of events, and appears to have been absolutely correct in his assessment that Sqn Ldr Farquhar would be awarded the DFC. On 1 March 1940 his immediate award of Distinguished Flying Cross was announced in the *London Gazette*.

All in all, it was a remarkable story although one element appeared in neither the newspaper, nor in Howell's letter. Apparently, when found in the company of the German airmen, and in flying kit, the hapless Farquhar was arrested as a German since his wrecked Spitfire was lying some distance away and out of sight of the arriving troops. It was certainly both a comedic episode and an extraordinarily dramatic arrival of an eagle. However, let us turn again to the subject of the Heinkel at North Berwick on 9 February 1940.

While Uffz Franz Wieners was being buried with full military honours at the Portobello cemetery in Edinburgh, the Heinkel 111 was carefully dismantled and transported to RAF Turnhouse where repairs were effected that allowed the bomber to be flown to the Royal Aircraft Establishment at Farnborough on 14 August 1940, via RAF Finningley, escorted there by two Hurricanes. Given the RAF serial number AW177 it was allocated, first, to the Air Fighting Development Unit at RAF Duxford but returned to the RAE on 6 October 1940 before being assigned to 1426 (Enemy Aircraft) Flight back at Duxford on 7 December 1941.

Here, it joined part of what became known as the German Flying Circus, or, colloquially, sometimes the 'Rafwaffe'. It was operated by the flight for almost two years in this capacity, but on 10 November 1943 it was lost in a tragic accident at the USAAF base at Polebrook. Coming in to land, and with eleven people on board, Fg Off F. A. Barr was alarmed to see a Junkers 88 heading straight towards him from the opposite end of the runway. This was Junkers 88 A-5 HM509 (see Chapter 11), also of 1426 Flight. Taking avoiding action, Barr had no option but to open the throttles and turn steeply to port but the aircraft stalled and crashed on the airfield perimeter, bursting into flames. Sadly, Barr and six of the ten passengers on board were killed in the crash in what was the worst single accident sustained in Britain during the often risky business of flying captured enemy aircraft.

The arrival of the Heinkel 111 at North Berwick was the first of a long line of Luftwaffe aircraft that came as arriving eagles which would later be flown for evaluation by the British. In time, the majority of significant types operated by the Germans would be acquired, although this does not include the very wide variety of aircraft types obtained by the Allies as they swept through Europe capturing enemy airfields and equipment; those war prizes are outside the scope of this book. By the time the North Berwick Heinkel arrived, the RAF had already obtained a flying example of the Messerschmitt 109 from the campaign in France but had to wait until July 1940 before procuring an airworthy example of the Messerschmitt 110.

Inevitably, and as with all the incidents detailed in this book, there were dramas of various kinds when Oblt Friedrich-Karl Runde of 4.(F)/14 bellied-in his Messerschmitt 110 C-5 at Goodwood in West Sussex on the morning of 21 July 1940 after being engaged by Hurricanes of Red Section, 238 Sqn, flown by Flt Lt D. E. Turner, Plt Off C. T. Davis and Plt Off J. S. Wigglesworth ten miles south west of Middle Wallop.

Whilst the Me 110 had been engaged on a photo-reconnaissance sortie (a single camera was installed instead of the two 20mm nose cannon) it had stumbled across a solitary Hawker Hart, K6485, of No 1 Service Flying Training School, RAF Netheravon, on a cross-country exercise with Royal Navy trainee pilot Leading Airman John Arthur Seed at the controls. Obviously, there was no contest. In what was an entirely one-sided engagement which resembled target practice, the Hart was shot down in flames by Oblt Runde over RAF Old Sarum. Seed jumped, but died of his injuries. However, retribution was swift when Turner, Davis and Wigglesworth found the Me 110 and chased it back to the coast at 2,000ft, this time engaging in their own target practice and managing to stop both engines.

Runde was able to make a good forced landing in a field of root vegetables at Home Farm on the Goodwood Estate near Chichester, where the *Sussex Chronicle & Gazette* of 26 July was later able to report that the two crew, 'an officer and a sergeant', were captured by a milkman called 'Reg' and a farmer's daughter called 'Betty'. Going on, the newspaper reported:

Messerschmitt 110 C-5 of 4.(F)/14 at Goodwood, West Sussex, on 21 July 1940.

'They were taken over by the RAF and later brought to a neighbouring railway station. On the platform the officer shook hands and saluted punctiliously the WRAF driver of the vehicle and paid the same courtesies to the officer in charge of the escort party. The two prisoners were kept separate, and on the train the officer was put in a first-class carriage and the sergeant in a third-class carriage, both with separate escorts.'

From the shooting down of an un-armed training aircraft and to their capture by an elderly milkman and fourteen-year-old farmer's daughter, Oblt Runde and Fw Willi Baden had had an eventful first and last operational sortie over the British Isles. Although for their aircraft, 5F + CM, Werke Nummer 2177, it was by far from its last flight over England. Given its condition, the aircraft was a prime candidate for flight test evaluation by the RAF and it was accordingly transferred to the RAE at Farnborough and repaired utilising parts cannibalised from a Messerschmitt 110 brought down at Wareham on 11 July 1940.

Messerschmitt 110 now RAF serial number AX772.

Given the RAF serial number AX772, and re-painted in RAF colours, the aircraft first flew with the RAE on 25 October 1940 and went into operation with 1426 Flight, the Air Fighting Development Unit and later the Central Fighter Establishment before being put into storage for the RAF Air Historical Branch until 1947 when it was scrapped.

For the various Luftwaffe crew members and their machines detailed in this chapter, the war was over. However, and for as long as the war would continue, RAF intelligence would seek the acquisition of every type of enemy aircraft for evaluation, be that by fair means or by foul.

Oblt Friedrich-Karl Runde.

CHAPTER 15

A Miscellany of Eagles

THROUGH VARIOUS MEANS, THEN, BOTH nefarious and simply arising from the fortune of war, the RAF had thus far acquired flying examples of the Me 109, Me 110, Ju 88 and He 111 and although the Dornier 17 and Junkers 87 Stuka had thus far eluded them as flying examples, a Ju 87 had fallen into British hands on 18 August 1940. Virtually undamaged, this Junkers 87 B-1 of 5./StG77 landed with minimal damage at Ham Manor Golf Course, Angmering, and was earmarked for flight testing. However, the aircraft was so badly stripped by souvenir hunters that it was reduced to a skeletal state and ended up being taken away by the RAF's 49 Maintenance Unit from Faygate before eventual processing and being reduced to scrap aluminium at the vast dumps of wrecked aircraft now being assembled.

Of course, in order to keep captured enemy aircraft examples flying, there was always a need for spare parts and other 'consumables' and thus the ever-growing mass of crashed Luftwaffe aircraft provided a useful spares source. Onto these scrap heaps, too, were thrown numerous Dornier 17 hulks and although many seem as if they might potentially have been capable of return to flight, none ever were made airworthy.

Throughout the Battle of Britain and the summer and autumn of 1940, the collection grew and almost exclusively comprised Messerschmitt 109s and 110s, Junkers 88s, Heinkel 111s, Dornier 17s and Junkers 87s. Most of them, though, ended up joining the Ju 87 Stuka from Angmering as they transited through the RAF 49 Maintenance Unit depot at Faygate before onward transmission to the aluminium smelters. Some, though, had another temporary life in store and although only very few airframes were selected to be made airworthy, other reasonably intact aeroplanes had a further use as they could be used for public exhibition to raise money for Spitfire Funds or War Weapons Week displays.

Into this category fell the Messerschmitt 109 E-4 shot down at the pre-war civilian aerodrome near the village of Penshurst, not far from Tunbridge Wells. Its arrival was not without some unusual drama.

Although Sqn Ldr Andrew Farquhar's attempt to capture a Heinkel 111 crew ended in a somewhat ignominious failure (Chapter 14), on 27 October 1940, during the very closing stages of the Battle of Britain, Plt Off Peter Chesters, a Spitfire pilot with 74 Sqn, achieved what Farquhar hadn't and reported thus of his engagement with a Me 109:

"The enemy which I attacked was diving down to the clouds and I followed him. He saw me and tried to get on my tail. I managed to turn inside him and put a burst into his engine, causing it to stop. I jockeyed him earthwards, and he landed on Penshurst aerodrome with his wheels in the up position. I landed on the same aerodrome."

Upon landing, Chesters officially captured the pilot of the Messerschmitt 109, Fw Lothar

Junkers 87 B-1 of 5./StG77 was shot down but landed with minimal damage...

Schieverhofer, before handing him over to a local military unit and then taking off for his home airfield, along with trophies collected from the downed German fighter. His deed was probably unique during the history of the Battle of Britain, and although rather less reckless than Farquhar's efforts given that this was actually an established landing ground, it perhaps demonstrated a flair and panache typical of the pilot involved. Sadly, those attributes were perhaps what led him to execute a foolhardy low-level victory roll above RAF Manston on 10 April 1941 in

...however it was pillaged extensively by souvenir hunters and also set alight, thus denying the RAF an opportunity to flight test an otherwise pretty much intact example of the Stuka dive-bomber.

celebration of his victory over another Messerschmitt 109. Misjudging his height, Chesters' Spitfire crashed onto the parade ground at Manston and he was killed instantly.

As for Lothar Schieverhofer's Me 109 E-4, this was Werke Nummer 3525 of 3./JG52 and although not extensively damaged it was not required for return to flight but had potential for exhibition purposes. Collected from the crash site and taken to 49 MU at RAF Faygate it was later used in a War Weapons exhibition at Horsham in West Sussex and at a number of other provincial venues. While by this stage of the war Lothar Schiverhofer's Messerschmitt 109 might have been considered rather 'old-hat', a few weeks later, a somewhat unusual if not exotic addition to the collection of enemy aircraft arrived in Britain.

Although this book is primarily about arriving Luftwaffe eagles, an exception must be made for the inclusion of a Fiat CR-42 bi-plane fighter that ended up landing on the Suffolk coast on 11 November 1940 during what was an ill-fated daylight operation by the Italian air force (Aero Italiano) against east-coast targets. In truth, though, this was an arriving falcon, since the Fiat CR-42 was given the name Falco by the Italian air force.

Badly mauled by RAF fighters, the formation of Fiat BR.20 bombers and their fighter escorts were dealt a heavy blow and sustained several losses, including a CR-42 of 95ª Squadriglia, 18° Gruppo, 56° Stormo that ended up with a

The majority of arriving Luftwaffe eagles ended up being processed for scrap and re-cycled back into the British aviation industry in the form of raw material. Here, at a processing yard, fuselages of Dornier 17s and other aircraft await their turn in the smelter

When Fw Lothar Schieverhofer of 3./JG52 was forced down onto Penshurst aerodrome near Tunbridge Wells during combat on 27 October 1940, his Messerschmitt joined the travelling 'circus' of shot down Luftwaffe aircraft that toured Britain to aid local Spitfire Funds and War Weapons Weeks. Here, Schieverhofer's Me 109 is transported on a civilian haulage contractor's lorry.

severed oil-line and crash landed on the shingle beach at Orford Ness at 13.45 hours. The aircraft tipped onto its nose, but was otherwise little damaged and its pilot, Sergente P. Salvadori, was captured unharmed.

The aircraft, MM5701, 13-95, went on to fly under evaluation at the RAE with RAF markings and the British serial number BT474 allocated to it. The Fiat continued to be operated until 1943 when it was placed into storage and is now on permanent exhibition in the Battle of Britain Collection at the RAF Museum, Hendon. The aircraft has since been re-painted to its original specification, exactly as it had been marked on 11 November 1940, and is rightly considered a unique survivor of the air war over Britain.

As the Battle of Britain ran on into the Blitz, so the 'supply' of downed Luftwaffe aircraft diminished significantly and once the Blitz, too, had wound down in May 1941 there was a further reduction in enemy aircraft landings in Britain. An exception to this general rule, though, was the arrival of another Junkers 88 A-5 whose crew had become confused by the RAF's Meacon radio countermeasures signal which they thought was Luftwaffe Beacon 173 at Audierne.

Sergente Pietro Salvadori of the Italian air force is taken in captivity as a POW.

With mist covering South Wales and Somerset, the Bristol Channel, ever-confusing for lost Luftwaffe fliers, was taken for the Brest Roads and, low on fuel, the 3./KG30 aircraft landed in error at RAF Lulsgate Bottom near Bristol. Uffz Wolfgang Hosie, Fw Paul Zimmermann and Ogefrs Franz Sander and Robert Riemann were all taken POW whilst their aircraft, 4D + DL, Werke Nummer 3457, became the RAF's EE205.

It was not just Luftwaffe bomber pilots in the west of England who were getting confused by false direction-finding beacons or misunderstandings as to where they were, geographically. Further east, a trio of Luftwaffe fighter pilots were also caught out during the spring and early summer of 1943 and landed intact at RAF airfields in Kent.

Whilst the major 'secrets' of the Focke Wulf 190 had already been laid bare by Oblt Armin Faber's arrival at RAF Pembrey on 23 June 1942 (see Chapter 10), it is always desirable, if not essential, for intelligence services to get updated on new models, equipment etc in use by the enemy. However, the RAF could not have imagined that they would be the welcome beneficiaries of the 'London bus syndrome' where, after waiting for one for a long while, several all arrived at once! In this instance, the 'London buses' were Focke Wulf 190s that arrived during 1943, and on 16 April, 20 May and 20 June of that year.

The employment of the Fw 190 on 'tip and run' raids against targets in the south and south east of England that had persisted throughout 1942 and early 1943 had noticeably been reduced during the early spring of 1943 and this was largely due to Luftwaffe intelligence believing that

Tipped onto its nose on the shingle beach at Orford Ness, this was Salvadori's Fiat CR-42.

the vast majority of such attacks had failed to achieve the intended results. However, such a reduction did not immediately herald the end of the Fw 190 raids although it *did* signal a shift in the way the Fw 190 force was employed against the British Isles.

Hitherto, the attacks had been in daylight. Now, the various Jabo Staffeln were being re-formed into a specialised unit, SKG10, or Schnellkampfgeschwader Gruppe 10 (literally, Fast Bomber Group 10). Their brief was to train for and undertake nocturnal attacks against targets in England with the first of these raids being attempted on the night of 16/17 April 1943. It was, pretty much, an unmitigated disaster for the Luftwaffe, and one that called into question the wisdom of operating single-seat fighter bombers at night. In fact, it was an operation that was doomed to failure before it had even begun.

Already, during the day on 16 April 1943, 2./SKG10 had lost Oblt Franz Schwaiger killed, with yet another pilot having to bale out after experiencing technical problems as the unit prepared for the operation scheduled to be flown that night. Then, taking off for the mission from Poix at around midnight, three of the unit's drop-tank-equipped Fw 190s collided, the accident resulting in the death of Oblt Fritz Trenn. Meanwhile, two further Fw 190s were damaged in take-off accidents. The operation had been a shambles before it had begun, and it doubtless led Lt Fritz Setzer of 5./SKG10 to feel vindicated in his view that such operations were nothing more than sheer folly. Events were already proving him right.

In total, a group of forty-seven aircraft are reported as having attempted the first night-fighter bomber attack against London but, aside from the losses before the operation had even really begun, four of SKG10's pilots became disorientated and lost in fog and poor visibility over southern England. The first loss over Britain involved the Staffelkapitän of 2./SKG10, Oblt Hans Klahn, killed when he apparently attempted to make a forced landing on Henhurst Farm at Staplehurst, Kent.

The aircraft was wrecked in a fiery disintegration that must have unsettled other pilots who were also attempting to get down at nearby RAF West Malling, apparently thinking they were over France. Of those, Ofw Otto Schulz from 7./SKG10 undershot and crashed, receiving very serious injuries in the process. Meanwhile, Lt Fritz Setzer had managed to land safely with his

The wreckage of Oblt Hans Klahn's aircraft, Staffelkapitän of 2./SKG10 at Henhurst Farm near Staplehurst in Kent.

already flak-damaged aircraft on the RAF airfield but, on taxiing in, his aircraft was fired on by an RAF regiment gunner, LAC Sharlock, from a Vickers machine gun mounted on a Beaverette airfield defence vehicle.

The shots struck the Fw 190 and set it fiercely ablaze, fatally injuring Setzer. His ominous predictions about such operations had come to fruition. However, one other pilot was still trying to get down – and to make sense of exactly where he was and what was going on.

Crossing the Kent coast, and releasing his drop tanks, Fw Otto Bechtold of 7./SKG10 flew on for an anxious forty minutes and became increasingly unaware of his position. Eventually, and after getting caught in searchlight beams, he ditched his bomb, reduced altitude and turned about to head back towards Poix. After about thirty minutes he saw searchlights pointing in the same direction and, with the anti-aircraft fire having ceased, he concluded these must be pointing towards an aerodrome. By now, low on fuel and convinced that he was over France, Bechtold lowered his undercarriage and landed at what he thought to be a German airfield. Instead, he was astonished to be met by an RAF airman and was duly apprehended at rifle-point by Gunner Lionel Barry of the 4th (Ulster) Light AA Regiment.

Fw Otto Bechtold's Focke Wulf 190 A-4/U8 is pictured at RAF West Malling the morning after its arrival and with instructions to 'Do Not Touch' scrawled in its lamp-black night camouflage.

Only two bombs are recorded as having fallen in the London Civil Defence region that night and, to further compound the disaster that had befallen SKG10, one other casualty was sustained with Fw Werner Ansrascheck of II./SKG10 failing to return home from the same operation. For Otto Bechtold, however, his flying days were over.

Not so, of course, for his aircraft: Werke Nummer 47155, a Focke Wulf A-4/U8. Now, the RAF had the latest Fw 190 variant to evaluate and to supplement the information already gleaned from Oblt Armin Faber's Fw 190 A-3. In its RAF guise as PE882, Bechtold's Fw 190 was operated by the RAE, and later by 1426 (Enemy Aircraft) Flight, until 13 October 1944 when it crashed into the garden of a house on the Stamford to Kettering road, killing Flt Lt E. R. 'Lew' Lewendon, the CO of 1426 Flight.

As if to emphasise the perils of operating the Focke Wulf 190 in the fighter-bomber role at night, I./SKG10 lost another Fw 190 A-4 (Werke Nummer 45838) on the night of 16/17 May 1943, but this time to the guns of a Mosquito night fighter of 85 Sqn flown by Fg Off J. D. R. Shaw and Fg Off A. L. Lowton with Uffz Wilhelm Schicke killed as his aircraft dived vertically to destruction at Higham, near Gravesend in Kent at 02.02 hours.

An RAF intelligence officer of A.I.1(g) picks amongst the pitiful shards of Uffz Schicke's Focke Wulf 190 A-4 wreckage for any useful information.

Such losses, however, were of rather limited value to RAF intelligence especially when the wreckages were so comprehensively destroyed. Incredibly, almost hot on the heels of Fw Otto Bechtold's arrival at RAF West Malling with a perfectly airworthy aircraft, two more Focke Wulf 190 aircraft arrived in Britain under broadly similar circumstances, both of them also undamaged.

Both were machines operated by SKG10 and had been on night operations to the London area. First, on 20 May 1943, came a Fw 190 A-4/U8 of 2./SKG10 that had become lost on the return journey and after crossing the English coast and proceeding out across the English Channel. Uffz Heinz Ehrhardt had received several vectors to get him home but, with fuel running low, he altered course and mistook the north Kent coast along the Thames estuary for the north coast of France and, believing RAF Manston to be St Omer, he landed there at 03.40 hours.

As he taxied in, a Hillman staff car screeched to a halt alongside and the startled pilot was

Uffz Heinz Ehrhardt posed somewhat reluctantly for a photograph with the Typhoon pilot of 609 Squadron the morning after his unintended arrival on their airfield.

bundled into the car by pilots and officers of 609 Sqn, some of whom would later pose for photographs with the disconsolate Heinz Ehrhardt outside the squadron's dispersal hut. Before he was taken away from Manston as a POW, though, the 609 Sqn intelligence officer and squadron historian, recalled how Ehrhardt was collected for the 'photo shoot from the quarters of 841 Sqn, FAA, where he was found sitting on a bed holding a gun as the RAF corporal guard explained its workings!'

Bechtold's aircraft, Werke Nummer 45843, later became PN999 with 1426 (Enemy Aircraft) Flight but was very soon joined on the Air Ministry's RAF inventory by yet another, this time a Fw 190 A-5/U8. Again, it resulted from a rather miserably failed SKG10 night sortie. It wasn't, though, quite the last Focke Wulf 190 to make a landfall at Manston.

On 30 November 1944, Dutch ferry pilot Johannes Kuhn didn't quite make it to the airfield at Manston but ended up, instead, executing a wheels-up belly landing in a field at Monkton Court Farm just outside the RAF Manston boundary. Unharmed, the defecting Kuhn was interned although the aircraft he arrived in, Focke Wulf 190 A-8, Werke Nummer 171747, White '13', of 3./Überführungs Gruppe West, was not of any value or use for flight evaluation by the RAF.

By now, a plentiful supply of aircraft of all types in perfectly airworthy order, were becoming available as former Luftwaffe airfields across Europe were being captured. However, and in common with much of the German hardware detailed in these pages, WNr 171747 ended up being displayed at the November 1945 exhibition of German aeronautical development at the Royal Aircraft Establishment, Farnborough.

On the night of 19/20 June 1943, yet another sortie by the I Gruppe of SKG10 ran into

Ehrhardt's Focke Wulf 190 A-5/U8 under the wing of a Junkers 88 also operated by 1426 Flight.

Dutch ferry pilot, Johannes Kuhn made this wheels-up landing near RAF Manston.

problems over Britain when it became clear that the weather forecast predicted for this operation was far from accurate as extensive low cloud was encountered. This made any accurate assessment of the raider's ground position, as well as any reasonable bomb-aiming difficult bordering on nigh-

Focke Wulf 190 A-5/U8 was test flown for a while (as here) however the aircraft was later grounded and became a source of spares for PN999.

on impossible. Already having ditched his wing drop tanks, Uffz Werner Oehme dumped his 250kg bomb randomly and turned about for a bearing that he thought would take him home.

Instead, the unfortunate Oehme now found that his wireless equipment had become unserviceable and he was not able to request a vector home. Lost, and again low on fuel, he managed to find RAF Manston where he observed a visual beacon that was flashing a signal broadly similar to that on his home airfield. Therefore, at 03.32, he landed, wheels-down, and experienced the same shocked surprise as had Bechtold and Ehrhardt upon discovering that this wasn't, after all, a Luftwaffe airfield.

Now the third Focke Wulf 190 on the RAF's inventory, this aircraft became PM679, and was a Fw 190 A-5/U8 sub-variant. It went on to fly with the Air Fighting Development Unit at RAF Wittering before being grounded and delivered on 11 July to 1426 (Enemy Aircraft) Flight as a source of spare parts for PN999.

Uffz Werner Oehme.

149

There would be no spare parts, however, to be derived from what was left of a German bomber shot down at Exbury House near Beaulieu in Hampshire during the spring of 1944. In any event, the RAF did not yet have an airworthy example of the type; a Junkers 188 E-1. It is, however, worthy of mention in this miscellany of arriving eagles given the unusual circumstances relating to the crew members on board and because of suggestions that they might well have been involved in a mass defection attempt.

By mid-April 1944 the organisation of Operation Overlord and the D-Day landings were in full swing, with men, equipment and material pouring into the area around the Solent. Almost every field, road and waterway was crammed to bursting point with the apparatus of a mass invasion and it was an important military area, and one that was highly sensitive to any prying Luftwaffe eyes.

Thus, when what turned out to be a Junkers 188 E-1 was tracked approaching the Isle of Wight at around 07.30 hours on 18 April there was immediate cause for concern. Travelling north west, it then turned northwards over the island between St Catherine's Point and The Needles at an altitude of around 4,000ft before crossing The Solent, down to about 1,000ft. Now, it flew a circuit of the northern part of the Isle of Wight, firing clusters of red flares as it did so before completing the circuit and heading back out across The Solent again. Now, engaged by anti-aircraft fire, the flak bursts attracted the attention of four Typhoons of 266 Sqn which were airborne from their new base at RAF Needs Oar Point. The four fighters roared in to engage the raider with Flt Lt A. V. Sanders closing to 200ft, pouring 100 rounds of 20mm cannon fire into the bomber, resulting in strikes on the port wing root and cockpit. At once, fire and smoke poured out of the bomber and as Sanders passed over the aircraft he saw pieces falling off it.

Flt Sgt D. H. Dodd then made a firing pass, also loosing off another 100 rounds, until the Junkers 188, now over the western end of the Isle of Wight, made a turn to starboard and descended in flames across The Solent to crash near Beaulieu. After the aircraft had been examined by RAF intelligence officers it was established that no less than seven bodies were in the wreckage; Uffz Hans Czipin, Uffz Johann Krauss, Uffz Robert Schultes, Uffz Hans Ehrhardt, Uffz Eitel Wysotzki, Gefr Kurt Edgar Vester and Ogefr Leonhard Schwingenstein all of 2./KG66. Why, though, so many men on board what was a four-seat bomber? The answer, in fact, might be far less curious than the subsequent defection stories would have one believe. However, perhaps the jury is still out?

Although drawing towards its conclusion, the 'Little Blitz', or Operation Steinbock, was still underway and KG66 were one of the units engaged on sorties that were part of the overall operation. Sometimes, however, aircraft were transited during the day to forward airfields that were nearer to the target for the following night, and this would often result in bombers being ferried across France on positioning flights and carrying ground crews who would service the aircraft at that forward base. And this is exactly what was happening here.

On board, apart from the normal crew complement, were an 'extra' radio operator plus two ground crew; a radio engineer and a maintenance engineer, Vester and Schwingenstein respectively. Exactly what happened on board Werke Nummer 260523, Z6 + EK, is uncertain although a reasonable guess might be that the crew simply flew a reciprocal course by accident, thus ending up over the south coast of England. If, however, theirs had been a deliberate defection plan they could hardly have chosen a more unfortunate spot as their landfall, bristling as it was with prickly and trigger-happy defences.

Question marks as to whether or not this was a defection flight, or simply a case of navigational error, were clearly evident in the RAF's A.I.1(k) [now A.D.I.1(k)] report which is reproduced in full at Appendix IV. In it, the reader will note the opinion of other POWs from this same unit that those on board were defecting and they point to the firing of red Verey lights as an indicator of this.

On the other hand, the fact that the Junkers 188 shot back at the attacking Typhoons might well be a contra-indicator of any such intent. That said, it was the author Nevil Shute, then a locally-stationed Royal Navy officer (actually Lt Cdr Nevil Shute Norway) who wrote of the event in an unpublished Ministry of Information article:

'What duty brought these seven NCOs to England in full daylight, without bombs, and at that suicidal height? Why seven? Or had they stolen the machine, and were they trying to escape to England to surrender? It may well be that we shall never have the answers.'

Junkers 88 G-1 night fighter landed in error at RAF Woodbridge, Suffolk, during the early hours of 13 July 1944.

In that closing comment, Nevil Shute had certainly hit the nail on the head, but in a blurring of fact with fiction he later wrote, loosely, of the very same event in his novel *Requiem for a Wren*. In it, seven men were shot down in a German bomber by Wren Janet Prentice who had been manning a Bofors gun on the Beaulieu river. In the novel, Prentice's joy at destroying the enemy aircraft turns to sorrow when she discovers the seven men on board were escaping, albeit that Shute has them as Poles and Czechs who had stolen the Junkers 188 rather than Germans who were defecting in it. All the same, a question mark about a real event had been placed in the public domain through a fictional story that did have some loose basis in fact. Little wonder that the jury is still out.

The last Luftwaffe arrival in this tale of arriving eagles was that of a Junkers 88 G-1 night fighter of 7./NJG2 that had landed during the early morning hours of 13 July 1944 at RAF Woodbridge in Suffolk. Operating from Twente in the Netherlands, the aircraft (4R + UR, Werke Nummer 712273) had been on a night-fighter patrol out over the North Sea looking for incoming or home-going RAF bomber streams when the crew managed to fly a reciprocal compass heading and ended up over Britain. Low on fuel, the crew spotted RAF Woodbridge, ironically an emergency airfield where bombers shot about by night fighters such as this Junkers 88 would make often desperate landings. Uffz Hans Maeckle and his crew of Ogefr Olze and Ogefr Mockl were so disorientated that they later claimed that they thought Woodbridge was, in fact, Venlo in the Netherlands.

The aircraft they had so obligingly delivered turned out to be an extremely significant intelligence prize, and was flown with Spitfire escort to RAE Farnborough two days later.

The Junkers 88 was fitted with the very latest radar sets; the FuG 220 Lichtenstein SN-2, FuG 227 Flensburg and FuG 350 Naxos equipment. This apparatus had been lately troublesome to the aircraft of RAF Bomber Command on their nightly raids into enemy territory. RAF intelligence were completely unaware of the very existence of the FuG 227 and FuG 350 systems, although the FuG 220 Lichtenstein had already been captured in the Dyce Junkers 88 (Chapter 13). Both of these other sets homed onto the British radar transmissions from RAF bombers, with the FuG 227 homing onto the RAF's 'Monica' tail-warning radar and FuG 350 locking onto the H2S radar bombsight transmissions. Within ten days, a jamming device had been created for the FuG 227 and the removal of 'Monica' sets from all RAF bombers was ordered, thereby entirely neutralising the very purpose of the FuG 227. Meanwhile, operational tactics were changed to avoid the unnecessary use of the H2S sets in order to minimise the effectiveness of the FuG 350 equipment.

Sometimes, as this capture amply demonstrated, Luftwaffe technology was ahead of that of the Allies but all it took was a lucky break like this to turn the tables again. In this instance, it is certainly the case that the apparent navigational error of Uffz Hans Maeckle's crew saved countless lives of RAF Bomber Command aircrew as these were crews who, until now, had unwittingly been using defensive radar equipment that was actually guiding enemy night fighters onto them.

It is tempting to wonder whether it was the case that the Allied invasion of Europe in June 1944 had in any way influenced the 'navigational error' of Maeckle's crew just a little over a month past D-Day. Similarly, there might be the same kind of link made to the accidental arrival of the two Me 109 G-6 aircraft at RAF Manston just one week later, on the night of 20/21 July (see Chapter 9). Certainly, things were getting very difficult for the German armed forces across the board, and a willingness to simply give up on the part of some individuals is surely understandable.

Now, Luftwaffe aerial activity against the British Isles rapidly drew down as 1944 progressed and as the beleaguered and decimated German air force struggled to maintain fronts in the east and the west and in defence of the homeland. No further enemy aircraft arrived in the UK that were of any particular significance or interest, but as Europe was finally liberated and Germany defeated, countless aircraft types became available for evaluation when they were found, abandoned, at surrendered airfields and factory sites. Many of these were shipped back to Britain or the United States to be tested and examined for scientific and technical purposes, and for the advancement of the Allied post-war aerospace industries. But that is another story.

CHAPTER 16

Kidnap Hitler!

IMPROBABLE, IMPOSSIBLE AND IMPLAUSIBLE ARE perhaps three words that might adequately describe an apparent plan to abduct Hitler and bring him to Britain during early 1941. Indeed, it was a scheme that led the then deputy chief of the air staff, Air Vice-Marshal A. T. 'Bomber' Harris, to hopefully suggest "…the story, that appears too fantastic for words, might have a fortunate outcome".

The origins of this fascinating story go back to December 1940, and the whole saga was detailed in a series of truly extraordinary 'Most Secret' letters and memos exchanged between senior RAF commanders during the early part of 1941 and today held in The National Archives, Kew, in file AIR 16/619. The inscription on the cover of this incredible record is marked rather incongruously as 'German Deserters; Enemy Aircraft Landing in UK', thus giving nothing away as to the highly unusual content of this very ordinary-looking buff-brown folio.

Air Vice-Marshal Arthur Harris, more famous as 'Bomber' Harris, deputy chief of the air staff during 1941.

In his opening memo of 21 February 1941, Harris sets out to Air Marshal Sholto Douglas, C-in-C RAF Fighter Command, the background to this case and reminds Douglas of a discussion the pair had had earlier that month when Harris explained that a Bulgarian by the name of Kiroff had approached the air attaché in Sofia claiming to be the father-in-law of Hans Baur, Adolf Hitler's personal pilot.

The story spun by Kiroff was that Baur had become disaffected by the war and, evidently, by the Nazi regime to the extent that he was prepared to defect to Britain whilst flying his Focke Wulf 200 Condor (Hitler's personal transport) and with the Führer on board! According to Harris, Kiroff's story had checked out 'with one or two exceptions' and since he had not asked for money a decision was taken to act upon the information on the basis that it was both credible and the defection attempt seemingly viable.

Really the senior staff officers at the Air Ministry could hardly do anything but act as though it might be credible. After all, to have dismissed it as nonsense would have been a dangerous path to follow because clearly there were nuggets of apparently verifiable information in Kiroff's tale. The risk of ignoring it was simply too enormous to take. As Harris pointed out "...this flight might have so much importance for all of us". Consequently, he issued specific instructions which were passed to Kiroff for onward transmission to Baur as to how his momentous flight to Britain should be conducted. Those instructions read as follows:

'(i) Aircraft must approach coastline and make steep descent to Lympne aerodrome with wheels down. The exact position is seven miles due west of Folkestone.

(ii) Pilot should fire not less than four red flares at thirty-second intervals when approached by British fighters.

(iii) As soon as aircraft lands engines should be stopped and put out of action.'

Air Marshal Sholto Douglas, then C-in-C of RAF Fighter Command.

So much for the guidance issued to Baur, but what of British preparations for this unusual German arrival?

Clearly, it was vitally important to ensure non-interference from RAF Fighter Command and thus urgent consideration had to be given in the form of new standing instructions dealing with how RAF fighters should approach any such arising. Consequently, and almost immediately after the communication from Harris on 21 February, HQ Fighter Command issued the following orders to its fighter squadrons should a Focke Wulf Condor be seen:

'An aircraft [of this type] seen approaching Lympne during daytime is at once to be closed on by our fighters. If accompanied by enemy fighters these are to be destroyed or driven off. The aircraft itself is not to be attacked unless:

(i) it fails within five minutes to fire four red flares, or,

(ii) it proceeds inland beyond circuit radius of Lympne, or,

(iii) it attempts to get away towards the French coast in which case it is to be shot down.

'During its approach and landing the aircraft is to be held covered by the AA defences. Directly it lands, it and all its crew are immediately to be seized. Opposition may be encountered. Our fighters are to remain airborne and patrol over the aerodrome until the aircraft has been seized.

'The aircraft is on no account to be allowed to take off again. If this is attempted it is to be disabled or destroyed by the AA defences or by fighters should it take to the air.'

A Focke Wulf 200 Condor, similar to the type that was allegedly to be used in bringing a kidnapped Adolf Hitler to Britain.

There is very much a presumption that the RAF fighters should succeed in 'destroying or driving off' the fighter escort. However such escort would surely be skilled, experienced, determined and present in some strength. On the ground, too, there naturally had to be preparations for the arrival of this very important visitor.

RAF Lympne, which had been selected as Baur's place of arrival in Britain, was not exactly a front-line station albeit that it was very much at the forefront of Britain's defence and having taken a pummelling during the Battle of Britain, it was utilised as a forward satellite airfield for the Biggin Hill sector. In practice, and since the air attacks on the airfield during August 1940, it was little used until well into the spring of 1941 although it remained as an established and occupied RAF station under the command of Sqn Ldr D. H. Montgomery.

As with all operational RAF stations it had ground defence forces along with anti-aircraft protection – although it was quickly judged that the existing defensive measures might not be adequate to deal with the eventuality of Hitler's arrival. Consequently, the arrangements for providing armed defensive personnel and equipment were considerably beefed-up for what was, in effect, a quiet back water of a station. Almost certainly, disclosure of the identity of the anticipated arrival was on a strictly 'need-to-know' basis and not even Montgomery, the station commander, had the slightest inkling as to who or exactly what the hurried security arrangements were all about – just that there was an anticipated defection.

Indeed, and whilst Sholto Douglas, the C-in-C Fighter Command, was in the know it appears from correspondence that not even Air Vice-Marshal Trafford Leigh-Mallory was aware of the full facts, and he was the C-in-C of 11 Group Fighter Command on whose 'patch' the drama would be played out. Again, he only knew about a likely defector.

The alleged point of arrival for what would have been the greatest kidnapping of all time was RAF Lympne on the Kent coast.

Back in Sofia in early March Britain's man there had had further contact with Kiroff, who claimed to have since been to Vienna to meet with his son-in-law, Hans Baur. Baur had understood perfectly his instructions from the British and passed back some information relating to his proposed flight. Three aircraft[11], he claimed, always accompanied him on his flights and kept at a distance unless he signalled them. For that reason he preferred not to fire flares but had instead prepared a number of yellow metal plaques bearing the initials 'A.B.' (possibly intended to be 'H.B.' for Hans Baur, although specified as 'A.B.' in a memo from Harris on 7 March 1941) which he would drop over Lympne. He also asked that one red light should be shown on the aerodrome and, further, stated that the timing was likely to be on or after 25 March 1941 between 5 and 6am or 6 and 8pm. The timings, it was concluded, were Central European Time since blackout ended at 6.23am GMT on 25 March and began again at 7.21 that evening.

On the ground at Lympne in the early part of 1941 the defences comprised four Bofors guns as anti-aircraft and ground defence weapons, and in addition, the RAF airfield defence force provided one Armadillo Mk III armoured car equipped with a COW gun – although at 1 March this was shown as 'unserviceable'. The RAF defenders also held twelve .303 rifles and one revolver (with a further twelve revolvers ordered in early March) and operated four Hispano 20mm gun posts.

11 Given the status of the passenger on board it does seem doubtful that such a small escort might have accompanied the aircraft, especially in or near airspace that might potentially be rather more hostile than over Germany itself. In fact, the possibility of Hitler flying anywhere near risky airspace seems most unlikely and it was not explained in any of the secret memos etc where Hitler was likely to be flying from or to during the kidnap attempt. It seems inconceivable that others on board the Fw 200, realising that something was amiss, would not have taken some measures to try to prevent Bauer's actions unless they, too, were complicit in the supposed plot.

Amongst the RAF fighter squadrons who were unwittingly on 'Hitler watch' during early 1941 was 91 Sqn, then operating its Spitfires from RAF Hawkinge where this photograph of A Flight pilots was taken at around the same time.

As to soldiery, seven officers and 150 ORs of the 70th Buffs were employed on 'inward defence', equipped with sixteen .303 Brownings, seven Vickers guns, two Boys anti-tank rifles, one Bren gun, three light automatics and twelve .303 Lewis guns. The local army units were also required to provide three Bren carriers and six 25lb field guns to supplement airfield forces. All told, it was quite a formidable force to protect an otherwise relatively insignificant and little-used airfield.

There was little doubt, surely, that if the Focke Wulf Condor did arrive then it would be quickly disabled and its occupants taken. There could be no question that the Condor should be allowed to leave once it was on the ground. Clearly, destruction of the aircraft and the likely death of those on board would have been the outcome should it have attempted to do so. However, the airfield defenders would have been in for a very considerable shock indeed had they bundled aboard and discovered the identity of the passenger.

Quite what the depth of involvement of British intelligence was in this whole pantomime is unclear from the National Archives file, and nothing with an intelligence service source is included. Whilst all of the pages are consecutively numbered there are gaps which suggest that some papers have certainly been 'weeded' before the file was downgraded to an open status in 1972 and eventually released some years later.

Certainly, there are blanks in our knowledge about this very strange case although one intelligence officer who was involved was Air Commodore Boyle, then head of RAF intelligence, and he described the plot as "a fantastic story". It was also an account which led Harris to remark: "This is an event we hope for, but do not expect."

Of course, one can speculate forever on what the true story of the kidnap plan really was but it is certainly the case that Boyle was involved in the 'Double X' Intelligence Committee which specialised in relaying misinformation to the Germans. However, it is difficult to see how this could somehow have fitted into that scenario. Rather than speculate, we need to stick to the facts so far as we know them.

Sholto Douglas wrote again to Leigh-Mallory on 19 March 1941 setting out some detail as to how Hitler was to be transferred from Lympne to London. In his communication, which was copied to the station commander at RAF Lympne, Sholto Douglas avoids any mention as to the identity of the expected occupants only describing them as '...persons of importance'. In detail, the instructions were now set out thus:

Hans Baur, Hitler's personal pilot.

'All persons taken from the enemy aeroplane are to be promptly put under guard and removed from the precincts of the aerodrome to safe custody. Any persons of importance, to a maximum of two, are to be removed immediately under the charge of the senior officer with an armed guard by car direct to Air Ministry, Whitehall, where report is to be made to DCAS or director of intelligence (Air Commodore Boyle) or to director ground defences (Air Commodore Sanders). A car for this purpose is to be kept ready and a spare car and motor cycle to proceed in company with it. The Air Ministry (one of the individuals noted above) is in the meantime to be notified of the action taken. A further report to sector and group is then to be made.'

For the purposes of transporting Hitler to London, Sqn Ldr Montgomery had been provided with a Ford V8 Touring Box Car and two motor-cycle outriders from No 4 MT Section, Abbey Road, London. All were kept on twenty-four-hour stand-by for what would be their epoch-making

Adolf Hitler with his trusted personal pilot, Hans Baur.

assignment, albeit that their task remained wholly unknown to the MT crews. Surely, had they known, they simply wouldn't have believed it.

Throughout March and April, and then into May, a close watch was kept at RAF Lympne for a mysterious German arrival which, of course, never came. Correspondence to Leigh-Mallory on 19 May stated that: 'In view of recent events … the special arrangements are to be kept in being for another fortnight from 17 May.' What, exactly, were the 'recent events' to which this memo referred?

It is difficult to conclude anything other than that Leigh-Mallory was referring to the unexpected and dramatic arrival of Rudolf Hess in Scotland on 10 May 1941. Quite why it was that this incident should have had any impact upon decisions now being taken in respect of the possible arrival of Hitler at Lympne is unclear. Whatever the obtuse reasoning might have been, there had clearly been some connected if not tenuous thinking by the powers that be.

Whilst the likely arrival by air in Britain of Adolf Hitler had seemed almost laughably risible to senior RAF officers during early 1941, although they couldn't ignore its possibility, they would surely have been equally incredulous had it been suggested that Rudolf Hess, Hitler's deputy, would soon fly himself to Scotland. But here they were, just weeks later, and with Rudolf Hess in British custody.

Nevertheless, on 28 May 1941 the incoming deputy chief of the air staff, Air Marshal Norman Bottomley, wrote the final memo in the whole tale and stood down the operation that had been set up by his predecessor, Air Marshal Harris. To all intents and purposes the Hitler abduction plot was dead and buried and no more time or resources were to be allocated to it.

Making sense of it more than seventy years on is somewhat difficult, and rather like trying to complete a jigsaw puzzle with a large proportion of the pieces missing. Baur remained as Hitler's personal pilot throughout the war, and was even with him at the very end when the Führer committed suicide in his Berlin bunker. Trying to flee the city, Baur was captured by the Russians and taken prisoner before enduring ten years of captivity. Released in 1955 he then wrote his life story: *Hitler at my Side*. Not surprisingly, no mention is made of any planned defection to Britain. Additionally, Baur is surprisingly vague about day-to-day events and his part in them during the late 1940 and early 1941 period. In his writings, in fact, there is virtually nothing recorded about the period in question although this alone is hardly evidence of anything sinister; intriguing rather than significant.

It would be very easy to fall into the conspiracy theory trap, here, and to come up with a baseless conclusion as to the reasons behind Baur's lack of any commentary covering the period of interest. However, when the author contacted Hans Baur at his home near Frankfurt in 1991 he was happy for arrangements to be made for him to be interviewed about his time as Hitler's pilot.

Willingly, Baur also sent the author a personally signed and dedicated copy of his book but when he was later interviewed and confronted with the direct question about the kidnap plot he flew into a towering rage. Nonetheless, his reaction was not one that indicated this to be the first he had ever heard of such a suggestion, although it quickly became clear that merely raising the matter had effectively ended the interview. "These are lies! All lies!" he fumed, as his elderly wife earnestly protested that he was a "good and true" German. Her inference, here, was given a very clear emphasis by the back-lit bronze bust of Hitler, prominently displayed in a place of reverential honour in Baur's sitting room.

Moreover, Frau Baur was fiercely adamant that his three wives had *all* been Bavarian. None had been Bulgarian, she said, remarking, "such a thing is just mischievous nonsense", before hissing disgustedly, "and to even *think* that he would have married a Bulgarian!"

Of the other key players in this curious affair, Trafford Leigh-Mallory was killed in a flying accident at the war's end and Sholto Douglas died in 1969 long before the files of the kidnap plot were released into the public domain. In his book *Years of Command*, published in 1966, he makes absolutely no mention of the extraordinary affair. However, there is a very clear explanation for this. In 1966 the file of documents that are now publicly available at Kew were still very much on the 'secret' list, and thus Sholto Douglas could not write about them, bound as he was by The Official Secrets Act.

As for 'Bomber' Harris, again no mention is ever made of the plot in any of his writings and, so far as is known, he was never asked about it in his lifetime. Quite why this whole scenario was apparently kept in-house by senior RAF commanders is equally unclear. In the existing documents at Kew there is absolutely no indication that any of this went outside the senior RAF circles, and yet it is hard to believe that it didn't. Surely, the British security agencies would have all been alerted? And wouldn't the prime minister have been informed about this as a matter of the utmost importance?

Quite possibly it is the documentation that would have laid a trail to the security services and to the prime minister himself which was extracted from the file. If not, then the existing documents seem to indicate that the RAF were keeping this entirely in-house. Although it is pure speculation, if this were the case it is quite easy to see the kudos that would surely be gained by suddenly 'producing' Herr Hitler like a rabbit out of the proverbial hat. As with all that is to do with this case, there are many more questions than there are any credible answers or explanations.

As to Squadron Leader Montgomery of RAF Lympne, he is long since deceased and, in any event, he would never have been privy to the truth behind the peculiar set of circumstances in which he had become unwittingly embroiled during the early part of 1941. If there was anything to this story at all, then the truth of it died with the pre-war Lufthansa captain, Hans Baur, when he passed away, aged ninety-five, at his Herrsching home in March 1993. Truth, as they say, is often stranger than fiction. Although this particular eagle never arrived it is surely the ultimate 'What if?' scenario of World War Two.

APPENDIX I

List of Luftwaffe Arrivals in Britain Test Flown for the RAF

Messerschmitt 109

Model	Werke Nr	German call sign	RAF Serial	Circumstances of acquisition	Fate
E-3	1304	White 1	AE479	Aircraft of 1./JG 76 flown by Fw Karl Hier, captured by the French near Wœrth, 22 November 1939; handed over to the RAF 2 May 1940.[12]	Sent to the US in April 1942; crashed at Wright Field 3 November 1942
E-4/B	4101	Black 12	DG200	Damaged by a Spitfire of 66 Squadron and belly-landed at RAF Manston. Pilot Wolfgang Teumer (of JG51) taken prisoner of war, 27 November 1940.	Repaired using parts of other aircraft and tested by Rolls-Royce. In February 1942 passed to research and development at Hatfield for propeller tests then to the Aeroplane and Armament Experimental Establishment (A&AEE) at Boscombe Down before delivery in March 1942 to 1426 Flight. In 1943 retired from use as more recent Me 109 models had been acquired. Selected for long term preservation as a museum aircraft. It was eventually moved to the Royal Air Force Museum, Hendon in 1978, where it is currently on display in the Battle of Britain Hall.

12 NB: Although this Messerschmitt 109 was not actually downed over the British Isles it was the first of its type to come into RAF hands and is thus included here. Other enemy aircraft types captured in the Middle East and Mediterranean were also brought to Britain and test flown by the RAF, but are not included in this table since they do not form any part of the basis for this book which looks, specifically, at enemy aircraft that were downed on British soil during the 1939-1945 period.

Model	Werke Nr	German call sign	RAF Serial	Circumstances of acquisition	Fate
F–2	12764	< +	ES906	Originally of I./JG 26, flown by Gruppenkommandeur Hptm Rolf Pingel, it suffered engine failure while attacking Short Stirlings and belly-landed near Dover, 10 July 1941.	Repaired by the RAE and evaluated by the AFDU in October 1941. Crashed near Fowlmere, 20 October 1941 during test flight, killing Polish Air Force pilot F/O Marian J. Skalski.
F–4/B	7232	White 1	NN644	Originally flown by Uffz Oswald Fischer of 10.(Jabo)/JG26, damaged by anti-aircraft fire during an attack on a Royal Navy corvette and belly-landed at Beachy Head, 20 May 1942.	Flown until the end of the war.
G-6/U2	412951	White 16	TP184	Lt Horst Prenzel, Staffelkapitän 1./JG 301, landed at RAF Manston by mistake after a Wilde *Sau* sortie over the invasion area against night bombers on 21 July 1944. Another Me 109 also attempted to land, but crashed.	Written off in a take-off accident at RAF Wittering, 23 Nov 1944.

Focke Wulf Fw 190

Model	Werke Nr	German call sign	RAF Serial	Circumstances of acquisition	Fate
A–3	135313		MP499	Oblt Armin Faber, Gruppe Adjutant of III./JG2 'Richthofen' became disoriented after shooting down an RAF Spitfire over Start Point, Devon. Attempting to return home, he flew north instead of south and landed at RAF Pembrey on 23 June 1942.	Struck off charge, 18 Sept 1943.

Model	Werke Nr	German call sign	RAF Serial	Circumstances of acquisition	Fate
A-5/U8	2596	White 6	PN999	Originally of I./SKG10, flown by Uffz Werner Oehme; landed in error at RAF Manston, 20 June 1943.	Despatched to store at 47 MU Sealand in July 1946.
A-4/U8	7155		PE882	Originally H+ of II./SKG10, flown by Uffz Otto Bechtold. Disorientated en route and running short of fuel, force-landed at RAF West Malling, 16 April 1943.	Crashed 13 October 1944, killing Flt Lt E. R. Lewendon, 1426 Flt.
A-4/U8	5843	Red 9	PM679	Originally of 2./SKG10, flown by Uffz Heinz Ehrhardt, accidentally landed at RAF Manston, Kent on 20 May 1943.	Last flight was June 1944 when shortly after take-off the aircraft suffered a major engine failure and forced landed. Was used for spares for PE882 and PN999.

Junkers Ju 88

Model	Werke Nr	German call sign	RAF Serial	Circumstances of acquisition	Fate
A-1		9K + HL	AX919	From 3./KG51 and landed near Bexhill, 28 July 1940, after becoming lost and low on fuel.	Test flown until June 1941 then used as source of spares for other Ju 88s.
A-4		4D + DL	EE205	Formerly of 3./KG 30, landed by mistake at RAF Lulsgate Bottom, after a night raid on Birkenhead on 23/24 July 1941.	Appeared in the 1943 film The Adventures of Tartu.
A-5	6073	M2 + MK	HM509	Originally of KuFlGr.106, accidentally landed at RAF Chivenor, 26 Nov 1941.	Damaged by a ground-loop on landing, 19 May 1944; although repairable, cannibalised for spare parts instead.

Model	Werke Nr	German call sign	RAF Serial	Circumstances of acquisition	Fate
G-1	712273	4R + UR	TP190	Night fighter of III./NJG 2 flown by Obgfr Maekle and equipped with FuG 220 Lichtenstein SN-2 radar and homing devices FuG 227 Flensburg and FuG 350 Naxos. Landed in error at RAF Woodbridge, Suffolk on 13 July 44.	Scrapped, Oct 45.
R-1	360043	D5 + EV	PJ876	Lichtenstein BC radar-equipped night-fighter Junkers Ju 88 of 10./NJG 3 flown to RAF Dyce, Scotland by defecting crew, 9 May 1943.	Preserved in the RAF Museum.

Me 110

Model	Werke Nr	German call sign	RAF Serial	Circumstances of acquisition	Fate
C–4	2177	5F-CM	AX772	Originally of 4.(F)/14 intercepted by RAF fighters while on a reconnaissance mission on 21 July 1940. Forced down near Goodwood racecourse, Sussex. ~	Royal Aircraft Establishment repaired this aircraft and after handling trials, was flown to the Air Fighting Development Unit at Duxford in October 1941. In March 1942 AX772 was transferred to 1426 Flight until moving to the Enemy Aircraft Flight of the Central Flying School at Tangmere in January 1945. It was stored at 47 MU Sealand in November 1945. Scrapped in 1947.

Fiat CR42

Model	Werke Nr	German call sign	RAF Serial	Circumstances of acquisition	Fate
Falco	MM5701	13-95	BT474	Made a forced landing on the beach at Orford Ness due to engine failure, 11 Nov 40.	Preserved in the RAF Museum.

Model	Werke Nr	German call sign	RAF Serial	Circumstances of acquisition	Fate
He 111					
H-1	6853	1H + EN	AW177	Originally of II./KG 26. Landed in a field near North Berwick on 9 February 1940 after being damaged by a Spitfire.	Crashed at RAF Polebrook on 10 November 1943 while carrying a number of 1426 Flight ground crew as passengers. The pilot, Fg Off Barr, and six others were killed, four were injured.
Go					
145	B	1115	SM + NQ	Landed on Lewes racecourse after pilot became disorientated over English Channel on 28 August 1940.	Flight tested Dec 1940/Jan 1941 and then allocated to ground use by RAF Maintenance Command.

RAF Air Intelligence
(Departments A.I.1[g] and A.I.1[k])

RAF Air Intelligence Organisations

At the outbreak of war the Air Ministry had already recognised that there was a requirement for formalised intelligence training and had thus established a number of courses to teach RAF volunteer reserve officers the art of intelligence analysis. Much of this early training was very simplistic and did little more than introduce those to be employed to the structure of the organisation and where its various sources originated, although by June 1940 the RAF's intelligence organisation was established as a directorate within the department of the chief of the air staff. At this time, the Directorate of Intelligence was headed by Air Cdre A. R. Boyle, CMG, OBE, MC and the branches within his command that are broadly relevant within the context of this book are A.I.1(g) and A.I.1(k).

Air Intelligence A.I.1(g)

The A.I.1(g) department was solely concerned with the technical examination of downed enemy aircraft and with a HQ working out of a requisitioned school at Wealdstone, Harrow, under the command of Wg Cdr J. A. Easton. Once an enemy aircraft was reported down within the British Isles a technical intelligence officer was tasked with a full examination of the wreckage and compilation of a report on the aircraft, its condition and any notable features. Matters such as armament, armour, various manufacturers' details gleaned from data plates and also camouflage and marking were all carefully recorded. Even in cases where the aircraft had been totally destroyed, burnt-out or even buried, a report was still filed on whatever there was left of the aircraft to note down.

In the event that unusual equipment etc might be located in a wrecked aircraft, those items might be forwarded to other specialists for scientific or technical evaluation. Although the Wealdstone school was the A.I.1(g) HQ, officers were posted out to RAF maintenance units the length and breadth of the country. The various MUs had responsibility for the eventual collection of wreckages within their operational areas, but the wreck could only be moved after it had been inspected by the A.I.1(g) officer. The intelligence officer's pro-forma inspection check list Form 'C' (known colloquially as the Alpha-Omega Form) is replicated at Appendix III along with a sample A.I.1(g) summary report. The originals of the inspection summary reports may be found at The National Archives, Kew, under AIR 22/266.

Air Intelligence A.I.1(k)

Working hand-in-glove with their sister organisation, A.I.1(g), the A.I.1(k) section of the RAF's Directorate of Intelligence was tasked solely with the gathering of intelligence from POWs or, in some instances, from papers etc collected from fatalities found in wrecked enemy aircraft. Working under the command of Gp Capt S. D. Felkin, the section also had field officers posted out at RAF airfields around Britain. It was their task to interrogate prisoners as swiftly as possible after capture, or to look for papers, maps or identity discs associated with the casualties from enemy air losses.

Initially, prisoners were transferred to the Tower of London for full interrogation but the section later based itself at Trent Park, Cockfosters, London. Often, very little information was gleaned from security-conscious prisoners but in some cases a great deal was revealed. Such information was frequently of great interest in determining German battle strengths, tactics, operation orders, bases, organisational structure and even matters regarding Luftwaffe personalities who were not yet prisoners. Thus, in certain cases, much was known about some individuals when they were later captured. A specimen A.I.1(k) report for the period covered in this book is reproduced at Appendix III, along with an order issuing instructions for dealing with enemy airmen upon capture.

APPENDIX III

Specimen RAF Intelligence Reports from A.I.1(g) and A.I.1(k)

Every enemy aircraft that came to earth in Britain was subject to a technical investigation and report by officers of the RAF's A.I.1(g) intelligence section. The format was always identical and based upon the compilation of leading particulars gleaned from each crashed aircraft. Whatever the con-dition, a report had to be submitted. Reproduced (right) is the pro-forma check list used by the A.I.1(g) officers. Listing points A to O it was, inevitably, called the 'Alpha-Omega' Form.

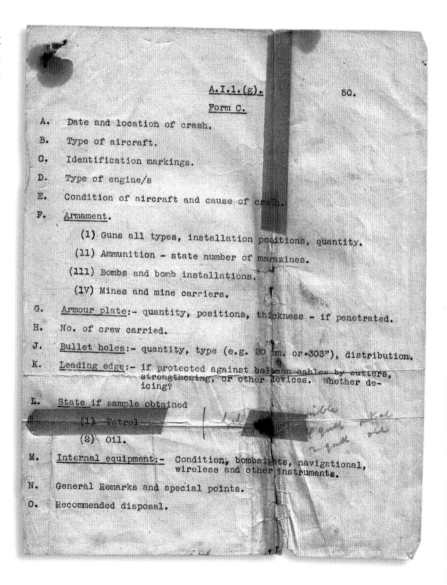

A.I.1.(g).   50.
Form C.

A. Date and location of crash.

B. Type of aircraft.

C. Identification markings.

D. Type of engine/s

E. Condition of aircraft and cause of crash.

F. Armament.

    (1) Guns all types, installation positions, quantity.

    (11) Ammunition – state number of magazines.

    (111) Bombs and bomb installations.

    (1V) Mines and mine carriers.

G. Armour plate:- quantity, positions, thickness – if penetrated.

H. No. of crew carried.

J. Bullet holes:- quantity, type (e.g. 20 mm. or .303"), distribution.

K. Leading edge:- if protected against balloon cables by cutters, strengthening, or other devices. Whether de-icing?

L. State if sample obtained

    (1) Petrol

    (2) Oil.

M. Internal equipment:- Condition, bombsights, navigational, wireless and other instruments.

N. General Remarks and special points.

O. Recommended disposal.

169

And this is the transcript of a typical report of the period, in this instance detailing the crash of the Messerschmitt 109 at Penshurst on 27 October 1940 which is covered in Chapter 15.

'Report 3/121
'Me 109 E

'Crashed on 27.10.40 at 0915 hrs at Penshurst Aerodrome, Kent. Map Reference: Q.9866. Markings: 4 + (4 in orange); rudder, nose and spinner, yellow. Airframe made by Henschel F.W. licence Messerschmitt; Order No 68708/240. Engine DB 601 made by Henschel Werke, Cassel. Engine No. 30713. Following fighter action, pilot made good belly landing. About forty .303 strikes are evenly distributed over airframe, and there is one hit in the magneto. Armament: 4 x MG 17s. All belts are practically full. Armour: cross bulkhead in fuselage, pilot's head protection and curved piece. Aircraft was fitted with bomb gear, but no bomb rack. Pilot prisoner.

Signed

J. A. Easton
Wing Commander'

Whilst the RAF's A.I.1(g) section concerned itself with purely technical matters relating to downed enemy aircraft it was the A.I.1(k) section that dealt with matters appertaining to the crew, whether they be captive or casualties.

The following is a sample of an A.I.1(k) report that is typical of the period, in this instance dealing with the captured pilot of a Messerschmitt 109 of 5./JG27 who had been shot down over Maidstone the next day, 28 October 1940.

50490

A.M.

A.I.1.(k) Report No. 818/1940.

THE FOLLOWING INFORMATION HAS BEEN OBTAINED FROM P/W.
AS THE STATEMENTS MADE HAVE NOT AS YET BEEN VERIFIED,
NO MENTION OF THEM SHOULD BE MADE IN INTELLIGENCE
SUMMARIES OF COMMANDS OR LOWER FORMATIONS, NOR SHOULD
THEY BE ACCEPTED AS FACTS UNTIL COMMENTED ON IN AIR
MINISTRY INTELLIGENCE SUMMARIES OR SPECIAL COMMUNICATIONS.

PLACE, DATE and TIME: East of Maidstone on London Road. (R 1577).
                        28/10/40.   1400 hours.

TYPE and MARKS: Me.109.   2 +

UNIT: 5/J.G.27.

IDENTITY DISC: 53537.

FELDPOSTNUMMER: 36660.

AUSWEIS: Grey, issued at Merseburg on 17/8/40.

START and MISSION: Started from the Calais area, at 1330 hours,
                     on "Free-Lance" patrol.

- - - - - - - - - -

        This aircraft was flying in the last Kette of a fairly
large formation. They flew up the extreme east of Kent, and made
a sweep over the Thames Estuary towards Gravesend, at 26,000 feet.

        He was attacked from behind and above by Fighters which
dived out of the sun, and which he never even saw. The engine went
out of action almost immediately, and the pilot baled out. The
aircraft, which was only delivered 10 days ago, crashed and was
completely wrecked.

        P/W, who had a total of 1½ years service, had not taken
part in the Polish or French Campaigns, and had indeed only recently
joined his Unit. He had made about 30 War Flights against this
country.

MORALE:-   Very good.   Firmly convinced of the outcome of the
                        War. Made disparaging remarks about
                        British Fighter pilots, stating that on
                        previous occasions he had sighted Fighters
                        which did not attack. This man is
                        reported as being a particularly unpleasant
                        type of German.

PILOT:-

Unteroffizier Artur GONSCHOREK - 23 (1½) - Slightly wounded.

- - - - - - - - - -

                                        S. D. Felkin,
                                        Squadron Leader.

A.I.1.(k).
28.10.40.

RAF A.D.I.1(k) Intelligence Report
Junkers 188, Exbury, 18 April 1944

This was the detailed report on the crash of the Ju 188 at Exbury, Hampshire, on 18 April 1944 (see Chapter 15) compiled by the RAF's intelligence department A.D.I.1(k) [formerly A.I.1(k)] and is typical of many such reports compiled on the background of Luftwaffe losses over the British Isles. The reports analysed all information gleaned from such incidents and often cross-referenced with other similar crashes to build as complete a picture as possible of Luftwaffe tactics, units, personnel, equipment etc.

SECRET

SECRET.   A.D.I.(K) Report No. 170/1944.

THE FOLLOWING INFORMATION HAS BEEN OBTAINED FROM P/W. AS THE
STATEMENTS MADE HAVE NOT AS YET BEEN VERIFIED, NO MENTION OF
THEM SHOULD BE MADE IN INTELLIGENCE SUMMARIES OF COMMANDS OR
LOWER FORMATIONS, NOR SHOULD THEY BE ACCEPTED AS FACTS UNTIL
COMMENTED ON IN AIR MINISTRY INTELLIGENCE SUMMARIES OR SPECIAL
COMMUNICATIONS.

PLACE, DATE AND TIME: Exbury, near Beaulieu,Hants.(U.8619)
                             18th April 1944, 0745 hours.

TYPE AND MARKS: Ju.188 Z6 + EK

UNIT: 2/K.G.66.

DISC: One: 55511 (= 2/K.G.6)
                             Three: 55512 (= 3/K.G.6)
                             One: 62724 (=6/K.G.26)
                             One: 2A/Flg.Ausb.Rgt.31
                             One: 7.Flum.Ers.Komp.306

FELDPOSTNUMMER: L.36596 T. Paris (=2/K.G.66)

AUSWEIS: Five: Green, issued by Fl.H.Kdtr.A.231/XII
                                    (=Bretigny) on 23rd and 29th May,
                                    8th July and 28th August 1943.

START AND MISSION: ---------

------- --------------------

1.   It is understood from British sources that this aircraft
was first picked up halfway between Le Havre and St.Catherine's Point,
flying North-West at a height of 4000 feet. It continued on this course
until midway between St.Catherine's Point and the Needles, and then turned
Northwards over the Isle of Wight, flew over the Solent at a height of
1,000 feet, and crossed the Hampshire coast near Exbury.

2.   Shortly afterwards the aircraft turned E.S.E. and flew a
complete circuit of the Northern part of the Isle of Wight, firing clusters
of red verey signals. On completing this circuit near Cowes, it headed
North-West to make landfall once more near Exbury. It was engaged by A.A.
and by a section of Typhoons, and was shot down in flames.

3.   The wreckage crashed into a pond and when a search was
made no less than seven dead bodies were found. From various papers and
from a P/W of the same unit it is clear that they comprised a crew of four
who had joined 2/K.G.66 from 3/K.G.6 on 5th March 1944, a member of another
crew of 2/K.G.66, and two members of the technical ground staff of the
Staffel.

4.   The P/W from 2/K.G.66 states that it is normally strictly
forbidden to carry more than a crew of five in a Ju.188. He himself had
had seven in his aircraft on one occasion, however, during a dawn move
from Montdidier to Soesterberg in readiness for an attack on London on the
same night, when members of the ground staff accompanied the crews; he
suggests therefore, that the present aircraft was in course of making a
similar move from its base at Avord.   Several maps from the Z6 + EK had
tracks from Avord to Soesterberg, and A.D.G.B. was therefore advised of this
possibility.

5.   It remains a puzzle as to why the aircraft flew over to
England. The P/W from the same unit was convinced that its occupants
intended to desert and the height of flight, the firing of red verey signals
etc., are consistent with this.   On the other hand it is unlikely that

- 2 -   SECRET.

seven people, some of whom were ground staff, should plot to desert and
manage to get into the same aircraft. It is understood that there was
very thick ground mist at the time of the flight and it is conceivable
that the crew had completely lost their bearings; they returned the fir
of the Typhoons which intercepted them.

6.   Amongst a mass of papers, only three were of particular
interest. The first of these, carried by the ground W/T mechanic, was
list of the aircraft of the Staffel, showing their works numbers and th
W/T apparatus with which they were equipped. This is reproduced in
Appendix I.

7.   A second document was a British 1:500,000 Gee map of
Paris-Geneva, marked Series 3, Plotting Series Sheet N.E.45$\frac{1}{2}$/2; it bore
the name of Leutnant Korte, who was shot down and killed in the Z6 + HK
on 24th February. This map has been sent to A.I.4.(b).

8.   The third paper was a note that Feldwebel Rauckfuss and
Oberfeldwebel Fellner were to be collected from the 2nd Staffel orderly
room at 0745 hours on an unspecified date to make an Ypsilon-Flug
(Y-procedure flight) with Oberleutnant Reimers of the 1st Staffel.
Recent P/W of both 2 and 5/K.G.66 have stated that the 1st Staffel oper
with the 'Y' procedure.

```
CREW:    Unteroffizier    Hans  CZIPIN  - 13th July 1922.............Dead
         Obergefreiter    Johann KRAUSS - 24th June 1920.............Dead
  W/T    Unteroffizier    Robert SCHULTES - 26th May 1924...........Dead
  W/T    Obergefreiter    Hans Ehrhardt - 20th March 1922...........Dead
Gunner Unteroffizier      Eitel  WYSOTZKI - 7th May 1921 ...........Dead
  W/T   )
        ) Gefreiter       Edgar  VESTER - 3rd September 1923 .......Dead
Mechanic)

1.Wart(?)Obergefreiter            SCHWINGENSTEIN...................Dead
```

A.D.I.(K)   S.D.Felkin
19 April 44.   Wing Commander.

DISTRIBUTION:
        Air Ministry: A.C.A.S.(I); A.C.A.S.(Ops); A.D.I.(Sc); A.I.1.(
A.I.2.(b); A.I.2.(g)(3); A.I.3.(4); A.I.4.(b)(6); A.M.W.R.(3); C.A.S.
C.T.D., D.D.C.P.; D.D.I.(2); D.D.I.(3); D.of I(0); D.of I(S); V.C.A.S
80 Wing.; A.I.2.(a).; D.G. of S.; D.of Radar.; D.of Tels.; Tels 2.

        Commands. A.D.G.B.(5); A.E.A.F.(3); S.H.A.E.F.; Bomber (2).;
Coastal; Eighth Air Force (4).; Ninth Air Force (5).; A.F.H.Q.(3).;
M.A.A.F.(Rear)(3).; M.A.A.F.Air Command Post.; M.A.T.A.F.; R.A.F.(M.E
2nd T.A.F.

        War Office. M.I.19 (For W.O. Distribution)(11); G.S.O.1., C.S.D
(U.K.)(4).

        Miscellaneous. ETOUSA(G.2.P.W. & X Det.M.I.S.(5); M.I.B., 80
100 (SD) Group.; File.

APPENDIX V

Interrogation of German Air Force Prisoners

Dealing with Enemy Prisoners of War

The following is a procedural guide issued by HQ Fighter Command for dealing with enemy POWs taken from downed aircraft. Although undated, reference to the Tower of London would give this an early-war dateline.

INTERROGATION OF GERMAN AIR FORCE PRISONERS

A note of the essential procedure has been drawn up for the guidance of all concerned.

1. It is most important, in order to obviate collusion, for prisoners to be kept strictly apart from the first moment of their capture; to be dispossessed of all papers and equipment; and to be prevented from interfering in any way with their aircraft or remnants of it. Such equipment and papers should be handed to the Interrogation Officer.
2. The first authority, military or police, to contact the prisoners, should take them to the nearest military depot. Wounded or sick prisoners will be placed under guard at the nearest convenient hospital.
3. The prisoner should not be allowed to converse with, nor should they be interrogated by anyone except Royal Air Force interrogation officers.
4. A list is annexed of interrogation officers, with the headquarters to which they are attached. Military authorities are requested to telephone the duty intelligence officer of the nearest Royal Air Force Headquarters on that list immediately they receive information on the capture of prisoners.
5. The information obtained by interrogation is to be transmitted to the Combined Services Examination Centre at H.M. Tower of London and to RAF Commands.
6. On completion of primary interrogation, prisoners will be sent to the Tower under escort provided by the officer in command of the depot. Only prisoners in hospital are allowed to write letters before they reach the Tower. Any such letters should be handed to the interrogation officer.

Signed:
G. N. Douglas-Hamilton[13]
Wing Commander (INTELLIGENCE)
Headquarters, Fighter Command
STANMORE
FC/S 17627/INT.

13 Wg Cdr George Douglas-Hamilton, 10th Earl of Selkirk, KT, GCMG, AFC, AE, PC, QC(Scot), was the chief intelligence officer at HQ RAF Fighter Command.

Royal Aircraft Establishment

The RAE at Farnborough was the main British test centre for captured enemy aircraft throughout the duration of World War Two and in the years immediately afterwards. With the outbreak of war the technical staff at Farnborough became heavily involved with the investigation of crashed enemy aircraft and related equipment.

The RAE produced a series of technical reports on enemy aircraft and from June 1940 the experimental flying department became involved with the flight testing of captured aircraft, starting with the Me 109 E. Appraisals of flying characteristics, engineering features and quality and technical examination of instrumentation and equipment were all carried out at Farnborough and a large number of forced-landed aircraft were taken there for inspection. Not all of them, though, were subject to flight testing but were merely brought in for detailed examinations. Often, the testing would exhaustively look at construction methods, chemical analysis of oils and fuels and metallurgical testing of the materials used in construction. In fact, it is fair to say that no stone was left un-turned by the various sections at RAE; wireless and electrical, engines, instruments and aerodynamics.

The main flight testing work was carried out by the aerodynamics flight of the experimental flying department and the range of aircraft passing through the hands of the RAE during the period of the war was considerable as will be seen from the content of this book. However, and once the flight evaluation and other testing was done, the airframes were generally released to either the Air Fighting Development Unit or 1426 Enemy Aircraft Flight. Post-war, the RAE was heavily involved with testing large quantities of German aircraft and equipment brought back from Europe and Germany.

APPENDIX VII

Air Fighting Development Unit

The Air Fighting Development Unit (AFDU) was an air technical intelligence unit of the RAF which developed operational tactics against captured enemy aircraft through flight evaluation. It was based, variously, at the RAF stations at Northolt (where it was formed), Duxford and Wittering.

The Air Fighting Development Unit fell under the control of RAF Fighter Command and the Air Ministry and operated from RAF Duxford from late 1940 before moving to RAF Wittering in March 1943. From June 1941 the AFDU had operated alongside the Naval Air Fighting Development Unit (NAFDU) which had a broadly similar remit. These units were also tasked to carry out a variety of tests and evaluations on a wide range of fighter aircraft, aircraft modifications and new equipment prior to entering Allied service.

In the work that it carried out, the AFDU (and the NAFDU) had a distinctly separate role from that of 1426 Enemy Aircraft Flight which existed for exhibition and instructional purposes rather than for evaluation.

The units were absorbed into the Central Fighter Establishment and moved to RAF Tangmere in January 1945. The combined enemy aircraft resources of the AFDU, NAFDU and 1426 Enemy Aircraft Flight (see Appendix VIII) were subsumed into the Central Fighter Establishment until that unit's disbandment in December 1945.

1426 (Enemy Aircraft) Flight

The unit was established on 21 November 1941 at RAF Duxford and was made up of a small group of pilots who had previously been maintenance test pilots with 41 Group RAF. The purpose of the unit was to exhibit enemy aircraft to operational units in flying and ground demonstrations around Britain. Initially, it operated a Heinkel He 111 (AW177) that had been in British hands for two years, a Messerschmitt Bf 109 that had been captured during the Battle of France (AE479) and a Junkers Ju 88A-5 (HM509). The flight came under the operational command of 12 Group, RAF Fighter Command, with the first 'tour' of RAF airfields starting on 11 February 1942. Many of the aircraft detailed in this book were, at one time or another, on the strength of 1426 (Enemy Aircraft) Flight, with the unit moving from its RAF Duxford base to RAF Collyweston on 12 March 1943.

The aircraft in the unit changed throughout the war as further and later types came into the RAF's hands. They were then passed to the Air Fighting Development Unit at RAF Duxford (1940-1943) where they were extensively tested and evaluated against Allied types before being passed on to 1426 Flight. Several aircraft were lost to crashes or damaged beyond repair and then cannibalised for spare parts.

The flight ceased operations at RAF Collyweston on 17 January 1945, reforming at RAF Tangmere on the same date as the Enemy Aircraft Flight of the Central Fighter Establishment, which finally disbanded in December 1945.

APPENDIX IX

Royal Aircraft Establishment, Farnborough; Technical Report (extracts) on Focke Wulf 190 Aircraft

Newly captured or significant aircraft types (or related equipment) were sent to the Royal Aircraft Establishment at Farnborough for technical evaluation and reports, a case in point being the Focke Wulf 190 which landed at RAF Pembrey on 23 June 1942.

Reproduced here are edited extracts only from the secret technical report issued on the electrics in this aircraft, including some of the photographs incorporated in that report.

November 1943
Enemy Aircraft: Focke Wulf Fw 190 A-3
No. 313
Electrical Installation
Ref: EL/G.1943-44/7

Summary

The Fw 190 single-seater single-engined fighter aircraft has electrically-operated mechanisms for retracting the undercarriage, lowering the flaps and adjusting the tailplane incidence, besides the usual electric services as employed in other German fighters. There is a 2 KW engine driven generator and 24 volt nickel-iron battery. A plug and socket wiring scheme is used, designed by Siemens, for connections at wing roots and for the main distributor. There is extensive use of other types of plugs and sockets at other points where the aircraft structure can be broken down into component parts.

Report

1.) **General**

1.1 The Fw 190 is a single-seater, singled-engine fighter monoplane with a BMW 801 fourteen-cylinder radial engine. Except for the brakes, all the services which require power transmission are operated electrically, i.e. undercarriage retraction, flap operation and tailplane incidence adjustment. There is also an electric engine starter motor.

1.2 The aircraft appears to have been designed to simplify maintenance as much as possible. Most of the equipment is connected to the aircraft wiring by plugs and sockets to permit easy withdrawal and where parts of the structure are removable plug connectors are used in the wiring.

2.) **Section 'A'. General Services**

    2.1 The most interesting feature of the installation is the type 24 CL10 nickel iron battery. This has nineteen cells, of ten ampere hour capacity, with a moulded case. It is made by Deutsche Edison Comp. G.m.b.H. Berlin. A full report will be issued in due course.

3.) **Section 'B'. Engine Starting and Ignition**

    3.1 An electrically driven inertia type starter is provided. This is the first German single-engine fighter to be so fitted.

4.) **Section 'C'. Lighting**

    4.1 Normal navigation lamps are fitted, i.e. one at each wing tip and one white tail lamp. No landing lamp is fitted.

    4.2 The instrument board is illuminated by four instrument lamps; two lighting the upper panel and two lighting the lower panel which is set back from the upper one. The illumination may be varied by a switch dimmer.

5.) **Section 'D'. Heating**

    5.1 The heated pitot head, of standard design, is mounted on the starboard wing. There is an electromagnetic indicator on the instrument panel to show when the supply is switched on.

6.) **Section 'E'. Systems**

    6.1 Propeller pitch changing is effected normally by a hydraulic constant-speed mechanism, but by means of a switch in the cockpit the pilot can disconnect the hydraulic controls and vary the pitch by means of a switch and electric motor. The control switch is fixed conveniently in the throttle handle.

    6.2 Two electric immersed fuel pumps are employed, one in each tank. Electromagnetic indicators on the instrument panel show when the pumps are switched on.

    6.3 Tailplane incidence is adjusted by a jack operated by an electric motor. Two switches on the port switchboard control the motor, one tending to make the aircraft tail heavy and the other nose heavy. A brake on the motor is magnetically disengaged while the motor is running and brings the motor rapidly to rest when the current is switched off. The incidence indicator is of a standard type, with a potentiometer type transmitter and a ratiometer movement indicator.

    6.4 Undercarriage retraction is effected by two electric motors, one to each main leg. The tailwheel being operated by a mechanical linkage with the starboard leg.

7.) **Section 'L'. Distant Reading Compass etc**

    7.1 A standard Patin distant reading compass is fitted, with the master compass in the rear of the fuselage. The indicator is of the small dial type, PFK/f2.

    7.2 The turn and bank indicator is of the electrically operated type: Wel.

8.) **Section 'M'. Temperature and Fuel Indication**

8.1 An electric resistance thermometer is fitted for measurement of the engine oil temperature. No cylinder head thermometer is fitted, though there is provision for thermocouples on the engine.

8.2 An electric fuel gauge transmitter is fitted to both fuel tanks, but there is only one indicator with a switch to select the reading to either tank. The switch has a central 'off' position. A red lamp on the dashboard glows when the fuel level in the forward tank falls below a certain point.

9.) **Section 'N'. Camera Controls**

9.1 There is wiring for the operation of two cameras, one in each wing, but it is not known whether it is for gun cameras or reconnaissance cameras.

10.) **Section 'P'. Gun controls**

10.1 The armament of this aircraft comprises six guns: two MG 17 machine guns, two MG 151 cannon and two MG-FF cannon.

10.2 The installation of the synchronised MG 17 is standard, with pneumatic cocking controlled by an electromagnetic valve and electrical firing.

10.3 The two MG 151 are fixed in the wing roots and are synchronised through the propeller disc. Electrical ignition of the cartridges is employed.

10.4 The operation of the MG-FF is standard, with electropneumatic cocking and electrical release.

11.) **Section 'R'. Bomb Release**

11.1 Provision is made for an external bomb carrier, which can be a type ETC501 to take a 250 kg bomb, or possibly to take a number of 50 kg bombs.

12.) **Section 'S'. Bomb Fuzing**

12.1 Standard Rheinmetall-Borsig electrical bomb fuzing is employed, with a 24 volt battery in the radio compartment.

13.) **Notes and Comments**

13.1 The Fw 190 is of considerable interest in that it is the first German 'all-electric' fighter that has been examined and it is the first in which some approach to a plug and socket wiring scheme has been used.

Notes:
In its technical examination of the Focke Wulf 190 it is clear that RAE, Farnborough, were greatly impressed by the various innovations the aircraft embodied, not least of all its 'all-electric' design approach.

A large number of reports into this particular Fw 190 were produced by the Royal Aircraft Establishment into various aspects of this aircraft, its construction, its power plant and other principal elements. Once their technical appraisal was complete the RAE were able to pass this

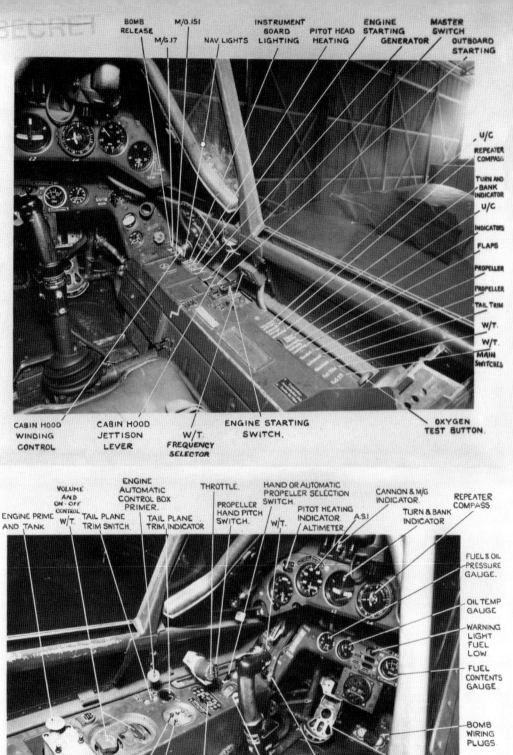

BOMB RELEASE

M/G.151

M/G.17

NAV. LIGHTS

INSTRUMENT BOARD LIGHTING

PITOT HEAD HEATING

ENGINE STARTING GENERATOR

MASTER SWITCH

OUTBOARD STARTING

U/C REPEATER COMPASS

TURN AND BANK INDICATOR

U/C INDICATORS

FLAPS

PROPELLER

PROPELLER

TAIL TRIM

W/T.

W/T.

MAIN SWITCHES

CABIN HOOD WINDING CONTROL

CABIN HOOD JETTISON LEVER

W/T. FREQUENCY SELECTOR

ENGINE STARTING SWITCH.

OXYGEN TEST BUTTON.

ENGINE PRIME AND TANK

VOLUME AND ON-OFF CONTROL W/T.

TAIL PLANE TRIM SWITCH.

ENGINE AUTOMATIC CONTROL BOX PRIMER.

TAIL PLANE TRIM INDICATOR

THROTTLE.

PROPELLER HAND PITCH SWITCH.

HAND OR AUTOMATIC PROPELLER SELECTION SWITCH.

W/T.

PITOT HEATING INDICATOR.

ALTIMETER

A.S.I.

CANNON & M/G INDICATOR.

TURN & BANK INDICATOR

REPEATER COMPASS

FUEL & OIL PRESSURE GAUGE.

OIL TEMP GAUGE

WARNING LIGHT FUEL LOW

FUEL CONTENTS GAUGE

BOMB WIRING PLUGS.

FOOT BRAKE RUDDER PEDAL.

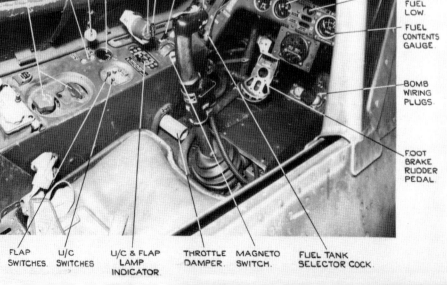

FLAP SWITCHES.

U/C SWITCHES

U/C & FLAP LAMP INDICATOR.

THROTTLE DAMPER.

MAGNETO SWITCH.

FUEL TANK SELECTOR COCK.

aircraft into the hands of the Air Fighting Development Unit who flight tested the Fw 190. Like the RAE, who were impressed technically, the AFDU were similarly impressed by its performance and reported on its appraisal against the Spitfire VB and IX, Mustang 1A, P-38 F and the prototype Griffon-engined Spitfire. The AFDU's test pilots quickly recognised the Fw 190's most outstanding quality was its remarkable aileron control which made it possible for it to change from a turn in one direction to a turn in an opposite direction with 'incredible speed'. This was a manoeuvre which, when viewed from the pursuing aircraft, appeared to be '…just as if a flick-roll had been made'.

The AFDU's advice to Allied pilots was that '…our aircraft must fly at high speed when in an area where the Fw 190 is likely to be met. This will give our pilots the chance of bouncing and catching the Fw 190 and, if bounced themselves, the best chance of avoiding being shot down.'

Bibliography

Air Ministry	*Manual of German Air Force Terminology*	(Air Ministry 1946)
Brettingham, Laurie	*Royal Air Force Beam Benders; No.80 (Signals) Wing 1940 – 1945*	(Midland 1997)
Brown, Capt Eric 'Winkle'	*Wings of The Luftwaffe*	(Hikoki 2011)
Butler, Phil	*War Prizes*	(Midland 1994)
Conyers Nesbit, Roy and van Acker, Georges	*The Flight of Rudolf Hess*	(The History Press 1999)
de Zeng, Harry and Stankey Douglas G.	*Bomber Units of The Luftwaffe*	(Midland 2007)
Goss, Chris	*Luftwaffe Bombers' Battle of Britain*	(Crécy 2000)
Goss, Chris	*Luftwaffe Fighter-Bombers Over Britain*	(Crécy 2003)
Harris, John and Wilbourn, Richard	*Rudolf Hess; A New Technical Analysis of the Hess Flight, May 1941*	(Pen & Sword 2014)
Hill, Robert	*The Great Coup*	(Arlington Books 1977)
Irving, Laurence	*Great Interruption*	(Airlife 1983)
Mackay, Ron	*The Last Blitz*	(Red Kite 2011)
Parker, Nigel	*Luftwaffe Crash Archive (Vols 1, 2, 3 and 4)*	(Red Kite 2013/2014)
Peskett, S. John	*Strange Intelligence*	(Hale 1981)

Quill, Jeffrey   *Spitfire; A Test Pilot's Story*   (Crécy 1998)

Ramsey, Winston   *The Blitz Then And Now (Vols 1, 2 and 3)*   (After The Battle 1990)

Rawnsley, C. F. and Jones, Ira 'Taffy'   *Tiger Squadron*   (W. H. Allen 1954)

Ross, David, with Blanche, Bruce and Simpson, William   *The Greatest Squadron of Them All*   (Grub Street 2003)

Sharp, C Martin and Bowyer, Michael J. F.   *Mosquito*   (Faber 1967)

Stanley, John   *The Exbury Junkers*   (Woodfield 2004)

West, Kenneth S.   *The Captive Luftwaffe*   (Putnam 1978)

Winslow, T. E.   *Forewarned is Forearmed*   (Wm Hodge & Co Ltd 1948)

Wood, Derek   *Attack Warning Red*   (McDonald & Jane's 1976)

Wright, Robert   *Night Fighter*   (Collins 1957)

Index

RAF Bases

RAF Squadrons, Units & Air Ministry Establishments

Messerschmitt 108 115-117

Messerschmitt 109 33, 38, 82-85, 87-93, 98, 113,
    118, 119, 122, 123, 124, 136, 139, 140, 162,
    170, 178

Messerschmitt 110 36, 37, 39, 41, 42, 43, 46, 71,
    73, 74, 75, 77, 78, 79, 80, 120, 121, 131, 133,
    137, 138

Mosquito 68, 115, 116, 128, 146

Miles Master 114

P-47 Thunderbolt 118

P-51 Mustang 118

Spitfire 12, 13, 79, 84, 87, 88, 90, 95, 100-104,
    115, 125, 126, 132-136, 139-141, 152, 162,
    163, 166

Typhoon 102, 147

Royal Navy Vessels

Belfast 11

Edinburgh 11, 16

Ganges 64

Mohawk 11

Southampton 16